JEAN-BAPTISTE CLÉRY
Eyewitness to Louis XVI & Marie Antoinette's Nightmare

H. Will Bashor, Ph.D. has taught at Ohio University, Ohio Dominican University and Franklin University, where he currently teaches Global Issues. He received his doctorate from the American Graduate School in Paris in 2005, and the DALF (*Diplôme approfondi de langue française*), the only French language diploma recognized by the French Ministry of Education, in 2006.

He is the author of *Oh, Léonard! Hairdresser to Marie-Antoinette and Other Sublime Ladies*, also published by Diderot Press.

Cover Art

Last Farewells of Louis XVI to His Family in the Temple Prison, January 20, 1793. Artist: Jean-Jacques Hauer. Musée Carnavalet, 23 rue de Sévigné, 75003 Paris.

From left to right: Temple Prison guard, Jean-Baptiste Cléry, Marie-Antoinette, Princess Marie-Thérèse, Louis XVI, Prince Louis Charles, and Madame Elisabeth.

JEAN-BAPTISTE CLÉRY

Eyewitness to Louis XVI and Marie-Antoinette's Nightmare

H. Will Bashor

Diderot Press
2011

First U.S. Edition
Copyright © 2011 by H. Will Bashor
ISBN: 978-0-615-58490-4

www.jeanbaptisteclery.com

To Bertina, Randall and Norma Blanche

CONTENTS

CHRONOLOGY

1759   Cléry (Jean-Baptiste Cant Hanet) born in Jardy, France.

1778   Princess Marie-Thérèse-Charlotte born on December 19.

1781   Prince Louis Joseph, *dauphin* of France, born on October 22.

1784   Cléry appointed as *barbier du roi*, the king's barber.

1785   Prince Louis Charles, Duc de Normandy, born on March 27.

1786   Princess Sophie-Hélène born on July 9; dies on July 19.

1789   Prince Louis Joseph dies on June 4; his younger brother,
        Prince Louis Charles, becomes dauphin; Versailles attacked;
        royal family forced to flee Versailles on October 6 and
        placed under house arrest at the Tuileries Palace.

1792   Tuileries attacked on August 8; the royal family imprisoned
        at the Temple Prison on August 13.

1793   King Louis XVI executed on January 21; the dauphin
        becomes the uncrowned Louis XVII; Cléry returns to his
        home in Juvisy on March 3; the dauphin separated from his
        family on July 3; Cléry arrested on September 15 and taken
        to La Force Prison; the queen guillotined on October 16.

1794   Madame Elisabeth, the king's sister, guillotined on May10;
        Cléry released from La Force Prison on August 10.

1795   Death of uncrowned Louis XVII, 10 years old, on June 8;
        Cléry arrives in Strasbourg on October 8; Princess Marie-
        Thérèse released from Temple, leaves for Vienna on the eve
        of December 19, her 17th birthday.

1797   Publication of Cléry's *Journal du Temple* prohibited in
        Vienna on November 30.

1798   Cléry's *Journal du Temple* published in London in August.

1809   Cléry, 50 years old, dies in Hetzing, Austria, on May 27.

PARIS MAP
18th Century

PROLOGUE
A Family's Honor

You denounce him, Monsieur? He is but one of the many defenders of the faith, a courageous and loyal man, a man who abandoned, without hesitation, his young wife and his children only to listen to the voice of devotion to his King.

–Daughter of Jean-Baptiste Cléry
Letter to Monsieur Lamartine, Rouen, April 18, 1847

While tending his family's garden one September morning in 1779, Cléry certainly never imagined that he was setting out on a journey that would take him from the quaint village where he was born to the magnificent courts of Russia, Poland, and England. But neither could the young farm boy have imagined that he would one day witness firsthand the horrific treatment of the royal family imprisoned in a dark medieval prison during the mayhem of the French Revolution.

Cléry, born Jean-Baptiste Cant Hanet, was the only personal servant to remain with King Louis XVI and his family in the tower of the Temple Prison. Although Cléry himself was closely scrutinized in the tower and even threatened with the guillotine, he managed to secretly record the guards' cruel and merciless treatment of the king, Queen Marie-Antoinette, their two children, and the king's sister.

Because of Cléry's courageous determination, we can relive one of the most moving and tragic stories in history. The servant's dedication to the royal family under such atrocious circumstances cannot be denied, yet rumors have since circulated that Cléry was also an agent of the revolution, spying for his master's enemies. These rumors haunted Cléry until his death in 1809 in Austria, where he was not only condemned to exile by the French government and estranged from his wife and family, but he was also snubbed by the royal family in exile as well. Cléry and his descendants were never able to clear his name, despite their determined and public protests. Doubts as to whether Cléry had been a sympathizer of the revolution followed him throughout his life and after his death.

Cléry's oldest daughter, Madame de Gaillard, wrote the following letter before her death in 1856 to Alphonse de Lamartine, an illustrious author of the 19th century who had accused Cléry of collaboration with the radical revolutionaries:

Monsieur Lamartine,

It has come to my attention that you have written about my father in your latest work, and I read the following lines with such painful bewilderment:

> Cléry, chosen by the mayor of Paris for his revolutionary viewpoints to be the deposed King's valet, and who was more devoted to his country than his master, allowed the tenderness of the King's sister Elisabeth and the heartbreaking scenes of the royal family imprisoned in the Temple to weaken his patriotism to the new republic and the revolution. His earlier passion for liberty made him remorseful, which soon led him to give unconditional support and assistance to the incarcerated royal family.

These few lines are simply untrue and slanderous! As daughter of the last servant to the martyred King, your prompt and severe retraction is owed to the memory of my father, to myself, and to my daughters.

No, Monsieur! Cléry was not chosen by Mayor Pétion as a spy! No, a thousand times no, my father never shared the sentiments of his revolutionary enemies before he was admitted into the Temple Prison to serve the royal family!

Assigned as valet to the young Prince, and, not as you claim, valet to the King, my father had no ulterior motive when he subjected himself to such cruel and agonizing captivity in the Temple to serve his masters. The courageous fidelity that he had shown them was only a result of his natural convictions. These convictions alone inspired him to address his appeal to the mayor of Paris, to be admitted to the Temple Prison to resume his service as valet de chambre to the royal child, being accustomed to his needs.

It was not, therefore, revolutionary sentiments, sentiments that he never had, that opened up the Temple Prison's gates for him; it was even less, as you claim, the remorse for his passion for liberty that dictated his admirable conduct in the Temple.

Monsieur, if you had read the « Journal of the Tower of the Temple » which my father published in London in 1798, you would have discovered his reason for serving his masters in the Temple. If you had read it, you would not have penned these deplorable lines, because you would have then known his true intentions.

You denounce him, Monsieur? He is but one of the many defenders of the faith, a courageous and loyal man, a man who abandoned, without hesitation, his young wife and his children only to listen to the voice of devotion to his King. And you dare, with these cold and uncompassionate words, condemn this man's admirable past?

Monsieur, I appeal to your Christian conscience, and to your honor as a Frenchman. Retract your statement at once, using all the means in your power to do so. Do not let it be said that the most unique example of loyalty in all history has been vilified by a French historian, a man who could publish such shameful defamation without any proof or any foundation.

A sense of loyalty and honor was the only fortune that Cléry had to his name when he was released from the Temple Prison, the only fortune that he had to bequeath to his daughters, and the only fortune that after more than forty years spent in exile and serving the daughter of Louis XVI, that I now have to leave to my family and my heirs. In the name of honor and truth, I entreat you to retract the lines that I have cited from your work.

The Widow De Gaillard (Cléry)
April 18, 1847

PART ONE

THE ROAD TO VERSAILLES

Chapter 1
The Prince's Promise

One day I will return, and you will hopefully show me more of your gardens. If that pleases you, I will then grant you a position as valet in my household at Versailles.

–Prince Louis Auguste to Cléry
Vaucresson, 1771

Two decades before the storm clouds of the approaching French Revolution began to gather on the horizon, Jean Baptiste Cant Hanet received a surprise visit that was going to change his life, and that of his family, for generations to come.

Jardy, the quaint but charming farm belonging to the Hanet family, was nestled in the wooded countryside near Vaucresson, a small village between Paris and Versailles. The great gate to the Jardy manor house was hung on large iron hooks, and secured with a lock and chain, opening to an almost magical dark leafy lane of shrubs and vines to the manor's courtyard. A small rustic fence separated at least a dozen acres of sculptured gardens from the courtyard. These gardens, laid out in geometric flowerbeds and pathways, were uncommonly beautiful and often attracted curious visitors from villages miles away.

The sleepy green rolling hills near the unique estate had for ages been the favorite hunting destination of the royal family, and the current monarch, King Louis XV, often indulged in the pleasures of the hunt in this idyllic region teeming with wild boar, rabbits, and deer. Moreover, the king used the elaborate hunt as an excuse to escape his dull and always pregnant wife, Queen Marie. Although he visited Marie everyday in her private chambers at the château of Versailles, he only remained with her for a few minutes as a matter of court etiquette.

The king's fancy for the queen, which was so intense in the early days of their union, eventually disappeared in time, and the queen finally detached herself from him, except for her duty to give him heirs to the crown. Her monotonous chilly tone, and her need to be lulled to sleep every night by storytelling, soon drove the king from his wife's bed. This alienation also drove him to spend his nights in the society of merry young women, and during the day he often used the hunt as an opportune time to meet his mistresses, far from the prying eyes of the queen. Although the king was not as promiscuous as his royal predecessors, his amorous encounters were made more public, and the king once called *le bien-aimé*, or the well-loved, would eventually become known as *detesté*, or simply hated.

The king's grandson, Prince Louis Auguste, was given the title *dauphin* because he became heir apparent to the throne when his father died five years earlier in 1765. The 17-year-old prince was just as passionate about hunting as the king, and he never missed an opportunity to join his grandfather on these gallant and extravagant occasions.

For centuries, French kings had claimed the right to hunt near Versailles as their royal prerogative. Although the king's subjects were punished if ever caught hunting on the royal domains, the king himself had free reign to hunt on their lands at any time. Furthermore, it was the duty of the king's subjects to assist him and his nobles on the regal chase. If it should ever become too late for the king to return to Versailles after hunting, his subjects were also required to prepare an elaborate feast for the entire hunting party, as well as provide everyone with lodging for the night.

Louis XV hunted at least three times a week, and afterwards he always enjoyed a lavish dinner, usually at Versailles, for the lords and ladies that had accompanied him on the outing. This was a costly affair for the monarchy, not to mention the cost of keeping the stables, boarding hundreds of hounds and employing an expert hunting staff, all to be ready at a moment's notice. The royal hunt was also a burden on the commoners who had to take valuable time away from their work and farms to appease the king. To add salt to the wound, the king's horses often trampled the farmers' crops or damaged their fences during the hunt.

When the royals arrived near Jardy one afternoon, however, it was a very special occasion for the young sons of Benjamin Hanet, the proprietor of the farm. The eldest son, Jean-Baptiste, 11 years old, was nicknamed "Cléry" to distinguish him from his grandfather, who was also named Jean-Baptiste. His brother, Pierre-Louis Philippe, one year younger than Cléry, was simply called "Hanet." Benjamin was especially proud of his sons' energy and endurance whenever they had the opportunity to follow the royal hunting party on foot. Hanet was more athletic and a more agile runner than Cléry, a reserved child who always preferred his father's library to the physical work that the farm demanded—the physical work that his younger brother revered.

Louis XV's hunting party

As the king's hunt approached the Hanet farm, a deer that was being chased by the royal hounds managed to find refuge in the manor's courtyard. The baying dogs and the frantic deer wreaked havoc, and to make matters worse, the boys' mother barely escaped being gravely injured in the path of the frightened animal. The king, his grandson the dauphin, and the royal entourage appeared an instant later in the courtyard on horseback.

When the hounds cornered the deer in the courtyard, it sprang on top of a pile of firewood and jumped the courtyard fence into the family's magnificent garden with the hounds trailing on its tail. The boys' father noticed, however, that the king's hunting party could not enter the small gate leading into the garden, so he ran to the house to fetch the key to the larger gate, despite the danger of being injured in the chaos. When he returned, he tried to open the lock with the oversized key, but the key became jammed in the lock. With a quick, forceful twist of the wrist he tried to open the lock, but he only managed to break the long metal key in half. Embarrassed and so disheartened about such an impatient maneuver, he sadly motioned to the king that the key was broken.

Acknowledging Benjamin's predicament and his humility, the king dismounted from his horse and shouted boisterously, "Oh well, kind farmer, we will just have to enter your garden on foot." The royals then made their way through the small gate to find the fallen deer surrounded by the hounds. Surprisingly, however, the deer was not the center of attention for the king and his guests; rather, the hunters were awestruck by the lavish and meticulously groomed garden that surrounded them.

Complimenting the proprietor of the farm on his artistic creation, the king stroked his chin as if he were trying to recall something. Somewhat puzzled, he mumbled: "I believe I know you. Is that possible?"

Benjamin Hanet bowed reverently and was quick to reply, "Yes, Sire, I cared for Your Majesty's gardens at Versailles many years ago."

The king's face lit up as he expressed his joy: "Oh! How could I forget! How are you, *Benjamin*? I am not so surprised then that this garden is in such an exceptional state. How content I am to see you once again. Come along, and introduce me to your family!"

Benjamin proudly escorted the king and several of his entourage into the parlor of the Jardy manor where his wife was nursing a baby girl. The king paid his compliments to Madame Hanet, asking her to remain seated, and he picked up the child that he found so pretty, giving it a small kiss on the forehead.

Upon leaving the room a few minutes later, he said to one of his valets, "Make sure that you indemnify this farmer for the damages that we have caused to the family's lovely garden." Stopping quickly, however, and feeling that he might have humiliated his hosts by simply offering money, he quickly pulled a gold *tabatière*, a richly decorated tobacco box, out of his pocket. He handed it to Benjamin's wife, saying: "I think that your husband would rather prefer this token of my appreciation here—above all others." It was a cherished gesture since a *tabatière* was normally given by French kings as a coveted sign of friendship, and Madame Hanet accepted it graciously.

"Sire, this is truly an honor," she said respectfully. "My husband often speaks of his service to Your Majesty in the Trianon gardens when he was a young apprentice."

The king nodded with a warm smile, and returned to his hunting party. Prince Louis Auguste had remained outside, however, admiring the gardens while the king paid his respects to the lady of the manor. The prince was so overwhelmed by the intricate landscaping that he asked Cléry to show him more of the estate before the hunt resumed. After a short excursion, the prince, who would one day be crowned King Louis XVI, smiled shyly at the young farm boy, and then mounted his horse.

"One day I will return, and you will hopefully show me more of your gardens," the prince said to Cléry. "If that pleases you, I will then grant you a position as valet in my household at Versailles."

Cléry, ecstatic with joy on hearing the prince's promise, dashed to the manor to tell his family about his rendezvous with the prince, the king-to-be that he would one day have the honor to serve at the château of Versailles.

Prince Louis Auguste

The very timid prince was the king's grandson, yet he was next in line for the throne. His father had died of consumption, the terminal stage of tuberculosis, at the age of 36. The prince's mother followed her husband to the grave five years later with the same illness. His two elder brothers had also died when they were children, thus leaving him heir apparent to the crown on the death of his grandfather. The prince's timidity may have been the result of the tragic loss of so many loved ones at such an early age, but it was also known that he was rather delicate and sickly as a child. Fortunately, however, in his teens he began to show signs of robustness and muscle strength, and hunting and shooting with his grandfather became one of his favorite pastimes.

Prince Louis Auguste

The prince faithfully kept a diary from the time he was 11 until the French Revolution when he ruled France as Louis XVI. The meticulous diary detailed his spending, his gambling, and even the results of his hunting excursions. On days that he hunted, he recorded the places where he hunted, the kinds of game he killed, and the quantity of each. He also noted where the hunting dinners were held and where he slept if he could not make it back to Versailles before nightfall.

Excerpt from Prince Louis Auguste's Diary

At the end of each year, he summarized how all of his days were spent. For example, he recorded the number of days he spent stag hunting or boar hunting by location. He was very careful to mark down the quantity of game he killed every month, and he even summed up the totals for the year. In December of 1775, he killed 1,564 head of game, and the total for the entire year amounted to 8,424. On the days that he killed no game, he wrote "*rien*" which meant "nothing." The following is an excerpt from his diary:

1. *Wednesday—Nothing.*
2. *Thursday—On horseback at the Porte du Main for a stag hunt. One taken.*
3. *Friday—Nothing.*
4. *Saturday—Hunted the roebuck at Butart. One taken, twenty-nine killed.*
5. *Sunday—Vespers (prayer meeting).*

These trifling and quite insignificant entries describing the most ordinary course of daily life are a striking contrast to the prince's later entries as king during the onset of the violent revolution.

Although the prince noted his day hunting on the Jardy estate in his diary, he never had the opportunity to return to visit the manor gardens as he had promised. Cléry, however, never forgot meeting the prince that day when the king's hunting party stumbled onto his family's farm, and he would never stop believing that he would one day serve his prince in the royal household at Versailles.

Unfortunately, Prince Louis Auguste could also never have imagined that this young farmer's son would 20 years later be his personal servant, a servant who would witness his terrifying ordeal in a revolutionary prison as King Louis XVI. Cléry would also be the very last person to receive the king's final embrace—or to hear his very last wishes.

Chapter 2
In and Out of Royal Favor

A servant's first obligation is fidelity. It is the foundation of society and especially that of the household where the father places his trust in his wife, his children, and his servants.

–Claude Fleury, L'abbé de Loc-Dieu
Treatise for Louis XIV, 1688

Many members of Cléry's family had served the royals at Versailles in one capacity or another for several centuries. His great-grandfather, Jean Hanet, had served King Louis XIV as a fencing master before retiring and purchasing the *seigneurie* of Cléry in Normandy, a tract of land with certain privileges and immunities, and hence the origin of the nickname "Cléry." One of his sons, also named Jean, served the monarchy as the king's stable master at Versailles. In fact, most of his 10 children had the honor of working at the grandiose palace at one time or another. One of them, Cléry's father Benjamin, made a name for himself at the château's Trianon gardens.

Benjamin practically grew up at Versailles caring for the exotic plants in the palace's greenhouses, and King Louis XV often referred to him as "my Benjamin" for his superb gardening skills. In fact, his work was so well-known that he caught the eye of Mademoiselle Marguerite Laurent, who lived in the nearby village of Vaucresson. Marguerite was known to be a lovely maiden from a very prominent family throughout the area.

However, Benjamin lost his favor with the court of Versailles because of a very unfortunate circumstance. When his older brother found himself in a military hospital and close to death, Benjamin decided to take leave from his position at Versailles to go to him— despite the fact that his father had previously disowned the wayward son. Benjamin received permission to take leave from his gardening, and, using up several years of his savings, he set out to bring his brother home.

The very same day that Benjamin left, however, a daughter of one of the king's servants was kidnapped. Because Benjamin was known to have brought her flowers on special occasions, all suspicion fell upon him. When Benjamin's father was served with a warrant for his son's arrest, he had no idea that he had left Versailles to rescue his older brother.

Two weeks later, Benjamin returned home with his brother, and he was able to prove his innocence in the bizarre kidnapping case. It was too late, however, to regain his position as gardener at Versailles due to his prolonged absence and, unfortunately, due to his guilt by association in the abduction of the young girl. Feeling unjustly punished, he decided to return to Jardy, which was his father's farm at that time, and devote his life to the work that he so enjoyed. In fact, within a year he was able to take over the farm's deed from his father and finally marry the lovely Marguerite in 1757. His eldest son, Cléry, was born two years later, and Hanet was born the following year.

In his *mémoires*, the younger brother, Hanet, tells an interesting story about his mother, Marguerite, which had a very notable effect on the family's position in society. One day in September of 1763, his mother was sitting in the grass in the shade of apple trees that lined the road leading to their farm. With her bosom uncovered, she was nursing a small child, and an "aura of happiness" reigned over the scene: She wore a straw hat, her long dark hair framed her sky-blue eyes, and her three small children sat peacefully next to her on the blanket in the fresh grass. At that moment two well-dressed ladies who were strolling down the lane remarked that the quaint scene was worthy of being painted. "Oh, my aunt, what a beautiful nursemaid," cried the youngest noble lady.

The boys' mother, Marguerite, was caught off guard with the arrival of the unexpected visitors. She began to get up, but the older beseeched her, "Please, Madame, please do not move. It is such a lovely sight watching you nurse the child." Moments later, the well-dressed ladies were joined by a small group of royal pages. Little did Marguerite know, but the surprise visitors were actually King Louis XV's daughter, his sister, and their personal servants.

When Marguerite finally stood up, the princesses noticed her natural stance, her motherly curves, and the freshness of her complexion. She answered the princesses' questions about her family and her life at Jardy with remarkable ease and simplicity. Since they were close to the family's beautiful gardens, Marguerite graciously invited them to take a stroll there, and the ladies gladly accepted.

Cléry's father, who was once a royal gardener at Versailles, recognized the princesses at once and offered them fresh flowers and fruit, which the ladies could not refuse.

Princess Marie Adélaïde, the king's daughter, was so impressed with Marguerite's charming persona that she asked her to become the nursemaid of the child she was carrying at the time. Marguerite, honored by the generous and honorable gesture, assured Her Royal Highness that she would be delighted to serve as her nursemaid. The princess then commented to her aunt that she hoped the royal physicians would not have to certify that Marguerite's milk was good, because "her health and that of her children attest to the fact." The princess then left with her royal entourage, telling Marguerite that she would soon have good news for her.

In fact, the good news arrived the following day. The princess's royal governess, Madame de Marsan, sent for Marguerite to come to the château of Versailles after hearing that she was "the most beautiful nursemaid that anyone had seen in such a long time."

According to court etiquette at the time, it was customary for the royal governess to choose four nursemaids at least two months before any princess was expected to give birth. Of the four maids chosen, the royal physicians had the duty of examining the maids' milk and then selecting one of the four to be the baby's nursemaid. This custom was honored not only to select the best maid, but also to be sure that the maid selected was capable of fulfilling her responsibilities. A humorous story circulated Versailles that the late King Louis XIV went through three nursemaids before a suitable one was finally found for him. Unfortunately, the prince was born with two front teeth, and he would bite the nursemaids to the point that they would refuse to nurse him any longer. When the fourth applicant was forewarned about the predicament, she said, "Afraid I am not! Bring me the child!"

When the young prince began to bite the maid, she brazenly broke court etiquette. She quickly smacked the prince's bottom several times and, from that time forward, he never dared to bite her again while she was nursing him. In fact, she later became one of his favorite governesses.

There was no doubt that Marguerite would be chosen to nurse the new addition to the royal family, but she had the misfortune one day to trip in a cluttered room, and she broke her two upper front teeth when she fell against the arm of a chair. Naturally, this would not have affected her role as nursemaid, but royal etiquette would never have allowed a "toothless" maid to nurse a royal child of France at the luxurious court of Versailles.

Madame de Maran's niece, the Princess de Guéménée, had noticed Marguerite among the four maids chosen, however. Despite the ruling of the royal physicians regarding nursemaids, she was so impressed with Marguerite that she decided to employ her as nursemaid to her first son, the Duke of Montbazon. She accomplished this by leaving her son with Marguerite at the Jardy farm, far from the court's eyes.

By nursing the noble lady's newborn, a baby that eventually became known as one of the most handsome princes at the court of Versailles, Cléry's mother earned her family many privileges as well as the protection of the very prominent and very grateful Princess de Guéménée and her husband. One of the privileges permitted the family to send Cléry and his brother Hanet to study in the village of Versailles and, according to the wishes of the generous princess, to later serve in the Guéménée affluent household.

When Cléry was 14 years old, he was the first to be sent to Mr. Guiné's private school in Versailles, and it was noted that he was a remarkable student. Cléry's brother Hanet remained on the farm, but when he became 15 years old, his father spoke to him on one occasion as he returned home from the fields: "Hanet, you should follow in Cléry's footsteps. Since the princess has sent him to school, he has made considerable progress. You know that the princess planned to take *both* of you into her household as servants."

Hanet, however, was not happy with his father's request. His only wish was to remain at Jardy and help his father with the farming and gardening, but his father was adamant. "Your younger brothers will soon be able to replace you here," his father continued. "We must also respect the good wishes of the princess, and in any event, it is far better to be connected to important people in these times."

He continued by saying that Hanet and Cléry would be more helpful "advancing the position of the family" by continuing their education for a highly coveted position with a noble family. Although dismayed, Hanet respectfully obeyed his father, and he joined his brother at Mr. Guiné's school one week later.

Benjamin's life was devoted to his five children. He had assembled a small library, and he took great care in his children's education. Hanet remarked that his father's favorite books were *La Maison Rustique (The Farm House)* and *Robinson Crusoe*. Although he wished his children to know a little about everything, he strongly emphasized the importance of agriculture and the mechanical arts.

When his wife Marguerite was reading a chapter of the Bible to the children one evening, Benjamin interrupted her to point out that the first real kings of the earth had tilled the ground. He, too, would read to them every evening a portion of *La Maison Rustique* and *Robinson Crusoe*, but always with similar commentaries.

"This book of *Robinson Crusoe*," he would say, "is the most useful work for man ever composed since writing was invented. He learns from it to provide for all his wants, and to be independent from the world. The farmer can do without the learned, the poet, and the musician, but none of them can do without the farmer."

Because Benjamin did not think it was enough for his sons to be acquainted with all the details of cultivation, he also taught them how to make all the tools required for common use in agriculture. Hanet wrote, "Such an education would only be despised by the frivolous; my father seemed to have had an intuition of the various fortunes in store for his children, and that they would be dispersed over the surface of the globe."

In fact, had Benjamin lived long enough, he would have seen the eldest among the isles of Courland, the youngest with yellow fever in the tropics, and his three children living in Prussia, Poland, and Hungary.

Fortunately, Hanet discovered that although Mr. Guiné had classrooms for his students, he also had a garden for their recreation. Hanet naturally preferred the rake and hoe to grammar and arithmetic. In fact, the school's garden became his refuge, and he spent more time in the garden than in the schoolmaster's classroom. Although Mr. Guiné was certainly disappointed that Hanet was neglecting his studies, the schoolmaster was also consoled by the considerable improvements made to his garden every day. When the boys' mother arrived at the school to take Cléry and Hanet to their new employment in the household of the Princess de Guéménée, it was obvious and unfortunate, however, that Hanet knew little more than he did when he left the farm a year earlier.

Although Cléry had improved immensely in his studies, the family was still concerned about Hanet's future in society which now depended upon his benefactress, the Princess de Guéménée. Upon their arrival at her extravagant residence, the princess was happy, however, to keep both handsome young men despite the younger brother's unsatisfactory record at school.

To everyone's astonishment, the princess had also just received the great honor of becoming the next royal governess to the "children of France." She would thus have the coveted and noble responsibility for the education and upbringing of the new king's children after his marriage to the Princess Marie-Antoinette of Austria.

The post of royal governess was very lucrative, but the arduous responsibility was demanding and time-consuming. The royal governess had to make all the arrangements for the education of the queen's children. Moreover, she had to keep guard personally over any new royal infant night and day for the first three years of its life, even sleeping next to the child behind a dividing screen to respect the child's privacy.

The princess immediately provided the brothers with money to purchase the proper attire needed for continuing their studies at the magnificent Hôtel Soubise in Paris. Being wealthy, she could afford to employ servants whose primary function was to display their masters' wealth and taste. The princess was undoubtedly preoccupied with the brothers' attire as well as their height and stature. In other words, the brothers were to be used as status symbols whose functions placed them in the public eye. Having the boys schooled, and clothed, in Paris could be considered nothing more but conspicuous consumption on a royal scale.

Cléry's remarkable progress at school in Paris impressed the princess immensely, and he was soon taken into the Guémenée household to become her personal secretary and librarian. Although Cléry could only be found in the library most of the time, he became so important to the princess that many felt it would be impossible to ever separate him from her service.

She decided to place his brother Hanet, therefore, in the royal household of Versailles as *valet de chambre*, or male attendant, of the first child born to the newly crowned King Louis XVI and Queen Marie-Antoinette. All royal children were customarily supervised by a *premier valet de chambre*, or first valet de chambre, two valets de chambre *ordinaries*, better known as replacements for the premier valet when needed, and 16 *quartier* valets which served in shifts, four at a time. Hanet was appointed one of the quartier valets.

Until the new prince or princess arrived, however, Hanet was to remain at the Hôtel Soubise in Paris and continue his education. This may well have caused jealousy on Cléry's part because he had always dreamed of serving the king at the château of Versailles ever since he met Louis Auguste when hunting at Jardy, but it appears that he was still quite content in the Guémenée household for the time being, enjoying the amenities and status of belonging to such a noble and well-known family.

The duties of the valet de chambre for the children of France included serving their meals, keeping up their rooms, providing exercise to increase their appetites, and helping with their lessons. King Louis XIV's valet de chambre actually slept in his room when he was a child and would read him bedtime stories so that he would be able to fall asleep. It was not uncommon for a *valet* to become tenderly attached to his young master in a fatherly manner and remain in his service until generously pensioned for his loyalty at retirement.

The valet de chambre was well compensated for his work, but the position also allowed the servant to earn favors from his master depending on how close the relationship evolved. If the servant and his master were on speaking terms, the servant could ask for a favor, directly or indirectly. However, if the servant had earned his master's trust and confidence, he was automatically awarded favors without ever having to ask for them. These favors often resulted in wealth, lucrative connections, honorable titles, and even land.

Masters and Servants

Being a personal servant for the Princess de Guéménée would have required Cléry to adjust to her household's strict code of etiquette with a time schedule that was quite different from the daily routine on the Jardy farm. He would most likely have been required to work but a few hours in the mornings, spending the rest of the day serving at the princess's table or her social gatherings as needed. Servants of his stature were normally free most of the day, and they would wait in antechambers for orders from their masters. Servants knew in advance the times when they were required to work, however, and they could thus circulate freely throughout the house or even leave the premises as they wished for taking walks, participating in games, or shopping in their free time.

Because servants of noble families were paid more than most lower class workers, they were often seen gambling in billiards cafés. Parisian police officers would arrest participants gambling in clandestine parties, but they usually tolerated it in gambling halls and billiards cafés. There was even a royal lottery at the end of the 18th century which many servants enjoyed playing with their excess earnings.

Common scenes of servants sitting on fences and loitering in the parks, combined with elaborate and expensive garb, would later be a cause for concern at the outbreak of the revolution. In fact, most servants were known to have an abundance of clothes, and they would change them according to the season or the circumstances of their service. Cléry's clothes cabinet could easily have contained a dozen cotton or silk shirts, four or five pairs of breeches and jackets, and even underpants for day and night attire; whereas, the poor laborer only had several rough shirts of hemp or linen, and normally wore no underclothes. Naturally, the lower class workers who were struggling for bread to feed their families found the blatant and lavish consumption of the aristocrats' servants abhorrent, to say the least.

A visiting Italian noble, Jean-Paul Marana, had earlier predicted that such excessive expenditure for clothing and keeping servants was a sign of a "dying city." He wrote to a friend in Sicily about the growing discontent with the high status of servants:

> Now that servants and coachmen wear scarlet and feathers, and their clothing is adorned with gold and silver, it is time for such luxury to come to an end. Nothing more can ruin a nobleman's taste for gold when he sees it on the backs of the most detestable creatures in the world.

What exactly was required of Cléry and Hanet as servants in the late 18th century? In one word, it was fidelity. During the reign of Louis XIV, the servant's first duty was *fidelité*. The following text prepared for the king claimed that "Fidelity is the foundation of society and especially that of the household where the father places his trust in his wife, his children, and his servants. If you remove that trust, then mankind sinks to the level of outlaws and horrible confusion, worse than the life of the most ferocious beasts."

Fidelity was commonly exchanged for favors, but there were other enticing benefits for Cléry to continue his tutelage under the princess. Servants learned to read, write, and sign their names. To provide consistency in their duties, they were provided with handbooks outlining proper service in their households. In addition to being paid well, they were clothed well, and provided room and board—often dining with their masters or being lodged in the château proper.

> Son premier devoir eſt la
> fidelité. C'eſt le fondement
> de toute ſocieté entre les
> hommes : & particulierement
> de la ſocieté domeſtique, qui
> ne ſubſiſte, que par la confian-
> ce qu'un pere de famille a en
> ſa femme , ſes enfans & ſes
> ſerviteurs. Otez cette con-
> fiance , la vie humaine n'eſt
> plus qu'un brigandage, & une
> confuſion horrible, pire que
> la vie des bêtes les plus farou-
> ches.

Claude Fleury, L'abbé de Loc-Dieu, 1688

To understand how well Cléry was compensated for his services, it would be essential to consider the average wages of other workers and the prices of goods that were available at that time in Paris. Laborers earned approximately 18 *sous* (French *cents)* per day compared to domestic servants earning 20 to 35 sous, depending on the social class of their masters. Cléry could easily have earned 28 to 30 sous per day from the wealthy, and generous, princess.

But what was a sous worth? Laborers earning 18 *sous* per day could possibly pay their daily rent (3 sous), purchase bread (14 sous), and possibly have one sous leftover. Cléry, on the other hand, would more than likely have received room and board, even if he was not housed in the princess's residence. Therefore, as most noble servants, Cléry would have had ample disposable income for gambling, entertaining, or even investing. In fact, many servants of noble families had invested their money with the house of Guéménée, but it is not known if Cléry did so. That Cléry would have fared well as a servant for a noble family is confirmed by the royal adviser Vauban:

> Domestics live the happiest of lives, given their lowly
> status. They never have to worry about paying for
> food or drink, their clothes, or their rent. They
> always appear more cheerful than their masters.

Moreover, servants were exempt from military service by working for prominent families in royal circles, families with pull that could easily have the military draft waived. As long as Cléry and Hanet remained in their positions, they could not be obligated to join the army to fight in the king's wars. Perhaps the most lucrative benefit of serving masters with royal connections was the ability to be promoted socially. Even a queen's hairdresser or a king's barber could retire with a social ranking that included an honorable position and title, royal privileges, and a very hefty pension for his loyal service.

Princess Guéménée's household could easily have employed up to 200 servants, mostly men, due to the added responsibility of caring for the first child of France. Court etiquette alone would have required the princess, as governess, to employ: 16 assistant governesses working everyday from 9 o'clock in the morning until 10 o'clock in the evening, nurse maids, assistants to dress and bathe the child, a premier chambermaid, 18 valets de chambre, two *garcons de chambre* or young valets, a porter, and a purser. Hanet was thus assigned to be one of the many valets de chambre when the first royal child arrived.

Pierre- Louis Philippe Hanet, Cléry's brother

Because both Hanet and Cléry were being groomed for positions in the public eye, their future roles depended on convincing the public of their master's superiority and wealth. Although they could be dismissed from their duties at any time, they would never be able to leave their positions without a loss of wages or possibly face prosecution. Male servants, depending on their loyalty and their income, commonly switched positions more than their female counterparts. However, servants in noble or royal households would normally remain until retirement. In any event, it was certainly easier for a male servant to accumulate wealth, but, as we shall see, it could also be more difficult for him to hold onto it.

Being in the public eye also required that should Hanet or Cléry marry, their marriages would have to be arranged, or at least the marriage contract approved, by their masters. Masters normally frowned on marriage because they feared that the servants' household duties would be disrupted. This was especially true of women servants due to pregnancy and nursing; however, marriage did not normally interrupt men's careers. In fact, wives normally contributed to the men's wealth in the form of dowries.

Chapter 3
Cléry's Uncertain Future

I am aware of the Princess's promise to appoint Cléry valet de chambre of the Dauphin, but Madame de Polignac has already promised it to another servant. There is nothing I can do to remedy the situation.

–Queen Marie-Antoinette
to Cléry's brother Hanet, Versailles, 1782

Cléry was somewhat taller than Hanet, but Hanet was still considered to be rather tall, and his height was befitting for his future calling. Hanet admits that he, although shorter, was "more robust and stronger" than his older brother. In fact, he was known to be very outgoing and occasionally reckless. Cléry, on the other hand, was more serious and more discreet in his social relationships. That is not to say that Cléry was not a brave man, because it was said that he would "stand proud and not back down from any adversary." In fact, Cléry would not hesitate to draw his sword when necessary, earning him the respect and admiration of all his contemporaries.

Modest and reserved, however, Cléry did not enjoy the more violent activities that Hanet preferred, such as fencing, dancing, playing billiards, and horseback riding, to name a few. Rather, he was completely satisfied to spend his time reading or visiting friends. Moreover, he did not share Hanet's expertise in weaponry as an interesting story attests. One afternoon Cléry invited guests to his somewhat stylishly furnished apartment for lunch. The fact that Cléry was entertaining in such a well-decorated apartment suggests that he had prospered well under the tutelage of the Princess de Guéménée, and was not uncommon for servants to form tight-knit groups, enjoying wine or *eau-de-vie,* a strong fruit brandy, in their private quarters or in taverns.

After a pleasurable meal, Cléry arranged for coffee to be served to the guests sitting in the parlor. A discussion of weapons arose when a certain gentleman began to brag about his prowess with the sword. Cléry, tired of the ill-mannered man's ranting, spoke up:

"I wager ten coins that my brother Hanet will get the first strike with his sword."

The gentleman accepted the challenge, and another guest was chosen to judge the match. Cléry leaned confidently against the chimney mantle with a cup and saucer in his hand, watching the men take their positions.

The match had barely started when Hanet made his move and struck with such a force that the gentleman fell over the serving table. Porcelain china and silverware crashed to the floor, and the ladies in attendance shrieked loudly, thinking that the pompous gentleman was certainly dead. The humiliated man was only slightly injured, however, except for his pride. Still standing with the cup and saucer in his hand, Cléry looked at the small gathering and calmly announced, "Tell me, was that not the best match that you have ever seen in your life!"

Jean-Baptiste Cléry, ca. 1781

Cléry may have appeared somewhat pompous from this story, but that may be attributed to his young age and his new status in Parisian society, a far cry from the country manor of Jardy. However, pomposity was not part of his nature. He was considerate, empathetic, and highly motivated to succeed in the ranks as a noble, and hopefully, royal servant. His brother wrote that "Cléry was studious, applied himself well to his tasks, and was very thoughtful." Cléry's greatest pastime was actually reading, spending most of his spare time in Princess Guéménée's library.

Hanet spent almost two years studying at the Hôtel Soubise while Cléry continued his service in the princess's household. One morning, Cléry entered his brother's room unannounced and much earlier than normal. Surprised, Hanet looked up from his bed and asked, "Why so early, dear brother? Is it April Fools' Day?" Cléry dropped a sack of coins on the table, and replied, "No, but you need to get out of your bed. Here is new clothing from the tailor, too. You shall begin your service in the Princess's household today!"

"Fine," replied Hanet yawning and smiling at the same time, "but why the money?"

"The money is from me, because it is time for you to start taking care of yourself," answered Cléry in a brotherly tone: You have led nothing but a life of leisure here in Paris, and the time has come for you to get serious about your future. Get dressed, and let us be on our way."

Later, when the brothers arrived at the Guéménée residence, the princess was resting on a chaise in her bedroom. It was customary at that time for aristocratic ladies to receive guests in their bedroom *à la ruelle*, the ruelle being the passage between the bed and the wall in which callers were received. She had not seen Hanet for almost two years, and she did not recognize him. Somewhat shocked to have a stranger in her presence, she asked Cléry, "What does this gentleman want?"

"Madame, this is my brother who you ordered to begin his service here today," replied Cléry.

Glancing at her lady-in-waiting, "What? This is Hanet?" the princess asked. "Julie, what kind of stories have you been telling me about Hanet? He does not look as if he were out every evening until all hours of the night!"

Addressing Hanet, the princess sternly said, "They say that you are not wise, that you sleep late, that you play billiards until early in the morning, and that you go to all of the shows in Paris."

Hanet knew that there was some truth to the gossip, but he thought he should at least partially tell the truth: "Me, Madame? All of the shows? I have frequented them at times, but only to accompany Mademoiselle Thiriot (an elderly and respectable governess of the court). If I play billiards, it is only with another valet de chambre, and if I am out late in the evening, it is only when I visit my dear mother in Vaucresson." The princess glanced at Cléry, and he nodded that what his brother said was true, at least partially true.

At that moment, the princess's husband, the honorable Prince de Guéménée, then entered the room and, tapping Hanet on the shoulder, said to the princess, "You know, Madame, this gentleman here is a friend of our children, and they enjoy his company immensely because they think he and I resemble each other." The princess examined Hanet's face, and asked her lady-in-waiting to bring her some miniature portraits of the family. Finding a portrait of one of her relatives, she agreed that there was some resemblance to her father-in-law. Surprisingly, the resemblance helped Hanet gain the princess's favor, and she welcomed him into her household.

Strangely enough, a day that began with reproaches from his older and wiser brother, Cléry, appeared to end on a happy note. He was now finally in the service of the Guéménée household with his older brother, but, unfortunately, his first day was not going to be like any other.

The princess spent most of the morning resting in her chambers. She read, she wrote letters, and she received guests there as was customary. Later in the day when Hanet returned with books from the library that the princess had requested, he noticed two refined women dressed in mourning who were asking to be announced to the princess. The lady-in-waiting told them that the princess was not available at the moment, but Hanet, not knowing the customs and etiquette of the house, went immediately to the princess's door and announced the visitors, accusing the lady-in-waiting of lying to them.

The princess, somewhat taken aback by Hanet's boldness, told her lady-in-waiting that she would receive the guests. When they entered, she nodded for Hanet and the lady-in-waiting to leave the room. Once in the hallway, the lady-in-waiting began to viciously chastise Hanet for overstepping his authority, "Only I have the honor to announce guests to the Princess in this household!"

Minutes later, Hanet saw the lady-in-waiting escort the two women into another parlor to serve them chocolate refreshments. The bell sounded for Hanet, and he entered the princess's chamber with a smile on his face, proud of what he thought was his good deed for the day. "Approach!" she ordered, in a very severe tone. "I am reprimanding you, because you deserve it. You must learn to respect the order of my household. Whenever a servant announces such guests to me, etiquette would never allow me to then refuse them an audience—even if I so desired."

Hanet, thinking he would be praised for his action, tried to defend himself: "Madame, if I may, these ladies would have left without you ever knowing who they were or why they requested an audience."

The princess swiftly replied, "How do you know that, young man? In fact, they had already written me that they were going to pay me a visit today."

"You should know," she continued, "that many people without titles or without any rights to my favors incessantly try to have an audience with me. It is good to see that you have a kind heart, Hanet, but you should also remember that I do know a little about what I am doing." Tears swelled up in Hanet's eyes, and the princess shook her head, but a smile slowly appeared on her face.

"The ladies that you announced," she said calmly, "are of noble birth, and they *were* worthy of my good graces. In fact, if it were not for you, I would not have been able to help them in their time of need. Please take these gold coins and give them to the ladies in the parlor without anyone seeing you, and do not say anything to anyone, *especially* Julie, my lady-in-waiting."

One can only imagine Hanet's relief. It was a lesson that he would never forget, but at the end of his first day he knew he would have to consult Cléry more often about etiquette and tradition in noble households. He would also have to borrow Cléry's handbook, a gift from the princess, on household service to learn that a servant was an important intermediary between his master and the public.

Fortunately, there was an abundance of manuals for domestics in the eighteenth century, depending on the social class of the household. Rules for valets de chambre, for example, could possibly have included the following:

- When cleaning the master's room, the valet de chambre does not arrange any papers, touch any boxes, and is not permitted even to open a book without grave consequences.

- The valet de chambre should never have his head covered in the interior of the master's house, nor should he ever be seated in front of his master unless so required to do so. When accompanying his master, the valet should always follow by walking behind his master, never at his side.

- The valet should never enter a master's chamber without being called upon. If there is pressing business, the valet will ask permission to enter before opening the door.

- It is indispensable for the valet to know how to read, write, and count. The valet can assist with the master's messages, copy notes and keep records, run errands, find addresses, get directions, and leave notes for other servants. More important, reading books is imperative to improve one's condition, allowing the valet to avoid the more dangerous diversions.

- The valet should be on time every morning to assist with the master's clothing, his beard, his hair, hot water in the winter, toiletries, soaps, perfumes, and powders. The valet must act diligently in silence, carefully shaving and arranging the master's hair.

- Always attentive, the valet must keep all of the master's clothing in order and his shoes well shined (see the manual for cleaning and removing stains from the shirt collar).

- The valet should, and must, ask his master for advice concerning his personal affairs; it is sign of confidence and affection. However, it should be asked in a certain manner such as: "Madame, could I speak to you about a personal matter?" or "Sir, could you please give me your opinion about an important matter?"

There is no doubt that Cléry and Hanet fared well in their new positions because in the months to follow, the brothers would follow the princess's family on vacation, take up residence in her beautiful manor Montreuil, and finally join her at Versailles in the royal household, the day they thought would never arrive. Hanet later wrote that, although he missed working on the farm, his years serving the princess were the happiest of his life. Cléry, too, was simply overjoyed, and his dream to serve the royal family was finally about to come true.

On the 19th of December 1778, Louis XVI and Marie-Antoinette announced the birth of the Princess Marie-Thérèse, also known as Madame Royale. Although everyone had prayed for a prince to carry on the royal lineage, the entire kingdom celebrated the birth of the royal couple's first child with exuberance. This was especially good news for the childless couple, because rumors were rampant about the queen perhaps being sterile.

The queen would have been somewhat disheartened at not providing France with the long awaited dauphin, the future heir to the throne, but she was happy to at least finally give France a royal child. The new princess, however, might have been aware of the family's initial dismay growing up; in fact, she once asked her father if he was disappointed when she was born. "I would not have wanted you any differently," he answered reassuringly.

The queen was known to be very strict with the young princess; she even refused to give the princess any lavish gifts one Christmas because so many other children were going hungry. However, she never loved the princess any less for not being a prince. In fact, the queen knew that if she had given birth to a son, he would have been taken from her immediately, kept in a separate household, and groomed to be king one day. As she held the princess in her arms, she remarked with tears in her eyes, "A son would have belonged to the state, but you will belong to me forever. You will receive all of my care, you will share all of my happiness, and you will soften my pain."

Because the Princess de Guéménée was determined to keep Cléry as a servant in her private household at Versailles until a dauphin was born, she sent Hanet to be one of the many *valets de chambre* in the newborn's household at Montreuil. Organizing a household was not an easy undertaking for any governess of France's children. It included the establishment of 15 to 20 distinct areas of responsibility such as the stables, the chapel, the bedchamber, the cellar, the wardrobe, the kitchen, the fruit room, the pantry, the fur room, the facilities, the council, and many other departments. The dignity of the princess as governess could not be suitably maintained without such elaborate undertakings. Staffing, supervising, and compensating the servants in each of these departments was an enormous task for the care of any royal child.

Due to the intense and time-consuming duties of the Princess de Guéménée, the two brothers were thus separated from each other for most of the next three years with Cléry employed in Versailles as the princess's secretary, and Hanet serving as Madame Royale's valet Montreuil. In 1781 Marie-Antoinette finally gave birth to the first dauphin of France, Prince Louis Joseph.

Princess Guéménée's Troubles

Being attached to the household of the Princess de Guéménée when she became royal governess to the queen's children was a chance of a lifetime for any servant, but there were risks involved. Should the governess ever fall from grace, it was known that her staff would go down with her.

One day the princess came very close to losing the royal family's favor. France had waited for a very long time to celebrate the birth of the young dauphin, the future king of France, but the entire court was in shock when they discovered that the prince one day came very close to being poisoned.

One of the princess's staff, Madame Duparc, who was in charge of preparing the dauphin's meals, decided to let her assistant prepare a *panade,* a soup made with bread crumbs. Instead of using the mortar and pestle to grind the bread, she used a wine bottle to roll the bread into fine pieces, obtaining the same result. The king and queen always tried to assist when it was time to feed the young prince, and on this occasion, they found the soup to be too hot for the child. Another servant took a spoonful to let it cool, but he noticed a strange coloring and odor, and he asked a doctor who was present to examine the soup.

The king and queen broke into tears when they were informed that there were splinters of green glass in the soup. Unaware of who might have been capable of such a deplorable act, the Princess de Guéménée felt responsible and immediately turned pale. Moments later she went into convulsions, fainted, and had to be carried away to her chambers.

Madame Duparc was dismissed from her duties in the royal household when it was discovered that she had been negligent in allowing her assistant to prepare the child's soup. Apparently, there were small bubbles that formed in the glass bottle when it was fabricated, and when the assistant rolled the stale bread with the bottle, the pressure caused the bubbles of glass to burst and become mixed in with the bread crumbs. The king and queen cried with joy that the young prince had escaped death, but the princess felt as if she had failed them in her duty as royal governess to the children of France.

The Princess de Guéménée came from a very honorable, wealthy, and noble family. Although there was no reason why she would not be worthy of the position of royal governess, she did have her faults. She gave extravagant parties at the Montreuil estate, often inviting the queen to join in at the gambling tables. Surprisingly, the princess had even once been caught cheating. She was convicted of the crime, but in aristocratic circles, she was nevertheless admired for her role in society and her duty as wife and mother. She was not punished for her crime, but ribbons were soon tied around the gambling tables to separate the players from the spectators, and to "render dishonesty more difficult."

Queen Marie-Antoinette frequented the Princess de Guéménée's parties quite regularly, because the king always retired very early in the evening. If the queen lost one evening at the tables, chances were she would win another night. In any event, the king was always ready to pay her debts. However, it could be said that the Princess was an unsuitable companion for the queen due to the late hours, the undesirable company, and the queen's chronically empty purse. The princess was also blamed for introducing the queen to Madame de Polignac, a woman who would eventually become incredibly wealthy, but at the queen's expense.

Princess de Guéménée with Madame Royale

The princess always dressed elegantly and hosted the grandest of parties in Paris, and money was never an object. Unknowingly, however, she paved the way for one of the most embarrassing and perhaps most disastrous bankruptcies in France, a scandal that would affect most of the nobles of Parisian society. In fact, people from all walks of life, from soldiers and servants to counts and dukes, had invested their savings in the house of Guéménée. Little did they know of the extravagant debts that the princess for years had accumulated, including such expenses as personally tailored boots and gowns, or even exquisitely designed wallpaper for the rooms of her estate.

The Prince and Princess de Guéménée were forced to sell their belongings including their residence at Montreuil, the manor that they had built near Versailles. To help the noble family, the king purchased the manor and gave it to his younger sister, Madame Elisabeth. Being only 17 at the time, the king would not let her sleep at the manor, however, until she had celebrated her 25th birthday.

In any event, the Guéménée dynasty was now in complete ruin. Court etiquette would not allow the Princess de Guéménée who was defamed by the bankruptcy to remain at Versailles as a royal governess to Their Majesties' children. She was immediately replaced with Queen Marie-Antoinette's newest friend, Madame de Polignac.

When the Princess Guéménée was taking leave of the court of Versailles, she bid her daughter-in-law, the Duchesse of Montbazon, farewell, saying: "I hope, despite this unfortunate event, that you are not any less happy with the name that you carry."

"No, Madame, as long as Monsieur Montbazon is an honest man."

Madame de Polignac

Many courtiers were upset with the queen's decision to appoint Madame de Polignac as governess to her children, because the position had traditionally required a person of higher nobility. Furthermore, the new royal governess began assigning her own servants to the newly administered royal household. She was unaware that the Princess de Guéménée had promised Cléry that he would one day be *valet de chambre* of the first prince born to the king and queen. Since his position was more or less guaranteed, the prior governess had also arranged for the marriage of Cléry to the court harpist, Mademoiselle Duverger, the daughter of a prominent innkeeper in Vaucresson.

Unemployed and therefore unable to marry, Cléry was understandably depressed. One afternoon, however, Hanet had just finished an errand for the queen when she asked him, "Tell me, what has happened to your brother since Madame de Guéménée has left the court?"

"Madame," he replied, "he was very disappointed to find out that he was no longer going to serve in Your Majesty's household. He was also looking forward to a very happy marriage that the princess had arranged for him. He is now without employ and a wife."

The queen nodded sympathetically, and said: "I am aware of the Princess's promise to appoint Cléry valet de chambre of the Dauphin, but Madame de Polignac has already promised it to another servant. There is nothing I can do to remedy this situation; however, I can promise him the position as valet de chambre to my very next child. Until that day he can serve the King as his barber." She added with a smile, "And then he shall surely be able to marry the Mademoiselle Duverger. I give you my promise."

Hanet's eyes filled with tears of happiness as he listened to the generous queen. He left immediately to tell Cléry the good news. When the queen gave France another prince, Louis Charles, in March 1785, Hanet and his family celebrated Cléry's new position as valet de chambre. Both Hanet and Cléry now served as valets to the royal children of France at the majestic château of Versailles.

There were two highly regarded departments of the royal household that allowed direct access to the royal family, the *bouche du roi* and the *chambre du roi*. The bouche du roi included those services for securing, preparing, serving, and tasting (for security purposes) the king's meals, including table settings and wine service. The chambre du roi, the department which employed Cléry and Hanet, consisted of those servants who had daily access to serve the royal family personally. These positions were extremely coveted and enviable. They included the valets, the governor and governesses, the pages, the barbers and hairdressers, the tailors, the doctors, the musicians, and those who cared for the dogs, the falcons, and the games played at court.

Personally, Cléry was ecstatic. The childhood promise made to him by his prince, now King Louis XVI, had finally come true. His life would be devoted to serving his king, and he took an oath that he would remain loyal to his master for the rest of his life.

First Impressions of the Queen

Queen Marie-Antoinette was not French; she was the daughter of the Austrian Empress Maria Theresa. Her marriage to Louis was a political move, because Austria had often been at war with France. In time, Marie-Antoinette became an enemy of France as well. To make matters worse, scathing pamphlets circulated long before the outbreak of the revolution that painted the queen as an adulteress, a lesbian, and even a scheming traitor. The grossly obscene booklets, certainly instigated by the king's jealous relatives and the appointment of the Duchesse de Polignac, upset the queen to such an extent that she tearfully wrote her mother in Austria about the growing abusive attacks:

> I thought that their insipidity and their bad style were sufficient to condemn them; for I am too young and too generous to fear the growth of such slander, which has not a grain of vital truth or wit to support it. These lies have their origin with my own nobility and disappointed courtiers.

Despite the treacherous slurs, however, Cléry and Hanet saw the queen in a very different light after entering the royal household at Versailles. Their queen was a woman who would take her children with her to help distribute coins to the poor. She was also a faithful patron of the *Maison Philanthropique*, a charitable foundation founded by Louis XVI which helped the blind, the elderly, and the underprivileged.

Libelous image of Marie-Antoinette

Like any royal court, nobles gathered for masquerade balls, lavish feasts, plays, and concerts. Every year at Versailles, however, there was also an extravagant fair where all the merchants of Paris were allowed to bring their best goods and wares for sale. The entire court enjoyed this colorful event, and their purchases were seen to encourage business and industry in France.

Cléry and his brother could not believe their eyes when they saw the variety of exclusive goods being displayed in the booths, especially one exceptionally large doll that had moving parts. They immediately thought of the young Princess Marie-Thérèse, knowing how much she loved such toys. Cléry inquired about the price and let the seller know that they were interested in purchasing it. The seller promised not to sell the doll until they returned with the money.

Hanet, Princess Marie-Thérèse's valet at the time, hurried off to find her chamber maids or her governess, so they could see the doll themselves. Excited, the maids ran to the booth with the princess, but they found that the toy was too expensive even though the princess fell in love with the doll. When they returned to the queen's chambers, the queen noticed that the princess had been crying, and she asked her daughter why she was so sad. "Oh, mama," she replied, "we just saw the most beautiful doll, but these ladies would not buy it for me."

Marie-Antoinette with the children of France: Marie-Thérèse,
Louis Charles, and Louis Joseph. The empty bassinet
represents Sophie-Hélène, who died days after birth.

The queen wiped her tears and said, "Well, if Hanet had been there, he surely would have purchased it for you." The queen was unaware, however, that Hanet was in the next room, and he was able to overhear her remark. He immediately scurried to the booth to buy the special doll himself, and he returned to the queen's chamber as quickly as possible.

Before entering, he announced a guest, calling the doll "Madame, the Countess of Miranda." The princess jumped with joy when she saw the doll, and Hanet said that he had never seen her so surprised. The queen, always ready to reward her servants for their zeal, immediately reimbursed Hanet very generously without even asking how much the doll had cost.

The queen was well aware of the value of her servants to the household, and Cléry noticed that the queen always made sure that they were never overburdened in their work. On one occasion, the queen accidentally left one of her Swiss guards on duty for more than 30 hours without dismissing him. When Cléry decided to let the queen know of the error, she cried, "Oh, my goodness, I totally forgot about him." The queen herself ran to relieve the guard who was on the verge of collapsing. She took his arm to hold him up, and she placed pieces of gold in his hand, "Go, get plenty of rest, my friend," she said. "If I can forget you for thirty hours, you certainly should be able to have plenty of time off from your duties to think about my remorse."

PART TWO

FROM PALACE TO PRISON

Chapter 4
The Final Days at Versailles

Get up, Madame! Do not stay here to dress yourself!
Hurry at once to the King's apartments!

–Lady-in-waiting to Queen Marie-Antoinette
Versailles, October 5, 1789

Cléry and his brother would spend the next four years as valets de chambre serving the queen's children at Versailles. The first two years were exceptionally happy. The queen now had three children and she was expecting another addition to the royal family. The king's subjects were happy, and their harvests were yielding more than enough wheat for the winter months.

Marie-Antoinette spent much of her leisure time at the Petit Trianon, a small château near the palace that Louis had given her as a gift. There she could escape the burden of her court responsibilities, and play with her daughter or dress as a milk maid in the idyllic setting. No one was permitted to enter the property without permission by order of the queen; even the king had to ask permission. Her favorites, the Princess de Lamballe and Madame de Polignac, however, were always welcome.

King Louis often visited the Petit Trianon as a spectator when the queen and her closest friends had parts in plays that were presented in its small theatre. "Oh, Louis, how good you are!" said the queen with tears in her eyes. "I know indeed how little pleasure you find in these foolish pastimes, and yet you sacrifice your own wishes and take part in our diversions."

"That is because I love you!" said the king with simplicity, and a smile of pleasure covered his good-natured face. "Yes, Marie, I love you tenderly, and it gives me joy to contribute to your happiness."

The queen gently laid her arm around Louis's neck, and let her head fall upon his shoulder. "Do you still know, Louis," she asked, "do you still know what you said to me when you gave Trianon to me?"

"Well..." said the king, shaking his head slowly.

"You said that I loved flowers, so you were going to present me with a whole bouquet, the Little Trianon!" she answered with a warm smile. "My dear sire," she added, "you have given me not only a bouquet of flowers, but a bouquet of pleasant hours, of happy years, for which I thank you, and you alone."

"And may this bouquet never wither, Marie!" said the king with a sparkle in his eyes.

Such were the happy times that the queen spent in Trianon, enjoying the simple, and undisturbed, country life far from the eyes of the court. She wrote her brother Joseph, "I feel more a Queen in my gardens than anywhere else. My trees and flowers do not fatigue me like the etiquette of court."

The queen even had a spinning wheel brought to the Trianon. Sitting upon a low stool, she would begin to spin her wool. How quickly the wheel would turn, as if it were the wheel of fortune— today bringing joy but tomorrow bringing only calamity. Times would soon not be so memorable for the queen.

Marie-Antoinette was known to be overindulgent; money was never an obstacle for her. She was known to have often purchased expensive diamond necklaces and bracelets, but on one occasion she curiously refused an offer to buy an exquisite necklace that was worth millions of French francs. A scandal soon evolved, however, in which the queen was unknowingly involved in, and accused of, purchasing the outrageously expensive jewels. Although a lengthy trial resulted in establishing the queen's innocence, witty songs and pamphlets portraying the queen as a spendthrift, and a prostitute, were rampant in the streets of Paris. This very public trial was the turning point in the happy lives of the royal couple at Versailles; it would also be the same, however, for Cléry and his brother as well.

Sadly, the dauphin was beginning to show signs of curvature of the spine. His body was also covered with tumors that tormented him to the point that the court physicians and servants were obliged to stay up with him throughout the night. Because the child's illness disrupted court etiquette, the king ordered that food and drink be served at night to the private chambers of the king, the queen, and all the royal children, which included two large pots of soup, two roasted chickens, eight freshly baked rolls, eight fresh eggs, and two bottles of the palace's best Bordeaux wine. Soon the practice was continued not only through the night, but in the morning and afternoon as well.

Although the routine feasts were provided with the best intentions, they soon became very costly. To make matters worse, anything that remained after the mealtimes was sold by the valets at a profit outside the palace. Hundreds of thousands of francs were being spent annually for the lavish meals; fortunately, Cléry and his brother were not involved in the abuse. Despite the fact that Hanet brought the unethical practice to the king's attention in a memo that he wrote to the governess, Madame de Polignac, the abuse continued for two years until the 8-year old Dauphin Louis Joseph died in 1789.

Louis Joseph's younger brother, Louis Charles, then became dauphin, the next male heir to the throne. Since Cléry had been the personal valet to Louis Charles, he thus became the personal servant of the dauphin, one of the most coveted positions at court.

In the meantime, Marie-Antoinette had given birth to Princess Sophie, but the young princess suddenly died when she was only 11 months old. Regrettably, the queen's subjects no longer mourned for the "children of France" as had been the custom for many centuries. Since the scandal of the diamond necklace, the ordinary Frenchman came to believe that the queen was the cause of the country's financial despair. Her subjects even shouted "Madame Deficit" when she attended the opera one evening, instead of the usual "Long live the queen!" More damning, she had also been falsely accused of sending large sums of money to her brother in Austria, France's longtime enemy.

Cléry and his brother had also suffered a great loss. Their father, Benjamin, passed away because of injuries sustained after a horseback riding injury. He had been injured while assisting King Louis XVI on one of the royal hunting outings near his home in Vaucresson, as was required of the king's subjects. When the king discovered that Benjamin was the father of two of his servants, the valets de chambre for Princess Marie-Thérèse and the Dauphin Louis Charles, he remembered that he was the farmer who broke the key to his courtyard gate at the Jardy farm when he was a young prince. From the time of the accident, the king regularly sent a courier to check on the condition of his servants' father before he passed away.

Cléry and Hanet were summoned to their father's bedside just before he died. Hanet arrived first, and Benjamin took his son's hand and put it on his heart, "I am finishing my career here at Jardy," he said. "You must promise me that you will take over for me here, and never abandon your heartbroken mother, your brothers, or your sisters."

"Yes, my father, yes!" cried Hanet. "I swear on this crucifix that you are holding in our hands." Although Cléry had not arrived in time to bid his father a final farewell, Hanet wrote that his father's dying eyes searched the room for Cléry before he closed them for the very last time.

Hanet took the solemn promise to his father very seriously. Although Cléry wanted to share Hanet's duties to take care of the family, Hanet convinced him that his father wanted Cléry to continue his service to the king in the royal household at Versailles. Since Hanet received the family inheritance, it was agreed that Hanet would care not only for his mother and brothers, but he would also support Cléry's wife and bring up his four children as well. Hanet told Cléry that he was determined to honor his father's last wishes and remain on the family's estate, convincing Cléry that he was destined to remain in the service of the royal family. That was Cléry's calling, his dream, and his lifetime ambition.

"There Is No Bread Today!"

The winter of early 1789 was long and treacherous. The royal family did their very best to help the poor. In fact, they often used their personal funds to help feed and clothe their subjects, but by summertime the people were in full revolt. About half of the workers of Paris and the surrounding areas were now unemployed. As a result, on the 14th of July, the Bastille, a fortress prison and a symbol of the monarchy's power, was ransacked by a crowd of irrational Parisians.

During the night of the 13th, the shops of the bakers and wine-sellers were pillaged. The Parisians were armed with muskets, pikes, and skewers as they forced open the doors of the shops and homes to get food, drink, money, and arms. To have arms for the following day was the desire of all the rebels; citizens and those in support of order needed arms to protect themselves from the rebels. There was a rush to the Invalides, where the magazines of arms were kept. This was the first violent action of the day. The mob carried off 28,000 muskets and 24 cannon. It was known that other munitions of war were stored in the Bastille, and the cry of "To the Invalides!" was soon followed by "To the Bastille!"

The Fall of the Bastille

The sole motive impelling this mob to the Bastille was the wish to procure arms. There were no cries for liberty from tyranny, for setting the prisoners free, or for protesting against royal authority. In fact, the capture of the Bastille was carried out amid cries of "Vive le roi!" At least a thousand men were thronging around the Bastille wildly. The garrison's leaders swore not to fire unless they were attacked, but the crowd was becoming more and more threatening. Suddenly, two daring rebels dashed forward and scaled the roof of the guard house, they shattered the chains of the drawbridge with their axes, and it fell. Soon afterwards the prison's warden and his guards were captured and beheaded, and their heads were paraded on the top of pikes throughout the capital's streets.

When the king learned that the Bastille had been taken, he was reported to have asked, "Is this a revolt?" and his informant replied, "No, Sire, it is a revolution." Little did the king know that his angry subjects' next plan of action was to march on the château of Versailles, and to force the royal family to return to Paris with them.

As the smoke cleared from the fall of the Bastille, Versailles soon became the object of the people's discontent. The Duchesse de Polignac, the children's governess, and other court favorites were forced into exile.

Bread was also becoming more and more expensive, and people waited in lines for the chance to purchase it, only to find on the 5th of October that the supplies of bread were finally exhausted. "There is no bread today!" cried the women in the streets.

Soon the fishwives and other women who worked in the market stalls stormed the Hôtel de Ville, demanding bread. They even broke into the town hall and managed to ring the *tocsin*, the bell which was used to sound an alarm that alerted the neighborhoods to join in the revolt. In their wrath, they managed to overtake the guards, take their arms, and begin their 14-mile march to Versailles on foot. Men tried to take control, but the women argued that "men did not know how to take action." Armed with pikes, axes, and knives, the increasing numbers of women made their way to the king's palace in Versailles, not at all hindered by the pouring rain.

à Versailles à Versailles *le 5 oct. 1789*

By 6 o'clock the next morning, the women had arrived in Versailles and they broke through the gates to the palace. They cut off the heads of two guards, and managed to break into the queen's apartment, yelling: "Kill the whore! Kill the whore!"

The queen had managed, however, to escape through a secret passage to the king's chamber, but his door was locked. The king's servants would not open it, thinking it was the violent mob trying to kill the king. Fortunately, the king's waiter, Louis-François de Turgy, recognized the queen's voice, and he opened the door for her immediately. The king and queen were soon joined by their frightened children. Turgy would never have imagined that, because of his courage that night, he would one day join forces with Cléry to help the royal family again.

Tens of thousands of the king's subjects gathered in the palace courtyard, calling for him to show himself to his subjects. He bravely went to the window to let his people see him, and curiously the mood changed when he appeared. "Long live the King!" shouted the crowd when he appeared on the balcony. The queen was also forced to appear before her subjects. With her son in her arms, she too received roars of "Long live the Queen!"

The Peasants' March on Versailles

Overnight, however, the crowd became more impatient and demanding. Shouts of "To Paris, the King must come to Paris!" filled the morning air. The king's ministers agreed that the royal family needed to comply with the people's demands to avoid any more bloodshed. The king, the queen, their 11-year-old daughter, their 4-year-old son, the king's sister Elisabeth, and the children's new governess, Madame de Tourzel, soon found themselves in the royal carriage surrounded by the fishwives and soldiers en route to Paris. It was one o'clock in the afternoon. A hundred deputies in other carriages followed in the drizzling rain.

A group of rogue rebels had set off two hours earlier, carrying the heads of the king's guards on pikes in triumph. The enraged group was so ferocious that it stopped on the way to Paris in the village of Sèvres, and forced a barber to dress the hair of the two bleeding heads. The army of fishwives and other women marched in front of the royal carriage, still drunk with fury and wine. Several of them walked near the king's carriage, singing vulgar tunes with gross gestures directed at the queen. Others yelled, "We shall have bread now that we have the baker, the baker's wife and the baker's boy."

Such was the trip of the disgraced royal family from Versailles to Paris on the 6th of October 1789. The procession of over 200,000 royal subjects filled the road for several miles. The eight-hour trip was accompanied by the firing of muskets and the chanting of vulgar, threatening songs before arriving at the Tuileries at 10 o'clock in the evening.

The drama of the Tuileries was about to begin. The first major compromising event in Cléry's life as valet de chambre of the dauphin occurred when the royal family finally arrived at the uninhabited palace, about 15 miles from Versailles. Cléry, separated from the royal family during the tumultuous riots, had been forced to follow this terrifying procession to Paris on foot. Exhausted, he was unable to arrive in time to fulfill one of his royal duties—to receive his young master, Prince Louis Charles, whenever he descended from his royal coach.

In Cléry's place, however, an unknown gentleman had fortunately taken the young prince in his arms when he was handed down from the carriage. The man placed the child on the front steps of the palace. When the queen descended from her coach and did not see Cléry, the crowd heard her pitiable scream of despair not knowing what had happened to her youngest child, the next heir to the throne of France. The frantic queen was soon consoled, however, when the unknown citizen took the prince's hand and made his way through the crowd to the queen. When Cléry finally arrived on the scene completely out of breath, the stranger, bowing with tears in his eyes, was presenting the prince to the very grateful queen. Not only did Cléry now understand the importance of always adhering to court etiquette, but he also realized how dearly the queen loved her children.

The first evening in the Tuileries was complete chaos. The medieval palace had not been inhabited for more than 100 years, and no preparations had been made for the royal family's arrival. It was out of repair, unfurnished, and undecorated. The doors would not lock, the paint on the floors was worn and cracked, and the tapestries were hanging in rags from the walls.

"Mama, everything is so ugly here," said the dauphin, "and I am hungry."

"My son," replied the queen, "Louis XIV lived here, and he liked it. We must not be more exacting than the great king." The queen could not restrain her tears when the dauphin complained of hunger.

Discovering that the young princess was dying of hunger too, the kitchen staff scurried off to prepare a meal for the family. Everyone had to do the best that they could to find a place to rest. The king whimpered, "Each one must arrange as best he can for himself." If lucky, the royals and their staff might have found an armchair, a chaise, or a ledge on which to sleep. The king and his queen were certain that they would manage this night in the strange environment, but they had no idea that they would never in their lifetime return to the luxury of their château in Versailles.

The next day the king accompanied the queen on a tour of the gloomy palace. They selected between them the rooms they wished to occupy and gave orders for such repairs as were absolutely necessary. Louis chose a suite of rooms on the second floor, with a couple of smaller ones below. He took for his bedroom the one that Louis XIV had occupied in his time. Marie Antoinette had her apartments on the first floor, level with the garden, comprising a bedroom, a dressing room, and a boudoir. Her children were upstairs close to the king. The king's aunts, who had accompanied the family to Paris, lived in Marsan's Pavilion, formerly occupied by the governesses of Louis XIV's children. A section of the Flora Pavilion was arranged for the Princess Elisabeth, the other for the Princesse de Lamballe.

During the week following their arrival in Paris, Louis and Marie-Antoinette received visits from most of the city's principal citizens, and they were all welcomed with kindness by the king, who seemed to have quickly forgotten the disturbances in Versailles.

From this point on, Cléry was required to live in Paris at the Tuileries Palace while the royal family was under house arrest. Cléry was only permitted to return to his family near Versailles on very special occasions. It is an understatement to say that he lived in constant fear for the lives of the royal family, as well as his own. His brother Hanet was no longer employed in the royal household; instead, he was forced to join the National Guard.

Since the fall of the Bastille, many members of the queen's intimate circle had been forced into exile. The Duchesse de Polignac, the former governess to the royal children since the financial ruin of the Princess de Guéménée, was forced to cross the border to Switzerland to avoid the wrath of the revolutionaries; in fact, there was a price on her head. A story in a French newspaper revealed the anger of the Parisians:

> Three days ago a child of four years old, but well taught and full of intelligence, made the round of the garden in full daylight, carried on the shoulders of a porter. He kept crying, "Decree of the French people: La Polignac exiled to a hundred leagues from Paris, Condé the same, Conti the same, d'Artois the same, the Queen...I dare not tell you the rest."

In the Duchesse's absence, the queen appointed the Marquise de Tourzel for the vacant post to care for the children. The marquise had always been extremely loyal to the family, and the queen was certain that she would never abandon her position as governess—despite any hardships to come.

Life, as the royals had become accustomed to at Versailles, would never be the same. Marie-Antoinette's hair began to turn gray since the shock of the violent attack on Versailles and the frightening trip to Paris. The king was no longer allowed to hunt, he had lost many of his royal powers, and he quickly gained weight resulting in his famous double chin.

The Family Flees Paris

For the next three years, the members of the royal family at the Tuileries Palace had no choice but to ride out the storm. Their former palace in Versailles had been ransacked and left in shambles. Moreover, their popularity had deteriorated immensely. However, the *Mesdames*, the king's old aunts, were known to have safely crossed the border, and plans were thus soon made for the royal family to flee from Paris.

The Swedish Count Axel de Fersen, supposedly Marie-Antoinette's lover, was in Paris, and he supervised the building of a strong *berline*, or traveling coach, and a lighter carriage capable of holding two ladies-in-waiting. The Marquis de Bouillé, the governor of Metz, had his soldiers ready to march at a moment's notice. Finally, passports were prepared for a Baroness de Korff, a Russian lady returning home with her two children, a governess, a maid-in-waiting, a valet, a courier, and other servants.

The queen confided in her 12-year old daughter, Marie-Thérèse, telling her that her little brother was to be dressed as a little girl. When she saw the prince, the princess giggled, crying out, "Oh, mama, how charming!" It was one of the few occasions that the family ever laughed under the tense circumstances.

The queen herself went with Madame de Tourzel, who represented the Baroness de Korff, and she saw the three safely into a coach waiting outside one of the courts of the Tuileries before returning to the palace. For greater precaution, the dauphin was placed on the floor of the coach, half hidden by Madame de Tourzel's skirts. No doubt he amused himself playing a game of bo-peep, and, being in disguise, he naturally supposed that he was about to take part in a play similar to those in the Trianon's theatre.

Madame Elizabeth, in a cloak and hood like Madame de Tourzel, and leaning on the arm of a servant, joined the party. As she entered the carriage, she accidently stepped on her little nephew who amazingly did not utter a cry. The king arrived in the round hat and *perruque*, or wig, of a valet. He also walked arm in arm with a servant. Fersen, as the coachman, was seated atop the carriage. The party was ready, but where was the Queen? Her companions waited almost an hour for her in desperate anxiety.

Inside the palace the queen's foolish preoccupation with her dressing case and the careful packing of her diamonds had aroused the suspicion of the sharp-eyed woman of her wardrobe who in turn told her lover, one of the National Guardsmen, about the queen's behavior. Information of the intended flight was then transmitted to Lafayette, the leader of the National Guard, who was in charge of the royal family's custody, but he did not believe the story at first.

To everyone's relief, the queen finally found her way to the coach in a plain gown and a gypsy hat, accompanied by one of her former body guards dressed as a courier. She represented the maid-in-waiting of the Baroness de Korff, and, ironically, had often played the part of such a character in her own theatre at Versailles.

Fersen immediately drove the party at great speed to a secret meeting place where the large berline awaited them. The travelers changed vehicles, abandoning the coach on the road, and Fersen, atop the large berline, conducted the party to the village of Bondy, where the smaller carriage with the maids-in-waiting had been sent in advance. Then the Baroness de Korff, her governess-companion Madame Rochet, her valet-de-chambre Durand, her waiting-maid Rosalie, and her daughters Amélie and Aglae, drove off in the summer night. For a time the royal family's plan was proceeding as planned.

The first of the relays of horses and escorts of troopers which De Bouillé had posted all along the road turned up at the town of Châlons, and the queen thanked God, albeit prematurely, that they were saved. Unfortunately, the soldiers' presence attracted attention, and did more harm than good. The men, while they waited, lounged about the villages, drank in the cabarets, and even quarreled with the villagers. Incredibly, the king would also look out of the carriage windows, and even descend from the coach to walk up the hills. As he did so, his placid features impressed the persons he encountered with a strange sense of familiarity.

Drouet, the postmaster of one of the villages, recognized the king from his likeness on an *assignat*, paper currency of the revolution. A fiery republican, the old man galloped on horseback to the next town through which the berline was to pass to warn the authorities. He did not make it before the royals, but he managed to reach the next town of Varennes before them.

The king was expecting more relays of horses, and additional troops, but when the berline stopped close to midnight on the hilltop above the sleeping town of Varennes, not a horse or rider was to be seen.

"Assignat" with portrait of Louis XVI

The horsemen of the berline waited for half-an-hour in doubt and dismay, because they were reluctant to drive on without fresh horses. The postmaster actually passed the royal carriage with his message, carrying it on to the Bras d'Or tavern where he whispered it in the inn keeper's ear. A group of villagers soon formed a barricade with wagons and barrels across the bridge over the river Aire where the royal party would need to cross.

When the berline at last arrived in the village, muskets were presented, passports were demanded, and the mayor arrested the travelers. The king took his children by the hand, the mayor offered an arm each to the Queen and Madame Elizabeth, and the royal family crossed the market square under the flickering light of the few torches which broke the dismal darkness. The group entered the mayor's house, and went upstairs to his living quarters, while the alarm was rung from the church spire, and alarmed patriots, roused from their sleep, flocked to the little square.

What could the queen do now but weep for the king and for herself, lay her weary children on the first bed that she could find, and beg the mayor, his wife, and his mother to save the lives of these innocent royal children. The family was amazed by the queen's bequest, but was definitely not unkind to her. In fact, the mayor's mother, unable to shake off the traditions of her youth, fell on her knees before the unexpected guests.

King Louis XVI captured in Varennes

When the news of the king's flight reached Paris, it excited the people into another one of their fits of madness, and the infection spread quickly. The Assembly issued an order to seize the king wherever he might be found, and to bring him back to Paris. One of Lafayette's couriers carried the decree to Varennes, where, after six hours of uncertainty amidst a crowd that was becoming more and more threatening, the king and queen awaited the will of the nation. Marie Antoinette heard the tidings with great despair, and she demanded to read the decree of the Assembly herself.

"The insolents!" cried the queen, throwing the decree down, which fell on the bed where the children slept. She quickly snatched it up and flung it on the ground. "It would soil my children's bed," she snapped angrily, "such vile debris."

The berline and its royal passengers returned to Paris among scores of thousands of National Guards, travelling so slowly that four days were spent on the humiliating journey. Two deputies, Pétion and Barnave, had been sent from Paris to guarantee the return of the king; they rode along with the family inside the crowded berline. Both were selected because of their hostile stance against the royals. The graying Pétion sat unmoved between the princesses Elisabeth and Marie-Therese, eating his food without ceremony and tossing his chicken bones past the king's face out of the window. He allowed Madame Elizabeth to pour his wine, calling on her to stop in a gruff voice. He also touted his republican opinions in reply to Louis's civil remarks, and in the heat of his argument pulled the dauphin's curly hair, who sat on one of the women's knees, until the child cried out with pain.

Young Barnave, however, declined to eat in royal family's presence. He was so respectfully attentive that the queen was touched by his generous sympathy. From that moment on, whatever opinions he had held formerly as a revolutionary, he strove to save the monarchy. Little did he know that in doing so, however, he was signing his own death warrant.

Like criminals caught red-handed, the king and queen arrived in Paris on a Saturday afternoon, six days after they had left it in disguise, only to find ferocious crowds assembled in the streets. One hundred thousand Parisians waited for a glimpse of the family, gloating and jeering at their misery. The watch on the prisoners at the Tuileries grew stricter than ever, and it was now maintained night and day.

King Louis XVI had lost the loyalty of his subjects, and he was being caricatured as a horned pig in pamphlets and in the press.

But Louis was by no means dim-witted; he was an avid reader, and he was fluent in English, Italian, and German. Nevertheless, it is well-known that he lacked self-confidence, and this has duly been noted as a key to his character and conduct throughout his reign. Even in Varennes, the king could possibly have saved the day by calling on his escorts to fight back the villagers in defiance and charge onward to the border. On the contrary, he sat at the villager's table and supped on cheese and wine. "This is perhaps the best Bordeaux that I have ever tasted," he remarked, complimenting his host.

Since the day Louis was crowned king, he had never felt at ease with the eloquently mannered nobles who surrounded him at his court. This feeling of apartness or oddness only enhanced his shyness, which he was never able to overcome. After the unsuccessful flight to Varennes, the king would never take an active role in his political or family life, leaving the queen to take the reins.

Caricature of Louis XVI

Unfortunately, the prior King Louis XV had never involved his grandson in public affairs, whether it was due to the prince's shyness or the king's lack of confidence in the boy. The prince's governor, the Duc de la Vauguyon, never inspired him to have confidence in himself when he was growing up. Nor did he teach him how to, one day, become the King of France. Louis XVI himself cried out, "They have taught me nothing!" when he ascended to the throne.

Louis not only lost the loyalty of his subjects and his noble courtiers, but he soon lost most of his royal functions when he signed the constitution that established a newly elected Assembly. Actually, the new government only allowed the king the right of veto. He would use this veto, however, to prevent 20,000 priests from being deported out of the country for political reasons, but his veto unfortunately met the backlash of an angry constituency. In response, the Tuileries was invaded on the 20th of June, and the king and his family were held hostage for hours because of his unrelenting stance. Although the king never retracted the unpopular veto, he did temporarily gain some favor for upholding the new French Constitution in doing so.

Unfortunately, the favor soon dwindled, and the king was soon seen to be counter-revolutionary for his refusal to give in to any of the Assembly's reforms. An organized insurrection was soon planned, and the mayor of Paris, Jérôme Pétion, sanctioned the distribution of arms to the angry Parisians. The relative calm at the Tuileries was soon to be shattered.

Chapter 5
August of 1792

"My children?" she cried, pressing them to her bosom. "No, I will not let them be murdered!"

–Queen Marie-Antoinette to King Louis XVI
Tuileries Palace, 1792

The Marquise de Tourzel, the new governess to the Dauphin Louis Charles after Madame de Polignac's departure, loved savoring the late afternoon sun and the sweet, pungent scent of lilacs in the gardens of the Tuileries Palace as she kept watch over her charge. The queen had especially asked the marquise to help the frail dauphin overcome his fear of loud noises such as barking dogs.

The dauphin had no suspicion of the misfortunes that were threatening the royal family since their arrival in Paris. In fact, the queen often remarked that he was like sunshine in the gloomy, damp palace, and that his merry little smile actually helped her learn to smile again. Fortunately, the strict adherence to house arrest orders was gradually relaxed, and the royal family was at least permitted to leave the humid, hot rooms and go down into the palace gardens, although still watched and accompanied by the National Guard.

There were even some periods when it appeared as if the throne might be reestablished with a portion of its dignity. The king had, in a sense, received forgiveness from the National Assembly by accepting the country's new constitution. Although most of his previous powers had been taken from him, he was still considered a figure head and he could still govern, but only according to the expressed will of the National Assembly.

Louis accepted the constitution as an effort to make peace with his people, and his subjects seemed grateful to him for his sacrifice. The queen was no longer insulted with obscenities when she appeared in the garden of the Tuileries, and it even became very fashionable in Paris to speak about the handsome young dauphin. In fact crowds would wait for hours outside the gates of the Tuileries to catch a glimpse of him working in his own little garden.

The dauphin had been given a small garden located by the small pavilion where his teacher, the Abbé Davout, lived. He himself worked and planted flowers in the space surrounded by a high wire fence, and every morning he would pick a bouquet and bring it to his "mama queen" after tending to a small family of rabbits that he had received as a gift.

The prince missed his larger garden at Versailles, but the little patch on the terrace of the Tuileries Palace delighted him, and every morning, when his study hours were over with the Abbé, he scurried to his little *Eldorado* to water his flowers and feed his pets. Parisians soon became even more enthusiastic about the royals as they marveled at the prince's sky blue eyes from behind the fence.

When the prince went into his garden, he was usually accompanied by a detachment of the National Guard that was on duty in the Tuileries. The dauphin generally wore the uniform of the Guard, and the people were delighted with the six-year old soldier. His picture was hung in all the shops, it was painted on fans and rings, and it was the fashion, among the most elegant ladies of Paris, and among the market women as well, to decorate themselves with the likeness of the dauphin.

The Parisians often remarked how he beamed and how his eyes sparkled when he entered his garden, always accompanied by an escort. At times when the size of the Guard was small, the prince would even join in the ranks of the regiment. One day, when all the guardsmen on duty wanted to accompany him in the garden, several of them were compelled to stand outside the fence. "Pardon me, gentlemen," said the dauphin. "It is a great pity that my garden is so small that it deprives me of the pleasure of receiving you all." Then he hastened to give flowers to everyone who was near the fence.

The interest in the dauphin was so great that Parisian boys envied the guards in his service, and they longed to become soldiers so that they might be in his regiment. There was, in fact, a regiment of boys formed, named the "Dauphin's Regiment," and citizens of Paris were all too anxious to enroll the names of their sons in this regiment, and pay the expenses of any equipment as well.

When this miniature regiment was formed, naturally with the king's permission, it marched to the Tuileries, in order to parade before the dauphin. The prince was so delighted with his new regiment that he invited its officers to visit his garden and admire his flowers.

"Would you do us the pleasure to be the colonel of our regiment?" one of the young officers asked the dauphin.

"Oh, certainly!" he answered.

"Then you should give up working in your garden and growing flowers for your mamma." said one of the boys.

"Oh!" answered the dauphin with a smile, "being a colonel will not hinder me from taking care of my garden. Many of these gentlemen have little gardens, too, as they have told me. They can follow the example of their colonel, and love the queen, and then mamma will receive regiments of flowers every day."

The majority of this regiment consisted, at the outset, of children of the highest ranks of French society, and it was therefore natural that they would want to pay some deference to their young colonel. But they were expressly forbidden by the king to show any tribute toward their young comrade. "For," said the king, "I want him to have companions who will stimulate his ambition; I do not want him to have flatterers, who shall lead him to live to himself alone."

Soon the number of little soldiers increased, because every family longed for the honor of having its sons in the Dauphin's Regiment. The people always thronged in the streets when the regiment practiced it exercises in the courtyard. It was a miniature representation of the French guards with the boys wearing their three-cornered hats and tailored white jackets.

The enthusiasm of the little soldiers for their colonel was so great that they wanted to give him a token of their affection. One day the officers of the regiment came to the Tuileries and begged the king's permission to give the dauphin a present, in the name of the whole regiment. The king gladly agreed to their request, and he himself conducted the little officers into the reception room where the dauphin was standing at his mother's side.

The little prince scurried to greet them. "Welcome, comrades, welcome!" he cried, extending his hand to them. "My mamma queen tells me that you have brought me something that I will like, but it gives me so much pleasure just to see you that nothing more is really needed."

"But, colonel, you will not refuse our present?" asked one of the boys.

"Oh, certainly not, for my papa king says that a colonel is not forbidden from getting a gift from his regiment. What is it?" asked the prince cheerfully.

Dauphin Louis Charles in his uniform

"Colonel, we bring you a set of dominoes, a set made entirely from the ruins of the Bastille," replied a little officer by the name of Palloy. He then handed the box to the dauphin, and repeated the following lines with a solemn look:

> Those gloomy walls that once awoke our fear
> Are changed into the toy we offer here,
> And when with joyful face the gift you view,
> Think what the people's mighty love can do.

The poor child! Even when the boys wanted to do their prince homage, they were actually insulting, even threatening, him. The present was offered to the dauphin with affection, but at the same time it was a legacy of the revolution. It mirrored the hate of the king's people that had destroyed the "dreary walls of the Bastille," walls that represented centuries of royal power. Fortunately, in his innocence and simplicity, the child saw nothing of the sting which, unknown even to the givers, lurked within this gift.

He enjoyed the gift like any other child would, and he listened with eagerness as the rules of the game were described to him.

It was a curious gift, indeed. All of the stones were taken from the black marble mantel of the reception room of Delaunay, the governor of the Bastille, who had been murdered by the people. On the back of each of these stones was a letter inscribed in gold, and when the pieces of the set were arranged in order, they formed the sentence: *"Long live the King, long live the Queen, and the Dauphin."*

The Parisian's Become Restless Again

The Marquise de Tourzel enjoyed occupying herself with the delightful dauphin and their daily promenade in the gardens of the Tuileries. On one day in particular she noticed that that the prince had his mother's large blue eyes, and how his long blonde curls framed his charming face. Dressed in his military jacket with golden epaulettes, he was kneeling in front of his rabbits as he knighted them one at a time with his intricately carved wooden sword. Cléry, his personal valet, smiled but cautiously kept an eye on the suspicious onlookers outside the garden gates—all wanting to catch a glimpse of the future king of France.

One of the soldiers guarding the royal palace watched as the dauphin fed his rabbits. He approached the prince and leaned over to pet one of them. Picking it up, he rubbed its ears as the prince proudly watched. Smiling, the soldier held the rabbit up high in the air for the onlookers to see through the garden fence. The rabbit gave a quick squeal, however, as the soldier snapped its neck with a quick twist of the wrist. The looming crowd roared with laughter as he tossed the convulsing animal to the ground. The laughter soon turned to obscenities, and the people began to shout vile insults against the royals.

The 7-year-old shrieked loudly as Cléry, who was standing nearby, and the marquise rushed to calm the prince before he dared to strike the guard. They each grabbed a hand and pulled him away. Leaving the small gate to his garden open, a few rabbits began to escape and the little prince stubbornly refused to leave his garden, not knowing the danger that prevailed. Throwing a tantrum on the spot, he stomped on his governess's toe. "What?" she scolded the child. "You, a Prince, who the whole world has their eyes upon!"

The dauphin lowered his head shamefully and then fell to his knees tearfully asking for her forgiveness. Cléry quickly helped him up and told them to hurry to avoid any further abuse by the guards who were beginning to congregate in the garden. The crowds were also becoming increasingly clamorous outside the palace gates.

Madame Tourzel and Dauphin Louis Charles

The royal family had been under house arrest for the past three years. A month earlier the family had tried to escape, but was captured just before crossing the French border. The failed escape only added fuel to the revolutionary fires. In the beginning of August, the fears of conspiracy and war on the borders further agitated the nation.

Once inside the palace, the young prince ran to the king's chamber. King Louis and Queen Marie-Antoinette were being briefed about a new conspiracy that was under way to besiege the palace. They were told that mobs of Parisians were gathering throughout the city, and royalists were clashing with the revolutionaries in the streets. On the queen's instructions, Cléry escorted the prince to his bedroom.

Once the prince was sleeping soundly later that evening, Cléry took the opportunity to leave the palace to get a better picture of the alarming situation. The palace courtyards were swarming with hundreds of Swiss Guards, originally placed there to protect and defend the royal family. Strong and resilient, the Swiss Guard was dedicated to the king; however, they also had become a symbol of the monarchy to the revolutionaries.

Cléry ventured into the city and discovered that the Parisians were menacing the royal guards in the nearby neighborhoods. He later returned to the palace only to find the entire royal court in an anxious, nervous mood. He spent the night talking to royal aides and, in particular, consoling Madame Rambaud who was a lady-in-waiting for the prince.

The royal family, however, was besieged with a crowd of onlookers in the king's bedchamber. The obstinate rebels broke tradition by sitting down in front of the king and by calling him "Monsieur" instead of "Your Highness." As a sign of disrespect, they also refused to remove their hats. Moreover, the king was not allowed to be dressed for bed by his courtiers, a royal custom enjoyed by the monarchs for ages. The queen and her entourage did not undress either. Only the children were able to slept that evening.

Unfortunately, Mandat, the general in charge of the king's guard was assassinated during the night. The next-in-command caused alarm for the royal family since he was known to be a weak leader with suspicious ties to the revolutionary government.

At 6 o'clock in the morning Cléry and Madame Rambaud followed King Louis XVI, Queen Marie-Antoinette, and their children, Prince Louis Charles and Princess Marie-Thérèse, into the gardens to review the troops. Most swore to defend the king amid shouts of "Long live the King! Long live the nation!" Some, however, murmured discontent with the royals. One soldier actually had the audacity to aim his canon at the king as he bid adieu to his royal guard.

After the royal family swiftly returned inside the palace, Cléry decided to venture into the surrounding neighborhoods of Paris again. He was soon confronted, however, with hoards of armed men carrying pikes, axes, and pitchforks calling on peasants to arm themselves and finally remove the tyrant Louis XVI from his throne. Understanding that a rebellion was looming, Cléry returned to the palace only to find that the royal guards were leaving the courtyards with sheer distress painted on their faces. More alarming, conspirators were rapidly infiltrating the grounds and menacing those guards still loyal to the king.

Although Cléry was able to enter the palace, he was refused entrance to the royal quarters, so he remained in the great hall with royal guards stationed at the entry ways and on the grand staircases. Knowing that the guards had been on duty all night long, Cléry enlisted other royal servants to bring them bread and wine and he encouraged them not to abandon the royal family. Danger was becoming more pressing as mobs of peasants began to occupy the palace grounds.

At 8 o'clock in the morning, the king received city officials who urged the royal family to accompany them to safer quarters at the National Assembly, which was within walking distance of the palace. The queen refused to leave, saying: "Never! Sooner than seek shelter among our cruelest persecutors, I would rather nail myself to these walls." She begged the king to use the troops to fight off the rebellion, but the king did not want the blood of his countrymen on his hands.

If the family members did not take refuge in the Assembly, the ministers told the king that they would not be able to guarantee their safety. The queen was told that she was risking the life of her family, her courtiers, and her servants. "Madame, all Paris is in march. It will be impossible to answer for the King's life—for yours—and for your children's," warned the official.

Crowds menace the Tuileries Palace

"My children?" she shouted, pressing them to her breast. "No, I will not let them be murdered." She then conceded, but added that the ministers would ultimately be responsible for the lives of the king and the dauphin. The king raised his head and, after a short pause, turned to the queen and said, "Let us go."

Only Madame de Tourzel and the Princess de Lamballe were permitted to accompany the royal family to the Assembly. The Princess de Lamballe was a young widow whose beauty and charms had drawn her to the attachment of Marie Antoinette. Little did she know that her affection for the royal family and her service and devotion to the queen, in particular, would cause the people to become so odiously suspicious of her. One of the other attendants was determined to disobey the king's order and leave the Tuileries Palace with the family. The young dauphin, however, tried to persuade him, "Stay here, because my papa and mama order it so—I beg you to stay, too."

By 9 o'clock, the royal family, the Princess de Lamballe, and Madame de Tourzel had no choice but to leave the palace due to the frantic chaos of the rebellious crowd trying to break into the palace. The royal *cortege* crossed the rooms, descended the main staircase, went out by the central gate, and then entered the gardens. The National Guards marched on the right, the Swiss Guards on the left. The queen followed the king, leading the dauphin by the hand. Madame Elisabeth gave her arm to the king's daughter, and the Princess de Lamballe and Madame de Tourzel followed closely behind. The Princess de Lamballe appeared to be the most dejected and the most frightened of the fleeing party.

The king walked erect and a serene expression, but sorrow was painted all over his face. The queen was in tears. From time to time, she wiped them and tried to put on a confident air which she was only able to maintain for a short while. A guardsman, misinterpreting the cause of her tears, said, "Your Majesty need fear nothing; she is surrounded by good citizens."

"I have no fear," the queen replied, laying her hand upon her chest. Nevertheless, the crowds could see that she was seen trembling.

Curiously, the dauphin did not seem frightened at all. He amused himself by kicking the small mounds of dead leaves along the way. "How many leaves there are!" remarked the king, trying to show his composure. "They are falling early this year." Little did he know that the monarchy, too, was about to fall.

Madame Elisabeth was calm and resigned to it all; it was religion that inspired her. She said, looking at the ferocious populace: "All these people are misguided, yet I wish them no punishment."'

The little princess wept softly as Princess de Lamballe said, "I am afraid we shall never return to the palace."

The crowd which thronged the terrace of the Convent of the Feuillants on the way to the Assembly greeted the advancing victims with derisive shouts. The king, nevertheless, preserved his unmoved attitude. As they approached the terrace, the mob became more turbulent, and their path was blocked. For ten minutes the party was obliged to remain at the foot of the staircase of the Feuillants amid furious cries: "Down with him! Down with him! Do not let them enter the Assembly!" When the mob caught sight of the queen, the uproar became deafening: "No women! We wish only the king, the king alone!"

A guardsman seized the royal prince, and took him in his arms. The queen, believing that he meant to carry her son off, uttered a terrible shriek, but the soldier lifted the dauphin above his head, reassuring the child and his mother that he was not going to harm the child.

Meanwhile the Assembly, notified of the royal family's arrival, sent a delegation of a dozen members to meet them. "Sire," said the deputy who led them, "the Assembly offers you and your family a refuge in its midst." The cortege resumed its march, but upon the terrace of the Feuillants the cries grew fiercer. Again the vicious crowd pressed upon the royal procession, forcing it to stop in its path. One of the wretched mob brandished a pike, and threatened the royal family with it, shouting, "Down with traitors! Down with them!"

A man broke loose from the group, and addressing the king said, "Give me your hand, Sire, and I will conduct you to the Assembly, but as for your wife, she shall not enter. It is she who has caused all the misfortunes of France."

One of the deputies ordered the National Guards to mount the staircase. He ascended it himself with the mob roaring about him. He took advantage of an opening in the crowd and was able to lead the royal family into the great hall of the Assembly.

Once inside, the king took his place by the side of the president while the queen and his family sat down on benches behind him. The soldier who carried the dauphin set him down upon the desk of the secretary, amid the cheers of the gallery. The child immediately jumped off the table and ran to his mother. "No, no!" a voice shouted. "The child belongs to the nation! The Austrian, however, she is unworthy of the confidence of the people!"

When calm was finally restored, the king addressed the Assembly, saying, "I have come in order to avoid a great crime, and I could not be better off than in your midst."

The National Assembly

Cléry Separated from the Royal Family

With the exception of only a few nobles, there were no faithful subjects left to be found in the Tuileries Palace after the royal family had escaped. The revolutionary commander reported that the palace was strewn with the naked, mutilated bodies of the Swiss Guard. Ferocious crowds of peasants had looted and ransacked the entire palace, leaving the floors covered with footprints in blood.

Cléry, separated from the royal entourage in the chaos, had tried to escape from the palace with Madame de Rambaud, the royal children's nurse, but all of the exits were barred. They finally found an open window in the queen's apartment, and they sprang from it onto the terrace below. Injured and limping, Cléry followed the crowds making their way to the Assembly, but he lost sight of Madame de Rambaud in the madness.

Within minutes, from the fire of canon and musketry, Cléry knew that the Tuileries Palace was being pelted with cannon balls and bullets. Along the route, he also noticed that angry rebels were stripping massacred royal guards of their arms. One even approached him, "What, citizen, you have no sword?" Handing Cléry a weapon, he accepted it without objection, because he knew that he would have met his death on the spot if the mob had any idea that he had been one of the king's loyal servants.

Tuileries Palace under siege by the revolutionaries

As the mob became more violent, Cléry saw several royal guards taking refuge in a stable nearby belonging to Madame de Rambaud's family, and he followed them. In his hiding place, he immediately destroyed his papers and his pass to the Tuileries Palace, which incriminated him as a royal servant. The owner of the stable spotted him and motioned him into the house where he stayed until later in the afternoon along with Madame de Rambaud who had arrived only minutes after him. She reported the horrors of the massacre: Men had been murdered, their heads were cut off their bodies, and their bodies were left in the gutters. The royal family had made it safely to the National Assembly, however, but was assailed with insults and threats all along the way.

The sons of the hospitable host returned to the home where Cléry was hiding, and reported that the king had been suspended of all his royal functions by the Assembly. He, along with his small entourage, was being closely guarded in a small cell there that the princess referred to as a "cage" in her mémoires that she wrote years later. Moreover, the family had to stand from morning until night with little food and water as they were verbally assaulted by the Assembly members. They spent the night in a nearby convent, the Feuillants, only to spend the next day again in front of the insulting assembly.

Since it would have been impossible to reach the heavily guarded royal family in the Assembly, Cléry decided his only alternative was to leave Paris to be with his wife and children in Juvisy. All of the routes leaving Paris, however, had been closed by the revolutionaries. He and Madame de Rambaud, accompanied by the sons of their host, decided to take an alternate route to Versailles first, where she lived. Along the route, however, they were stopped and threatened by rebels who asked why they were leaving Paris. They fortunately were able to convince the rebels that they were not shirking their duty and that they were indeed needed at home to care for their families. Also, their host's sons vouched for them, and they were finally allowed to proceed on their journey unscathed. They were grateful because many aristocrats and royal guards trying to leave the city were taken to a nearby prison or executed on sight.

Agathe de Rambaud

As soon as Cléry had safely escorted Madame de Rambaud to her family, he immediately set out for his own family in Juvisy, a village near Versailles. Arriving at 7 o'clock the next morning, Cléry had to be confined to his bed after such a long journey on foot and the injuries he suffered from jumping out of the palace window. He was also overcome by the sights and sounds of the Parisian massacre that he witnessed, leaving him in bed for three days with a high fever. "I was tormented to no end, fearing the worse for the King and his family," wrote Cléry in his mémoires. To continue his duty to his king, he also knew that he would again have to abandon his wife and his children.

Cléry had been married for 10 years to Marie Elisabeth Duverger, the daughter of one of the musicians for the royal court at Versailles. She, too, was a royal musician that not only played the harp at court but also had taught Queen Marie-Antoinette how to play it.

At home, Cléry's wife and four young children attended to his injuries and fever. The oldest, Bénédicte, was 9 years old, and old enough to understand the dire situation at hand. She also remembered seeing the fish mongers' wives with pikes, knives, and axes march on Versailles demanding bread three years earlier. She heard them calling for the head of Marie-Antoinette whom they blamed for the food shortage in Paris. Cléry's daughter had also seen the royal family removed from Versailles and escorted to Paris the following day. She soon realized that the royal family, and her father, would never return to their beloved palace again. Bénédicte's younger brothers, Charles and Louis, and her younger sister, Hubertine, were too young, however, to understand the complexities of the French Revolution, but they did miss their father who had spent most of the past three years in Paris serving in the royal household at the Tuileries.

Cléry's mother, Marguerite, was the matriarch of the family. She sat with Cléry in the afternoons as he convalesced and built up his strength. A royal supporter as well, she had served as nursemaid to the Princess de Guéménée; therefore, she understood Cléry's attachment to the royal family. She also knew that it was her husband's dying words that Hanet should care for the family, whereas Cléry should keep his position in the royal household.

If Cléry did not speak of the dangerous flight from Paris or the bloody confrontations that he had experienced, his mother would have been well aware of the riots and rebellions in the city. Her husband had died a year earlier leaving her with eight children, two of whom, as we have seen, were placed in the service of the royal household. Two of Cléry's other siblings had been sent to serve the

King of Prussia, and the others, being too young for service, were kept at home and supported by Cléry's older brother, Hanet, as promised.

Disregarding his family's concerns about his health, Cléry returned to Paris despite his own pain and suffering, only to find that the royal family had since been arrested and sent to the Temple Prison. He also had word from city officials that the king had chosen Monsieur Chamilly to be his personal valet, and he had chosen Monsieur Hüe to serve the young prince. The Princess de Lamballe, the queen's closest friend, and Madame Tourzel, the prince's governess, were allowed to accompany the queen to the prison along two of her ladies-in-waiting. Permission for the entourage to follow the family to the Temple was agreed upon only after a very heated debate in the Assembly.

The royal family transported to the Temple Prison

Disappointed, Cléry had lost all hope of continuing his service with his royal masters. If he had not been separated from the family at the Tuileries Palace, he surely would have had the honor to resume his service with the imprisoned king. After a week in Paris, Cléry decided to make arrangements to return to his home and family in Versailles, but his plans suddenly changed as soon as he was informed that all of the royal servants at the prison had just been removed and taken to another location, *La Force* Prison.

Not only was Madame Tourzel, her daughter Pauline, and Marie-Antoinette's most loyal friend, the Princess de Lamballe, separated from the royal family and imprisoned elsewhere, but they soon found themselves victims of the September massacres, when violent revolutionaries conspired to rid the prisons of thousands of jailed aristocrats. Although Madame Tourzel and her daughter had been secretly smuggled out of the prison by some mysterious benefactor, the Princess de Lamballe was not so fortunate. She was savagely murdered in the streets after leaving an impromptu trial one morning.

The Princess de Lamballe removed from the Temple

Cléry immediately paid a visit to his brother Hanet, who also showed interest in serving the royals again. Cléry told him, "Dear brother, I am determined to take any measures to devote my life to the King, but I cannot do so without your help, and your assurance that my wife and children will want for nothing." Hanet nodded, and Cléry continued, "You must swear, my dear friend, that you will take my place and never abandon them." Hanet answered, "I promise you."

"And remember the wishes of our father on his death bed," continued Cléry. "You were to take care of our mother and look after the entire family. Brother, with your skills in farming, no one can better take the place of our father than you."

In a grave tone, Cléry added, "I am your older brother, I am like a father to you, and I demand this sacrifice from you."

Hanet later wrote in his mémoires, "I swore to my brother that I would abide by his wishes, and God knows that I regarded my promise to him as sacred." Indeed, Hanet did commit his life to the protection of his and Cléry's family, saying: "After Clery's wife followed him to the grave, his children's well being have but proved that I kept my word."

Cléry's Plight to Rejoin the Royal Family

When Cléry heard that Mayor Pétion allowed Hüe, the king's former servant, to return to the Temple, he immediately tried every possible means to resume his place in the service of the young prince as well. However, Cléry had never met Pétion, and he was worried that his past loyal attachment to the royal family would preclude him from a position in the Temple.

To circumvent an interview with Pétion, he managed to get information about three of Pétion's closest associates. The first was a journalist, then a member of the Convention; the second was a justice of the peace of the Bonne-Nouvelle section of Paris where Cléry was living at the time; and the third was a military commander that Cléry had seen at the Tuileries on several occasions when he was *valet de chambre* to the prince. Cléry went to see these three gentlemen, and after informing them of his motives, he asked them to speak to Pétion on his behalf.

On the 24th of August, Cléry was presented to Pétion, who noted Cléry's request and promised to help him. However, after explaining the importance, and the danger, of serving the royal family in the Temple, the mayor told Cléry that he doubted if the Council of the Commune would approve. Cléry replied, however, that Monsieur Hüe had just been permitted to return to the Temple by the Council. He also added that if he were to receive permission from the Council, he wanted the mayor to get the king's consent as well before he entered the prison, to be sure that resuming his service with the prince was agreeable to the king. Pétion promised Cléry that he would speak with Manuel, the Council prosecutor, about the matter. This was the first and the last time that Cléry would ever see Mayor Pétion, who wrote the following letter to the King:

> Sire, the valet attached to the Prince-royal from infancy asks to be allowed to continue his service with him; as I think the proposal will be agreeable to you, I have granted his request.

The next day on the 25th, Cléry visited the mayor's office, but there was no message for him from the mayor. The following day he returned, and the mayor's secretary told him to report to the Temple Prison and to find Pétion's right-hand man, Manuel. When he arrived, he was told that Pétion had just sent Cléry's request to the king, and he should return later in the evening for a response. He returned at 7 o'clock and he was told that the king had agreed to his request; however, the king's consent was being sent to the Council of the Commune for final approval.

Cléry feared, understandably, that if the Council assembly had the opportunity to deliberate on the king's response, he would surely not be admitted to the Temple. He therefore immediately went to Manuel to tell him about his concerns. Fortunately, Manuel agreed, and he was able to retrieve the letter before it was read in the assembly, telling the Council that there had been a misunderstanding.

According to Mayor Pétion's direct orders, Manuel escorted Cléry immediately to the Temple on the 26th of August, two weeks after the royal family had arrived. Stepping out of the carriage, they proceeded to the gate of the haunting medieval fortress, an imposing structure on the Rue du Temple that was previously owned by the king's own brother. The towers of the Temple glowed faintly, being lit by lanterns in the cool autumn night. When Manuel knocked at the gate, the guard on duty slowly opened the door. Seeing Manuel, he motioned the two visitors into the courtyard where another guard accepted official documents from the mayor, allowing Cléry to enter the tower.

Cléry had finally arrived; he could now resume service with the king and his family. Unfortunately, however, rumors were circulating that Cléry had secured the position in exchange for favors to the revolutionaries. In fact, it was reported that Cléry's revolutionary outlook was the only reason why he was considered by Mayor Pétion, who referred to Cléry as "a man more devoted to the nation than to his master." This heinous rumor would haunt Cléry for the rest of his life; accusations from other city officials and even a fellow servant in the Temple would only incriminate Cléry more in the years to come. But was it a heinous rumor, or was there truth in the comment?

Jérôme Pétion de Villeneuve

It is understandable that Cléry's motives must have been a mystery to his contemporaries. Why would he ever want to return to the king's household in such a terrifying prison? After all, a majority of those who had previously served the king had already been imprisoned or executed for their royal ties—if they had not already left the country in exile. Therefore, one could speculate that Cléry's safety was perhaps more at risk outside the prison walls than within. Since many aristocrats, courtiers, and servants to the king had already lost their lives, it was possibly safer for Cléry to stay within the confines of the Temple where the royal family was intimately protected by municipal guards, rather than face the ruthless revolutionaries in the streets of Paris or the continued harassment at home in Juvisy.

More damning, Cléry's critics believed he was strategically serving two masters at the same time—to avoid the scaffold. On the one hand, he was valet de chambre to the heavily guarded king; on the other, he was the "*bon patriote*" who could spy on the royals for the revolutionary government, and save his neck in doing so.

Chapter 6
The Valet's Commitment

*"Be careful not to compromise yourself," said the
king. "If anything should happen to you, we should
then be left all alone, and I fear their intention is to
surround us only with strangers."*

–Louis XVI to Cléry,
Temple Prison, September 1792

Once inside the Temple walls, Cléry was thoroughly
searched and sternly lectured for half an hour on how he must
conduct himself while serving the royals in the prison. Climbing the
winding, corkscrew-like, medieval stairs, he entered the salon
upstairs where the royal family was having supper. He was so
overcome with emotion upon seeing the family in such unfortunate
circumstances that he had to take a deep breath to keep his
composure. Seeing her servant again, the queen smiled and gave
Cléry his first orders, "You will serve my son, and you will arrange
with Monsieur Hüe all that concerns us." Cléry wrote in his journal,
"I was so overwhelmed that I could hardly answer the queen."

Curiously, Cléry also remarked how ornately the dinner table
was prepared although the members of the royal family still had not
changed their clothes since the last time that he had seen them.
Ironically, peasants could be seen parading in the streets donning the
royal family's attire, attire they had ransacked in the royal wardrobe
of the Tuileries Palace on that fateful day when it was invaded.

The surroundings could by no means be described as
comfortable amid the tight security of the Temple, but apparently the
family dined very well. In the morning the steward provided the
prisoners seven cups of coffee, six of chocolate, a pot of double
cream, a decanter of cold syrup, another of barley water, three pats of
butter, a plate of fruit, six rolls, three loaves of bread, a bowl of
powdered sugar, and a salt cellar. Not all of this was consumed by
the prisoners; the remainder was given to the servants.

Dinner and supper were three-course affairs, which the
family was permitted to order on a daily basis. Bordeaux wine and

champagne accompanied the appetizers, soups, roasts, and desserts. One of the Temple guards described the dishes of the royal feast in detail:

> Supper consists of three soups and three courses. On days that are not fasting days, they are composed of two entrées, two roasts, and four or five side dishes. On fasting days they are composed of four entrées not made of meat, two or three of meat, two roasts, and four side dishes. Dessert is the same as for dinner but with coffee.

The increase in the number of dishes on fasting days was due to the fact that Louis XVI fasted regularly on the days prescribed by the church, but his companions did not. He alone drank wine while the others only drank water. Moreover, the prisoners' table service was all silver-plated which consisted of one soup-tureen, 18 spoons and forks, one gravy-spoon, one soup-ladle, eight coffee-spoons, two coffeepots, and 12 knives.

Whatever was leftover from the meals was first given to the personal servants of the royal family in the tower. They would then in turn give the remainder of the food to the servants in the kitchen and the pantry. One or two additional dishes were normally offered to the domestics along with a bottle of wine.

Not only did the revolutionaries blame the royals for the country's hardship and famine, but they added fuel to revolutionary fires by touting the enormous expense of keeping the royal prisoners in the Temple. Unfortunately, the posters that were hung in the streets of Paris did not exaggerate the numbers:

> Do not be surprised, Citizens, if food becomes dearer. The cannibals of the Temple Tower, whom you imagine are being treated like prisoners, only consume about one hundred pounds of beef and twenty-five pounds of bacon a day. Of butter, eggs, and milk the quantity used is about forty pounds a day.

When Cléry began his duties in the Temple, he was surprised to find that Turgy, one of the king's former servants at Versailles, was waiting on the family at the dinner table, because Turgy had not been one of the attendants authorized to accompany the king to the

Temple. It appears that Turgy was just as courageous and resourceful as Cléry. Not being able to obtain an entry pass to the Temple, he hurried off to the commissary-general of the royal household, Monsieur Chousy, to secure a position there. Chousy made inquiries, but he could only promise Turgy a pass for one day. Turgy understood, however, that once the king was in the Temple, it would be almost impossible to gain entrance because of all the formalities. He also knew that he would have to have references from these "enemies of the royal family."

Turgy turned to two of his comrades, Chrétien and Marchand, pleading: "Let us simply go to the Temple. Perhaps if we show a very bold front, they will let us in." After a lengthy discussion, they finally decided to follow Turgy to the Temple. They arrived at the Temple only to spot one of the king's attendants entering the Temple with a ticket in his hand. Turgy begged the guard to let him speak to the attendant, telling the guard that he and his companions had also belonged to the royal household. At first the attendant hesitated, but he finally answered, "Come with me, take my arm, and make your companions take yours. I will get you inside." To their astonishment, they were led to the Temple kitchen, where Turgy noticed instantly that there were no supplies at all.

The determined servant left the Temple to procure what was necessary to begin preparing meals for the royal family. He decided to use one door only, and he took the precaution to make sure that the porter and the guards on duty were well aware of his departure, and his position in the kitchen, so that he would be able to get back into the Temple when he returned.

Two days after their arrival, city officials entered the kitchen and asked who had admitted the three attendants into the Temple. Turgy answered that the Assembly committee, after making inquiries, had authorized them to take up their duties there. Satisfied with Turgy's reply, the officials left.

Officials from the Assembly arrived the next day to identify all the people who had remained with the royal family and to make a list of their names. They asked Turgy and his two comrades if they had been in the king's household prior to the Temple, and Turgy replied in the affirmative. "But who could have let you in here?" cried Chabot, the official in charge. Turgy quickly told him that Mayor Pétion, after making inquiries, had allowed them to enter.

"In that case," said Chabot, "it must be because you are good citizens. Remain at your posts, and the nation will take better care of you than that tyrant Louis ever did. The officials let the three attendants return to their work in the kitchen.

When Turgy was alone with his comrades, he noticed that they were quite alarmed. "Do you want to be the death of us all?" asked one of them. "You tell the town counselors that we were sent here by the Assembly, and you tell the deputies from the Assembly that we were sent here by the mayor of the city. We wish we were not involved at all!" They remained, nevertheless, by Turgy's side. The stroke was definitely a bold one, but it succeeded, and Turgy would remain in the Temple with his two assistants until the 13th of October 1793.

While in the Temple, the Turgy also played an important role, along with Cléry, in relaying information from outside the prison walls to the royal family whenever he left for kitchen provisions, sometimes three times a week. It should be remembered, however, that Turgy was not allowed to converse with the prisoners except for that which concerned his duties. He only worked in the kitchen and carried the meals to the rooms in the tower where the family dined. As personal valet, it was Cléry's duty to serve the meals himself.

One evening, after Turgy and Cléry had served the family's supper, the queen mentioned to Cléry that she, her daughter, and the king's sister, Madame Elisabeth, had been without their ladies-in-waiting for more than a week. The queen's hairdresser, Léonard, was also not allowed to enter the Temple. Knowing that Cléry had experience as the king's barber, she asked him if he would comb their hair—not knowing that this would be a valuable scheme allowing Cléry to relay messages among family members when they were later separated in different towers.

Cléry replied, "I would do whatever you desire of me, Your Highness." At that moment, however, one of the guards on duty approached Cléry brusquely and told him in a threatening manner that he had to be more circumspect in his conversations with the royals. Cléry had forgotten that he had been ordered only to address the royals as regular citizens because France no longer recognized royalty. In fact, the king was now referred to as "Citizen Capet" or "Louis Capet" because he was a direct descendant of Hugh Capet, the first king of the Capetian Dynasty dating from the 10th century. Referring to the king as "Citizen Capet" was a sign of disrespect, and the guards enjoyed humiliating the king in such a manner. In almost all circumstances the king ignored the comments and insults of the guards and city officers.

Cléry, however, was alarmed because he was beginning to notice that he was under constant watch by the tower guards, and nothing that he did seemed to please them. Knowing that he would be confined to the tower for the next eight days before a short leave, he often thought about his home and family in Juvisy. He also thought about happier days before the revolution when he and his brother were young servants at the court of Versailles. He had no idea that he was going to be the most important witness to the royal family's horrendous calamities that were about to take place in the following months in the Temple.

During the next eight days, he was also not allowed any communication with the outside world. Hüe was the only person in the tower who was allowed to ask for and receive any items that the royal family needed from outside the prison walls. Although Cléry had been one of the two ordinary valets to the dauphin, Hüe had held the post as principal valet. It was reported years later by Madame Hüe that Cléry was jealous of Hüe's role in the Temple as well as his level of responsibility. Otherwise, Cléry and Hüe shared all other duties for the royal family. The third valet, Villette, had applied for a position in the Temple, but Cléry was chosen before him.

Cléry's daily tasks quickly adapted to the royal family's routine. He dressed the king's hair in the morning and rolled it at night before the king retired. However, he was relentlessly watched by the municipal officers and guards whenever he was in the presence of the king and queen. He was also conscious of the fact that any irregularity on his part would have endangered his position in the Temple as well as his life.

All was relatively calm until the 2nd of September, when the king and his family went down as usual to walk in the Temple courtyard. These walks allowed the family to learn about current events since street criers shouted news outside the prison walls. That afternoon Cléry overheard a guard who was following the king tell one of his colleagues, "We did wrong to consent to let them walk this afternoon." Cléry had also noticed all morning how uneasy the prison staff had appeared, and the clamor of the crowds outside the gates was becoming increasingly deafening. The guards soon hurried the royal family back into the Temple. They were scarcely assembled in the queen's room before two officers who were not on duty at the tower entered unexpectedly.

One of them said to the king: "You are ignorant of what is going on. The country is in the greatest danger, and the enemy has entered Champagne. The King of Prussia is also marching on

Châlons, so you are answerable for all the harm that will come of this. We, our wives and children, may perish, but *you* will go first, before us. The people *will* be avenged."

The king empties his pockets for the deputies

Showing no emotion, the king responded in a composed manner: "I have done everything I could for the people. I have nothing to feel guilty about." Cléry was bewildered by the calm reaction of the king after such a threatening approach.

The officer then addressed Hüe: "The Council has ordered me to put you under arrest."

"Who?" asked the king.

"Your personal servant, Monsieur Hüe, is under arrest," answered the officer angrily. The king wanted to know of what crimes Hüe was being accused, but he could learn nothing from the officers. Cléry could see on the king's face that he was very concerned about Hüe's fate. The king strongly objected, telling the officers that Hüe was not guilty of any crime, but they ignored him and proceeded to take Hüe away. Fearing he would never see Hüe again, the king gave him a lock of his hair which the royal servant would cherish for the remainder of his days. It was not uncommon for the king and queen to give locks of their hair as remembrances to family and dear friends.

As the guards escorted Hüe from the Temple, one of the officers stopped and whispered to Cléry, "Take care how you behave, for the same thing may happen to you as well." Cléry froze in his tracks until the king called for him. He gave Cléry some of Hüe's papers, which were accounts of expenditures in the Temple for the royal family. Cléry asked the king if there was anything more he could do for him. The king hesitated and then replied, "The turmoil today has upset me immensely. Would you be so kind as to sleep in my room this evening?" Cléry nodded sympathetically, and he began to set up a small bed in the king's room.

The following day Cléry was helping the king dress when he asked Cléry if he had heard any news of Monsieur Hüe, or if he had any news about Paris. Cléry answered that during the night he had heard an officer say that the people were violently attacking the prisons. Whispering, he told the king that he would try to get more information.

"Be careful not to compromise yourself," said the king softly. "If anything should happen to you, we should then be left all alone, and I fear their intention is to surround us only with strangers." Cléry had thus ensured his position as the king's *confidant* despite rumors of his affiliation with the revolutionaries. However, Hüe's removal still raised eyebrows in the Temple. Why was Cléry allowed to enter the Temple, but Hüe was removed? Rumor had it that Cléry was thus Hüe's replacement, and in his place he would be able to spy on the activities of the royals for the revolutionaries. Although the king was locked up in the tower of the Temple, there was still the fear of the king rallying support from France's neighbors, and enemies, to put him back on the throne.

September Massacres

The inhabitants of the Temple were unaware of the massacres commencing on Sunday, the 2nd of September, and continuing until the following Thursday. This period could be considered one of the darkest and most revolting tragedies of the revolution. The wave of mob violence was responsible for executing half the prison population of Paris that was believed to be counter-revolutionary. Also, unknown to the royal family, the angry crowds had killed, disemboweled, and beheaded the Princess de Lamballe, the Queen's dearest friend, after she was turned out onto the streets following an impromptu trial.

The Princess de Lamballe attacked in the streets of Paris

These shocking atrocities were not merely the result of mob violence, but organized, or at least encouraged, by men who were leading the revolution such as Danton, the Minister of Justice, who cried, "We must have boldness, boldness, and always boldness" in the National Assembly. More than 1,300 prisoners were butchered, and it should be remembered that hardly any of the helpless victims had been guilty of anything which could be considered anything close to a serious crime.

Later that morning the king went to the queen's room to sit with the family. An officer approached Cléry and told him to go the king's room where he found several members of the Commune. One of them asked Cléry what the king had said about Hüe's removal, and Cléry answered that the king was very distressed about it.

"Nothing will happen to him," the official said, "but I am ordered to inform the King that Hüe will not return. You can warn the King about this." Cléry begged him to be excused from such a dreadful task, and added that the king wished to speak to the officials in regard to items which the royal family needed.

Cléry often asked to be excused from relating unfavorable news or decrees to the king. Although he was the king's servant, such reluctance raised eyebrows. Could Cléry have felt that he might lose the king's confidence by appearing too cooperative with the city officials? Also, one may ask why the officials would allow Cléry to refuse obeying their orders. Did Cléry have any special favors or privileges from the revolutionary committee?

The officer hesitated for a moment and then decided to go to the king on his own. He told the king about the Council's decision to detain Hüe indefinitely, but he added that another person could be sent as soon as possible if so desired.

"I thank you," replied the king, "but I shall only need the services of Cléry, my son's personal valet, and if the Council opposes it, I shall serve in that capacity myself." The officer said he would discuss the matter with the Council and he left the room. As Cléry showed him out, he took the opportunity to ask the officer if the disturbances in Paris were continuing. When the officer replied that the people would more than likely attack the Temple, Cléry trembled and turned pale. "You are charged with a difficult duty," the officer added. "You will need all of the courage that you can muster."

At 1 o'clock the king and his family asked if they could take their afternoon walk, but permission was refused. During the afternoon meal, the family heard the noise of drums and the shouts of the crowds in the neighborhood. The royal family left the dinner table in a state of anxiety and quickly returned to the queen's room to play a game of backgammon. In the meantime, Cléry went downstairs to dine with the gruff Tison and his hysterical wife, who were employed as servants in the tower.

Cléry and the Tisons were hardly seated when they saw a head dangling at the end of a pike in the window. Tison's wife screamed loudly, but the mob outside thought it was the queen's reaction as intended, and the barbarians laughed frantically. Thinking that the queen was still at the dining table, they had raised the victim's head even higher so that it could remain in her sight in the window. It was the Princess de Lamballe's head. Though bloody, it was not disfigured. Her blond hair, still curling, floated around the pike. In fact, the princess's head had been taken to a coiffeur to have the hair styled so that the queen would more easily recognize her best friend. One of the murderers later boasted of having cooked and eaten one of the princess's breasts.

Cléry ran immediately to the king's chamber. The terror had so changed Cléry's face that the queen noticed it immediately. Cléry thought it was important to hide the cause of his distress from the queen, but he wanted to warn the king and Madame Elisabeth of the horrific incident. Prison officers were present, however, so he dared not reveal any information about the Princess de Lamballe in their presence.

"Why do you not go to dinner, Monsieur Cléry?" asked the queen calmly. "Madame," Cléry answered, "I am not feeling too well." At that moment, an officer entered the room and spoke mysteriously with his colleagues. The king interrupted him and asked if he and his family were safe from the mobs.

"There is a rumor going around," the officer replied, "that you and your family are no longer in the tower. The people want you to appear in the window to be sure you have not escaped, but we shall not allow it. The people should have more trust in us."

The cries and shouts outside increased. Cléry and the family heard insults very distinctly that were being addressed to the queen. Another municipal officer came in, followed by four men elected by the people, to make sure that the king and his family were all still actually in the tower. One of the officials insisted that the royal prisoners should show themselves at the window, but the prison guards opposed it.

The official then said to the queen in the coarsest tone, "The guards are trying to prevent you from seeing the Princess de Lamballe's head, which has been brought here on a pike to show you how the people avenge themselves of tyrants. I advise you to show yourself to the people!"

The queen fell unconscious upon hearing the shocking news. Cléry rushed to help her, and Madame Elisabeth helped him place her into an armchair. The children burst into tears and tried to bring her around with their caresses. The official stood by watching with a smile, but the king approached him and said firmly, "Monsieur, you might have refrained from telling the Queen about that dreadful event." The man left with his comrades without a word—they had achieved what they were determined to do.

When the queen recovered, the family escorted her to Madame Elisabeth's room, where less could be heard from the mobs outside. Cléry remained a few moments in the queen's room. When he looked out the window through the blinds, he saw the Princess de Lamballe's head a second time. This time the man who was carrying it earlier propped himself upon a pile of rubbish so that the royal family could more easily see the head through the windows. Another man beside him carried the bloody heart of the unfortunate princess on a pike.

Princess de Lamballe's head outside the tower window

The two men and some followers wanted to break in the door of the tower to seize the queen, but a city official, Daujeon, chastised them: "The head of Antoinette does not belong to you. France entrusted the keeping of these great criminals to the city of Paris. It is for you to help us keep them confined until national justice avenges the people." It was only after an hour's resistance that Daujeon finally succeeded in making the unruly crowd leave the premises.

Later that evening one of the commissioners told Cléry that a mob had even attempted to enter the tower with the naked and bloody corpse of the Princess de Lamballe. They had dragged her body from La Force Prison to the Temple. Daujeon held the mob back at the Temple gates, but for almost six hours it was uncertain whether the royal family was going to be massacred or not. It appears that, although the government was calling for a complete end to the royal family, it did not know how to accomplish it and was hoping that it would be accomplished in hands other than that of the government.

All was quiet in the Temple neighborhood by 8 o'clock in the evening, but the rest of Paris was in tumult where massacres of the royalists and aristocrats continued for another four or five days. The young Princess Marie-Thérèse later wrote in her mémoires that the queen sobbed uncontrollably throughout the entire night. Cléry had an opportunity while undressing the king to tell him what he had seen that day and to give him more details. The king asked Cléry which of the officials had defended the royal family, and Cléry told him about Daujeon's courage. Although this official did not return to the tower until four months later, the king did remember his conduct and he thanked him then for his bravery that day.

Marie-Antoinette's room in the Temple

The scenes of horror which had taken place were soon followed by some tranquility, and the royal family again returned to its daily routine, which Cléry noted had been curiously adopted on entering the Temple Prison. Despite the harsh treatment by the jailors while confined in the medieval grotto, the family followed the same rules of etiquette and the same time schedule that they had enjoyed at the court of Versailles—regardless of 24-hour surveillance in such close proximity.

Chapter 7
Royal Delusions

My children, the summation of life is love, labor, and prayer.

–Marie Antoinette to her children
September 1792

The small tower in which the family was kept under surveillance was actually joined to the large tower but without any interior communication between the two. It formed an oblong square flanked by two small, corner towers. In one of these small towers was a narrow staircase that started at the second floor and led up to a gallery along the eaves. In the other tower there were small cabinets which were alike on each floor of the tower.

The Temple Prison's towers

The imposing structure had four floors. The first was composed of an antechamber, a dining room, and a cabinet constructed in one of the small towers, which was the library and archives of the Knights of Malta, holding some 1,200 to 1,500 volumes of books that King Louis enjoyed reading. He read at least 250 of them while in captivity.

The second floor was divided almost in the same manner. The largest room was the bedchamber for the queen and the dauphin; the second room, separated from the first by a small and dark antechamber, was the bedroom of the king's sister, Madame Elisabeth, and Princess Marie-Thérèse. It was necessary to cross through this room to enter the cabinet constructed in the small tower which served as a privy to the entire main building; it was shared by the royal family, the municipal officers, the guards, and the soldiers. This was quite a contrast with the queen's private privy with plumbing at the château of Versailles.

The king occupied the third floor and slept in the largest room. The cabinet of the small tower was used by him as a reading room. On one side was a kitchen, separated from the king's bedchamber by a small dark room, which was occupied at first by Chamilly and Hüe. It was later sealed up, however, when the servants were removed from the Temple. The fourth floor was closed off and locked up. There were also some kitchens on the ground floor that were never used.

The king usually rose at 6 o'clock in the morning. He shaved himself, and then Cléry arranged his hair and dressed him. Afterwards, the king went directly into his reading room. Because the reading room was very small, the municipal officer guarding the king had to sit in the bedroom with the door half open, so he would not lose sight of his charge. His Majesty prayed on his knees for five or six minutes, and then he read until 9 o'clock. During that time, Cléry would have straightened up the king's room and prepared the table for breakfast. Then Cléry would go down to arrange the queen's room.

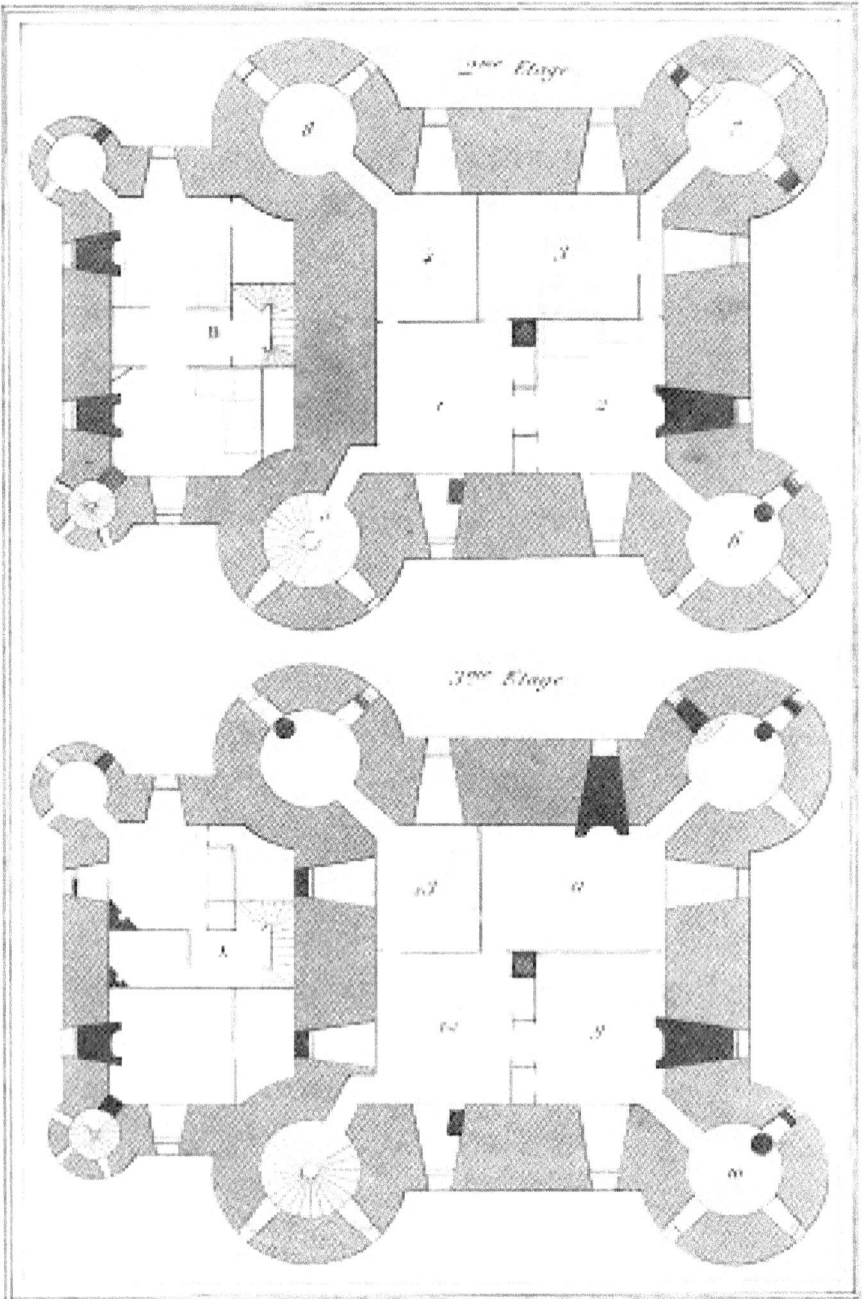

2me Etage

3me Etage

The Temple floor plan

The queen would never open her door until Cléry came to her room in the morning. This was to prevent any of the municipal guards from entering her bedroom. Cléry then dressed the young prince and combed the queen's hair. Thereafter, he went to perform the same service for the king's sister, Madame Elisabeth, and the young Princess Marie-Thérèse. Cléry used these moments in his service to tell the queen and Madame Elisabeth about the news he had heard and what he knew was happening in Paris. Cléry had a special sign which told them that he had something to tell them, and one of them would then talk to the municipal officer on guard to distract his attention.

At 9 o'clock the queen, her children, and Madame Elisabeth went up to the king's room for breakfast. After Cléry served them, he did the bedrooms for the queen and the princesses. The peculiar pair, Tison and his wife, only helped Cléry when he was cleaning the bedrooms.

The Tisons had not been placed in the Temple just to help the royal family. The couple actually served a more important purpose: They were to observe all that might escape the surveillance of the municipal officers and even to denounce the officers themselves if necessary. They were indeed spies, but Mrs. Tison seemed a rather gentle woman who trembled in front of her husband, a man whom the royal family found rough and unfeeling in nature.

Cléry found the Tisons to be incapable of showing any empathy for the prisoners and completely destitute of any feeling of humanity. Madame Tison eventually denounced the queen; however, that action was followed by a fit of insanity for her misdeeds and the guilt. There is evidence that the royals were aware of the role of the Tisons. On one occasion the couple became annoyed when a stranger had been admitted to the Temple to bring the princesses some clothes. They were upset because their own daughter, of whom they were very fond, was excluded from receiving any. Because Tison himself made some suspicious remarks that were reported to the mayor, the Tisons were immediately interrogated, making all sorts of accusations against the royal family. Although the family members were torn from their bed that very evening to allow the officials to search prisoners' rooms, the royal family nevertheless continued to treat them with the utmost respect.

There is also evidence that Princess Marie-Thérèse was suspect of Cléry when he first arrived at the Temple. This might have been the result of Cléry working side by side with the Tisons and the fact that he was the only royal servant who had escaped imprisonment, execution, or exile. Furthermore, the question arose why Hüe was removed from the Temple, but Cléry was permitted to stay. Rumors circulated that Cléry was Hüe's replacement simply because he was the mayor's spy.

The royal family would have been surprised, no doubt, that after being deprived of those servants who were most attached to them such as Hüe, the Commune would then consent to send Cléry to them. Furthermore, the family must have wondered why Cléry was even brought into the Temple, because Tison and his wife were sufficient to fulfill all of the duties required in the tower.

The Princess Marie-Thérèse, it is true, was always suspicious of Cléry's intentions. She remained persuaded that he was from the beginning a tool of the revolutionary party. Her respect for her father, however, prevented her from ever publicly avowing her sentiments about Cléry, but her opinion about him would never change on this subject.

At 10 o'clock every morning the king went downstairs with his family to the queen's room and spent the day there. He occupied himself with the education of his son, made him recite passages from the works of Corneille and Racine, gave him lessons in geography, and taught him to read maps. The precocious prince reacted perfectly to the tender care of the king. One of the guards remarked that his memory was so good that on a map covered with a sheet of paper he could point out the departments, districts, towns, and the course of the rivers of France.

The queen, on the other hand, was occupied with the education of her daughter, and these lessons lasted until 11 o'clock. The rest of the morning she spent sewing, knitting, or doing tapestry. At midday, the queen and the princess went into Madame Elisabeth's room to change their morning gowns.

At 1 o'clock, if the weather was agreeable, the royal family was escorted downstairs into the garden. Four municipal officers and a captain of the National Guard would accompany them. This stroll was obligatory to allow guards to search the family's rooms in the Temple. Since there were many construction workers about the Temple, the royal family was only allowed to walk in the alley lined with chestnut trees. Cléry was permitted to join the family during these walks, during which he made the young prince play ball or run for exercise. The noisy playtime also allowed the royals to speak freely among themselves without the officers overhearing them.

Madame Elisabeth, Princess Marie-Thérèse, Louis Charles, Marie Antoinette, Princess Marie-Thérèse and the King in the Temple Prison

At 2 o'clock they returned to the tower, where Cléry then served dinner. Every day at the same hour, Santerre, a general in command of the National Guard of Paris, came to the Temple accompanied by two assistants. Sometimes the king would speak to him, but the queen always refused to acknowledge him. He was an insolent man with a foul mouth. After the meal, the royal family returned to the queen's room where they usually played games such as backgammon and trivia. It was during that time that Cléry finally had the opportunity to have his dinner.

The guards often noted that the queen was haughty and obstinate, but in fact, Cléry attributed this to her being extremely reserved. Also, she had inherited her mother's pouty lips which gave her the air of being snooty. The guards were also taken aback by the family's tranquil demeanor in such treacherous circumstances. Despite mistreatment and verbal abuse by the guards, the royal family continued to play games, tell stories, and read as if they were still holding court at Versailles.

Cléry playing ball with the prince in the Temple courtyard

Around 4 o'clock, the king always took a short nap, and the princesses sat next to him with a book in their hands. Cléry noticed that the deepest silence reigned during the king's nap. "What a spectacle!" he wrote in his *Journal*. Cléry was serving a king that was pursued by hatred, a king that had fallen from a throne to a ragged, used armchair in a prison, yet a king that was still able to sleep and snore peacefully at will. His wife, his sister, and his two children often noticed the king's serene features as well, and they were always careful not to wake their master.

When the king awoke, conversation resumed. He would make Cléry sit beside him to give writing lessons to the young prince while he watched. After this lesson, Cléry took the little prince into his Aunt Elisabeth's chamber, where he made him play checkers or some other game.

At the close of the day, the royal family sat around a table while the queen read passages from books of history aloud or other chosen works suitable to instruct and amuse her children. Sometimes she would read unexpected scenes which reminded her of her own painful situation. Madame Elisabeth would also read in turn, and the reading lasted until 8 o'clock. Cléry then served the young prince his supper in Madame Elisabeth's bedroom. The royal family was present, and the king took pleasure in amusing his children by playing checkers, the medieval board game *tric-trac*, or the card game *picquet*.

After the prince's supper, Cléry undressed him, and the queen would hear him say his prayers. He said one prayer especially for the Princess de Lamballe; he would say another asking God to protect the life of Madame de Tourzel, his former governess. If the municipal officers were very near, however, the little prince took the precaution to say these last two prayers in a low voice. Cléry then made him go into the cabinet, and if Cléry had anything to tell the queen, he seized that moment.

Louis XVI, Marie-Antoinette, Madame Elisabeth, Marie-Thérèse,
and the Dauphin

Cléry would have to tell the queen what was written in the newspapers because the officials prohibited them in the tower. There was also a street crier who came every evening at 7 o'clock and stood near the wall on the rotunda side within the Temple courtyard, where he shouted a summary of what was taking place in the National Assembly, the Commune, and the armies. Cléry stationed himself in the king's cabinet to listen carefully and to remember all that he heard, so that later he could secretly relate it to the family later at an opportune time.

At 9 o'clock the king had his supper. The queen and Madame Elisabeth took turns to remain with the dauphin during this meal, and this was another opportunity for Cléry to speak without being overheard. Cléry then served the princesses *whatever* they desired for supper. Despite the family's mistreatment and cruel imprisonment, the meals continued to be extravagant affairs with wine and desserts. Turgy and his two assistants in the kitchen had been able to maintain their places in the kitchen under false pretenses. In addition to his kitchen duties, Turgy was also responsible for carrying the meals from the kitchen to the royal family's quarters which was quite a distance.

After supper, the king went up to the queen's room for a moment, gave her his hand to bid her goodnight as well as his sister, and he kissed his children. The king then went to his own room, retired into his cabinet, and read there until about midnight. The queen and the princesses closed the doors to their rooms, but one of the municipal officers remained all night in the little room between their two chambers. The other officer on duty followed the king to his room.

Cléry then placed his bed beside that of the king, but the king waited before going to bed until the municipal officers had changed and the new one came upstairs. If he did not know the replacement, he always told Cléry to ask him his name. The officers were relieved at 11 o'clock in the morning, at 5 o'clock in the afternoon, and at midnight like clockwork.

The routine just described was the way of life for the royal family that lasted the entire time that they were in the tower, from August 13th until the 29th of September—the day when the family would experience one of the cruelest moments of their captivity.

PART THREE

INTOLERABLE CRUELTY

Chapter 8

The Dog Days of September

The guillotine is here to stay, and is awaiting the tyrant, Louis XVI

–Poster hanging in the tower of the Temple

All was relatively calm until the 2nd of September, when the king and his family went down as usual to walk in the Temple courtyard. These walks allowed the family to learn about current events because street criers shouted news outside the prison walls. That afternoon Cléry overheard a guard who was following the king tell one of his colleagues, "We did wrong to consent to let them walk this afternoon." Cléry had also noticed all morning how uneasy the prison staff had appeared, and the clamor of the crowds outside the gates was becoming increasingly deafening. The guards soon hurried the royal family back inside the Temple tower. They were scarcely assembled in the queen's room before two officers who were not normally on duty at the tower entered unexpectedly.

One of officers, Mathieu, said to the king: "You are ignorant of what is going on. The country is in the greatest danger, and the enemy has entered Champagne. The King of Prussia is also marching on Châlons, so you are answerable for all the harm that will come of this. We, our wives and children, may perish, but *you* will go first, before us. The people *will* be avenged."

Showing no emotion, the king responded in a composed manner: "I have done everything that I could for the people. I have nothing to feel guilty about." Cléry, who was standing nearby, was bewildered by the calm reaction of the king after such a threatening remark by the bad-tempered officer.

Mathieu then looked away and said: "The Council has ordered me to put you under arrest."

"Who?" asked the king. "Me?"

"No, your personal servant Hüe is under arrest," answered Mathieu as he approached the servant.

"What has he done? Is serving his master to be his only crime?" asked the king in a severe tone.

"Yes," added Hüe, "what right do you have to arrest me, and where are you taking me?"

"I do not have to explain anything to you," replied Mathieu. "I have my orders."

Hüe wanted to go to his room first, but Mathieu grabbed him by the arm and said: "You are not going anywhere. You are my prisoner, and you can only go where I go."

The officers then proceeded to take Hüe away. When Hüe asked if he could take some linen and his razors with him, Mathieu replied: "Razors? Where I am taking you, you will be shaved, and I can assure you that the barber will not miss."

Hüe understood completely what Mathieu was saying but he kept silent, convinced that he was going straight to the scaffold. After going downstairs and passing the queen's chambers, he did receive permission from Mathieu to take some documents to the king before leaving the Temple.

"Poor soul," said the king to Hüe with a sympathetic tone after reading the papers. "The little bit of money that you had, you paid my expenses! And now you leave without a penny in your pocket?"

"Sire," answered Hüe with tears in his eyes. "I have no need for anything."

The entire family acknowledged Hue's good deeds and especially his fidelity to the king. Not being able to bear the family's sentiments any longer, he turned to the officers and said, "I am ready now to follow you." The officers escorted him downstairs and out of the Temple—Hüe would never see his master again.

As the guards escorted Hüe from the Temple, one of the officers stopped along the way to speak with Cléry, "Take care how you behave, sir, for the same thing may happen to you as well." Cléry froze in his tracks until the king finally called for him. He gave Cléry some of Hüe's papers, which were accounts of expenditures in the Temple for the royal family. Cléry asked the king if there was anything more he could do. The king hesitated and then replied, "The turmoil today has upset me immensely. Would you be so kind as to sleep in my room this evening?" Cléry nodded, and he began to set up a small bed in the king's room.

The king was understandably upset about Hüe's arrest because he had served as the king's doorman since 1787 before becoming the premiere valet de chambre of the dauphin. Also, unknown to the king, Hue had paid 526 francs for the king's expenses before he was arrested. In fact, if the king had been searched when he first entered the Temple, the officers would not have found one *sou* in his pockets. The king was penniless.

Although the Legislative Assembly had voted an annual sum of 500,000 francs for the expenses of the king in the tower of the Temple, the king had not received any money since he arrived there. Having no funds to pay for his domestics' services, food, and supplies, the king had asked Hüe to write Mayor Pétion for assistance. Because the mayor ignored his request, the king then took it upon himself to personally write the mayor:

> The King would be pleased if Mr. Pétion would send a reply to the letter written to him five days ago. This is the last day of the month, and he has received no money to defray his expenses. The King will be obliged to Mr. Pétion if he will let him know how much he is to receive, and send him an answer today. (Signed) LOUIS

On the 3rd of September Pétion sent his secretary to the tower to give the king a sum of 2,000 francs and receive a receipt. The king had requested the secretary to also pay Hüe 526 francs, which Hue had advanced him for his household expenses. The secretary promised him that he would do so, and the receipt was signed and dated on the same day:

> The King acknowledges having received from Mayor Pétion the sum of 2,526 livres, including 526 livres that the Municipal Commissioners were ordered to pay to Mr. Hue, who had advanced them to the King for his household expenses. (Signed) LOUIS

Despite the weeks of hardships, it appears that the king had been patient with the mayor for some time. It was only out of consideration for those in his employ that it was crucial for him to personally write the second letter himself.

Two thousand francs was all that was ever paid to the king, although the Legislative Assembly had authorized 500,000 francs. This was perhaps before the Assembly understood the real intentions of its leaders.

Caricature of royal family in the Temple Prison

Two days later, Madame Elisabeth told Cléry to collect a number of small articles that belonged to the Princess de Lamballe, items she had left in the tower when she was suddenly removed. Cléry made a package and addressed it, with a letter, to the princess's lady-in-waiting. Cléry heard later that neither the package nor the letter ever reached the unfortunate princess's servant. It was now becoming clear that the character of most of the municipal officers chosen to come to the Temple was indeed questionable.

One officer named James, an English language teacher, decided one day to follow the king into his little reading room and sit beside him. The king told him in a kind way that other municipal officers always left him alone there. He added that, with the door remaining half open, he would always be in his sight, and that the room was so small that two persons could not remain in it comfortably. James insisted, however, in such a harsh and vulgar way that the king did not object, but the king did give up his reading for that day. He decided to return to his chamber, but James joined him, however, and continued to torment him with the same tyrannical surveillance.

One day, when the king rose, he mistook the municipal officer on guard for the one from the night before, and he said that he was sorry his colleagues had forgotten to relieve him of his duty. The municipal officer answered the king's kind words with insults. "I come here," he said harshly, "to keep watch on your conduct, and not for you to take notice of mine." He then approached the king without removing his hat as a sign of disrespect and added, "No one, and you less than anyone, has the right to meddle with me." Undeterred, the guard was determined to remain insolent to the king for the rest of the day.

Another day, a commissioner was in the queen's room while Cléry was giving the young prince a writing lesson. He abruptly interrupted the lesson with a speech on republican education that ought to be given to the young prince; he also warned Cléry that he should substitute the prince's traditional books with the most revolutionary works available for the child to read.

Another commissioner was present when the queen was reading to her children a chapter from the history of France, a period when a French prince took up arms against his country. The commissioner rebuked the queen for trying to inspire her son with any feelings of vengeance against France, and he actually made a formal denunciation to the Council later that day. After that, the queen made an effort to choose her subjects in a way that prevented anyone from misreading her intentions. In such circumstances, the queen normally would have replied that she had always fulfilled her duty as queen to ensure that her son would one day be only the people's king.

The shoemaker Simon, a municipal officer, was one of six commissioners charged with the duty of inspecting the works and expenditures of the Temple. He was the only official who never left the tower. Moreover, he was the rudest of all the commissioners, and he never missed an opportunity to slight the royal family. He would often say to Cléry, "Ask Capet if he wants anything because I'm not going to make a second trip on the stairs." Cléry was forced to answer, "He wants nothing." Simon made it common practice to call the king by his surname, Capet, rather than "His Majesty." More disturbing, Simon would one day also be put in charge of the young dauphin.

Cléry made, by order of the queen, a multiplication table for the dauphin. Upon seeing the table, however, a municipal officer accused the queen of showing her son how to talk in ciphers or secret codes. Teaching mathematics to the prince from that day forward was strictly forbidden.

A similar accusation was made regarding the tapestries which the queen and the princesses had worked on since they were first imprisoned in the Temple. When several chair backs were finished, the queen directed Cléry to have them sent to their friend, the Duchesse de Sérent. The municipal officers, from whom Cléry asked permission, thought the designs represented hieroglyphics and that they were destined to open up secret correspondence outside the prison walls. Consequently, they obtained a decree which prohibited any work done by the princesses to ever leave the tower of the Temple.

Some of the commissioners never spoke of the king and queen, the prince, and the princesses without insulting them. The officer Turlot even told Cléry one day in threatening manner, "If the executioner doesn't guillotine that [expletive] family, I'll do it myself."

Whenever the king and his family went for a walk in the gardens, they had to pass in front of a great number of soldiers, some being posted in the interior of the small tower. They presented arms to the municipal officers and officers of the National Guard, who accompanied the king, but when the king passed them, they grounded their muskets or pointedly reversed them as a sign of disrespect.

One of the sentinels posted inside the tower wrote one day on the door of the king's chamber: "The guillotine is here to stay, and is awaiting the tyrant Louis XVI." When the king read the words, Cléry made a motion to erase them but His Majesty opposed it.

Rocher, one of the two porters of the tower, was a frightening man with a long moustache, a black fur cap on his head, a large sword, and a belt from which hung a bunch of big keys. He would present himself at the door whenever the king wished to go outside, but he would never open it until the king was close beside it. Then, under pretence of choosing the right key from his enormous bunch which he rattled with a frightful noise, he kept the royal family waiting. Then he would draw back the bolt with a bloodcurdling clash to frighten the children and their parents.

Afterwards, Rocher would hurry down the stairs and stand by the last door with a long pipe in his mouth. As each member of the royal family passed by him, he would puff bellows of smoke in their faces, especially those of the princesses. Some of the national guards who were amused by such insolence would gather near him and laugh loudly at each puff of smoke. Some, to enjoy the spectacle more at ease, would even bring chairs from the guard room, sit down, and obstruct the passageway, which was already very narrow, making it very difficult for the prisoners to pass.

During the family's daily stroll, the artillery men assembled to dance and sing songs, but their songs were always revolutionary and often very obscene. When the royal family returned to the tower, they were forced to endure the same insults. The walls were sometimes covered with the most indecent messages that were written in such large letters that they could not escape their eyes, such as: "We will put the fat pig on a diet" or "Strangle the cubs." On one occasion they drew a noose on which dangled a figure, and beneath it was written: "Louis taking an air bath." Another time they drew a guillotine with these words: "Louis spitting into the basket."

Thus, the little walk in the garden granted to the royal family in the afternoons became a cruel, terrifying affair. The king and queen might have escaped the torture by remaining in the tower, but their children, the objects of their tenderness, needed the fresh air after being confined to the damp, dark quarters of the Temple. It was for the children that the king and queen endured these innumerable outrages every day without any complaint.

Although the short daily walks in the garden were tarnished by the crude behavior of the guards, sometimes, however, they were an opportunity for signs of sympathy to be shown. Some of the sentinels on duty showed, even tearfully, how painful their duty was for them. Such signs of fidelity or pity softened the horror of the family's persecutions, yet they were very rare. One day, a sentinel took his place at the queen's door. He was dressed neatly but in a peasant's attire. Cléry was alone in the first room reading when the sentinel looked at him attentively with a sympathetic air. Cléry rose and passed before him, but the sentinel presented arms and said in a trembling voice, "You cannot go out."

"Why not?" Cléry replied.

"My orders are to keep you within my sight," answered the sentinel.

Cléry stopped in his tracks, and with a puzzled look on his face said, "But you are mistaken."

The sentinel looked surprised and asked "What, monsieur, are you not the King?"

Cléry shook his head and asked, "Then you do not know him?"

The sentinel answered in a loud voice, "I have never seen him, but I surely would like to see him removed from this treacherous place."

"Speak softly!" Cléry warned the young man. "I shall enter that room and leave the door half open. Look in and you will see the King. He is sitting by the window with a book in his hand." Cléry then told the queen of the sentry's desire, and the king, whom she informed, had the kindness to go from one room to the other and walk before him.

Cléry then went back to the sentry, who said, "Ah, monsieur, how good the King is! How he loves his children!" The guard was so moved that he could hardly speak. "No," he continued, striking his chest, "I cannot believe he has done us any harm at all." Cléry, fearing that the young man's excitement would compromise him, immediately too leave of him.

Another sentry, posted at the end of the alley where the royal family took their walk, still very young with an interesting smile, expressed by his looks as if he wanted to give the royal party some information. Madame Elisabeth, on the second turn of their walk, went near him to see if he would speak to her. Whether from fear or out of respect for the royal princess, he did not dare to do so, but tears rolled down his cheeks, and he made a sign to indicate that he had left a note in a rubbish heap near him. Cléry began to look for it, under pretence of finding some of the prince's toys, but the municipal officers stopped him and forbade him to go near any of the sentinels in the future. Cléry never discovered the intentions of that young man, but one could easily speculate that the note possibly pertained to a planned attempt to rescue the royal family from the prison.

If there were plans for the family to escape from the Temple, it is doubtful if Cléry would ever have been involved. He had only been recently admitted to the Temple, and the royal family may still have had questions concerning his fidelity. There is evidence, however, that plans had been submitted to the queen to escape the prison, and although she was pleased with the authors' daring, she would never have considered them without the help of the Chevalier de Jarjayes, the husband of one of her ladies-in-waiting who had completed secret and important missions for her and the king in the past. In fact, months later the Chevalier would procure signed passports for the family and have peasant clothing at their disposal for a planned escape. The long awaited getaway, however, was foiled at the very last minute.

Temple and the surrounding area

The family's daily walk for an hour also brought another kind of spectacle. A number of faithful subjects took advantage of that brief hour to get a glimpse of the king and queen by placing themselves in the windows of houses across the street which looked onto the courtyard of the Temple. Their good sentiments and their prayers were evident. On one occasion Cléry was certain that he had recognized the Marquise de Tourzel by the intent way she always watched the movements of the little prince whenever he left his parents' side. Cléry mentioned this to Madame Elisabeth, who had believed her to be a victim of the September massacres. Tears rolled down her cheeks when she heard her name. "Oh!" she cried. "Could she still be alive?"

The next day Cléry found a means to get more information. He does not disclose how, but he discovered that the Marquise de Tourzel had escaped the massacres and was actually living on one of her estates. He also learned that the Princess Tarente and the Marquise de la Roche-Aymon, who were at the Tuileries on the 10th of August, had also escaped danger. The safety of these persons who had been so devoted to the royal family gave some moments of consolation to the royal family.

The Monarchy Is No More!

On September 29th, at 9 o'clock in the evening, a municipal officer named Lubin, surrounded by gendarmes on horseback and a number of commoners, arrived at the Temple to make a proclamation in front of the tower. The trumpets sounded, and a great silence followed. When Rubin spoke, the royal family could distinctly hear the proclamation that royalty had been abolished and that a new republic had been established. Hébert along with other municipal officers happened to be on guard over the royal family that day. They were seated at that moment near the door, and they stared at the king with treacherous smiles. The king noticed them, but he had a book in his hand and he continued to read. There was no change in his demeanor. The queen showed equal firmness; she did not utter a word, nor make a motion, that could add to the enjoyment of the devious men. Finally the proclamation ended, and the trumpets sounded again.

Cléry went to the window and instantly all eyes in the courtyard turned toward him. The crowd mistook him for the king, and he was immediately confronted with vile insults. The soldiers made threatening gestures towards him with their swords, and he was obliged to retire from their view in order to stop the tumult.

That same evening Cléry informed the king that his son was in need of curtains and covers for his bed, since it was beginning to get cold. The king told him to write the request and he would sign it. Cléry used the same expressions that he had always used: "The King requests for his son …"

"You are very daring," said Hébert, "to use a title that has been abolished by the will of the people. As you have just heard tonight, the monarchy is no more!" He warned Cléry that it was in his best interest to refrain from using royal titles in the future.

Cléry defended himself by replying that he had heard a proclamation, but he did not know the subject of the order. "It is," Hébert said, "the abolition of royalty, and you can tell *monsieur* (pointing to the king) to stop taking a title that the people no longer will recognize."

"I cannot change this note," Cléry said obstinately, "because it is already signed. The King would ask me the reason, and it is not my place to tell him why."

"You can do as you choose," Hébert replied, "but I shall not certify your request for curtains and covers." The next day Madame Elisabeth interceded by ordering Cléry to write requests in the future for such purposes as follows: "It is necessary for the service of Louis Auguste, or Marie-Antoinette, or Louis Charles, or Marie-Thérèse, or Madame Elisabeth ..."

Up to that time, Cléry had been forced to make these requests quite often. The small amount of linen the king and queen had was lent to them by persons of the court during the few days they were at the Feuillants before they were brought to the Temple. They were unable to get any linen from the Tuileries Palace where, on the 10th of August, everything had been pillaged. In fact, the royal family lacked clothing of every kind, and the princesses mended what they had on a daily basis. Often Madame Elisabeth was obliged to wait until the king went to bed in order to darn his clothes. Cléry finally discovered after many requests that a small amount of new linen would be made for them. Unfortunately, the seamstresses had embroidered the linen with *crowned* letters, and the municipal officials insisted that the princesses pick out any and all symbols of royalty. They were forced to obey.

On the 26th of September, Cléry learned from a municipal officer that it was proposed to separate the king from his family, that an apartment was being prepared for him in the great tower, and that it was nearly ready for him. It was not without precaution that Cléry announced this new tyranny to the king. Cléry, by his demeanor, let the king know how much this news upset him. "You could not give me a greater proof of your loyalty," said His Majesty. "I know that you will not hide anything from me, and I expect to know everything. Try to learn the day of this cruel separation from my family and inform me of it."

On the 29th of September, at 10 o'clock in the morning, five or six municipal officers entered the queen's room where the royal family was gathered. One of them, Charbonnier, read to the king a decree of the Commune that ordered "the removal of paper, pens, ink, pencils, and written papers, whether on the persons of the prisoners or in their rooms; also from the *valet de chambre*, and all other persons on service in the tower."

Charbonnier added, "If you have need of anything, however, Cléry will come down and write your requests on a register which will be kept in the council chamber." The king and his family searched their persons and gave up their paper and pencils. The commissioners searched all the rooms and closets and then carried off the articles as designated in the decree. Cléry learned from a member of the delegation that the king was to be transferred that very evening to the great tower. He found a way to inform the king with the help of Madame Elisabeth.

After supper, as the king was leaving the queen's room to go up to his own, a municipal officer told him to wait because the council had some news for him. A quarter of an hour later, the six municipal officials who had carried away the papers and other items, entered and read to the king a second decree of the Commune, which ordered his removal to the great tower. Although already informed of that event, the king was still greatly affected by the news.

Separation of the king from his family with Cléry in the background

The entire royal family was in a state of distress. The king, in bidding them good night, left them in the utmost state of apprehension and uncertainty. This separation, forecasting as it did so many other misfortunes to come, was one of the cruelest moments that Their Majesties had yet experienced in the Temple.

Cléry followed the king to his new prison quarters. The apartment of the king in the great tower was not ready; there was only one bed and no other furniture in it. The painters were still at work, which caused such an odor that Cléry feared His Majesty might become ill. They intended to give Cléry a room very far from that of the king, but he insisted vehemently on being as near as possible to the king. He passed the first night in a chair beside His Majesty, but the next day the king, with great difficulty, obtained a room for Cléry adjoining his own.

The Temple Prison

After the king had risen, Cléry wished to go into the small tower to dress the young prince, but the municipal officers refused. One of them said, "Neither you nor your master are to have any communication with the other prisoners. He is never to see his children again."

At 9 o'clock the king asked to be taken to his family. "We have no orders to allow that," replied the commissioners. His Majesty objected, but they did not reply. Half an hour later, two municipal officers entered, followed by a servant who brought the king a piece of bread and a carafe of lemonade for his breakfast. The king expressed his desire to dine with his family, and they replied that they would have to make an inquiry. "But," said the king, "my valet de chambre Cléry can surely go downstairs. He was given the care of my son, and nothing prevents him from continuing that service."

As they left the room, the commissioner replied, "That's not a decision that we can make."

Cléry was sitting in the corner of the room, and he was overcome with sorrow and was fearful for the lives of the royal family. On the one hand, he saw the suffering of his master; on the other, he thought of the young prince, abandoned perhaps to strangers. The municipal officers had already talked of perhaps separating the young prince from his parents altogether. Would the child have to leave his cherished dog behind as well?

Coco the Dog

There is little information about Coco, the little spaniel that belonged to the children of the Temple, and the stories to be found are conflicting. One story reveals that Coco had originally belonged to the dauphin, yet there is no mention of the dog ever being attached to the dauphin while he was imprisoned in the Temple. Another story indicates that the first dauphin, Louis Joseph, had a dog by the name of Moufflet that was passed on to his younger brother Louis Charles, whereas Coco was actually Marie-Thérèse's dog, a gift from one of the kinder prison guards.

Yet another version claims that Coco was King Louis XVI's dog. It is doubtful, however, that Coco ever belonged to the king, because he did not like domesticated animals such as cats and dogs. He took pride in his hunting dogs, but only as long as they were cared for by his hunting staff. One day, while the king was taking a stroll at the Feuillants when the family was in captivity at the Tuileries Palace, he came across a young lady who was taking her small dog for a walk. When she recognized the king in front of her, she hastily stooped down to call her dog so that it would not inconvenience His Majesty. When the dog turned to run towards the young lady, Louis XVI was standing nearby. Surprisingly, he raised his cane and he began to beat the dog severely. Although the lady cried out with tears rolling down her cheeks when she discovered that the dog had died, the king appeared somewhat enchanted by what he had done, laughing loudly "like a farmer" as he continued his stroll.

Coco, the mystery dog of the Temple

The king was known to be a kind and benevolent man, but he obviously did not understand or care for animals as was the fashion in Paris at the time. One of Marie-Antoinette's ladies-in-waiting later wrote that each of the princesses had always kept a favorite dog with them at all times. She added, however, that Louis XVI would never have kept a dog in his room.

A Glimpse of Hope

Cléry could not stop thinking of the queen's suffering when she was told that the king was being moved to another tower in the Temple. He was also distressed about his master's sorrow. Perhaps the king was not fond of animals, but Cléry was well aware of the king's compassion for his subjects, and his servants. The next morning the king approached Cléry, holding in his hand the bread the guards had brought him for breakfast. He offered him half, saying, "They seem to have forgotten your breakfast this morning. Take this, and the rest will be enough for me." Cléry refused, but the king insisted. Cléry could not restrain his tears, and when the king saw them, his own eyes filled up with tears as well.

At 10 o'clock, several municipal officers brought the painters to continue their work in the king's new chambers. One of officials said to the king that he had just seen his family having breakfast, and everyone seemed to be in good health. "I thank you," said the king, "and I beg you to give them some news of me. Tell them that I am well."

Before the officer left the room, he continued, "Can I not have a few books which I left in the queen's room? You would do me a great pleasure if you would send them to me, for I have nothing to read here." The king named the books that he wanted, and the municipal officer consented to the king's request. However, since he did not know how to read, he proposed that Cléry should go with him to fetch the books.

Cléry gladly took advantage of the man's ignorance, and he blessed Providence for that moment of consolation. The king charged him with certain orders, but his eyes told him the rest. Cléry found the queen in her room with the children and Madame Elisabeth. They were weeping, and their grief only doubled when they saw Cléry. They asked a thousand questions about the king, but Cléry could only answer them with reserve and very carefully because the municipal officers were present. The queen, addressing the officers with sobs of grief, requested to be with the king at least a few moments a day and during meals.

"Well, they shall at least dine together today," said a municipal officer, "but as our conduct is subordinate to the decrees of the Commune, tomorrow will be another matter." His colleagues agreed with him.

The afflicted family was overcome with joy knowing they would be with the king again, even for a short while at dinnertime. The queen held her children in her arms, and Madame Elisabeth raised her eyes to heaven thanking God for the unexpected mercy. Not only could Cléry not hold back his tears, but some of the municipal officers had to wipe their tears as well.

One of them, however, the shoemaker Simon, said aloud, "I believe those [expletive] women will make me cry, too." Then turning to the queen he added, "When you murdered the people on the 10th of August, *you* did not cry, madame."

Cléry cringed when the queen dryly replied, "The people have certainly been greatly deceived about our sentiments, sir."

Cléry then gathered the books the king had asked to be brought to him, and he carried them upstairs to him. The municipal officers went along to inform the "citizen Capet" that he might again see his family. Cléry said that he supposed he could continue to serve the young prince and the princesses, and the officials consented.

When he returned to the princesses, he had an opportunity to inform the queen of what had just taken place and also how much the king had suffered after being separated from her and the family.

The municipal officers served dinner in the king's room where his family was finally permitted to join him. After dinner, they showed the queen the apartment that was being prepared for her in the great tower, above that of the king. She begged the workmen to finish it quickly, but it would still be three weeks before it was ready.

In the meantime, nothing more was said about the decrees of the Commune, and the royal family continued to meet to have their meals together and to take their walks in the courtyard. Nevertheless, it was feared that communication would become even more difficult when the family was split up and forced to live in separate towers of the prison.

Chapter 9
Cléry's Dilemmas

Cléry asked my father to forgive his past conduct, for which my father's bearing in prison and my aunt's exhortations had made him feel remorse.

–Mémoires of Princess Marie-Thérèse,
1792–1795

Cléry continued his services for the king and queen as well as the young prince and princesses; the daily routine remained much the same. The king's lessons to his son were not interrupted. However, the royal family living in two separate towers made the surveillance by the municipal officials more difficult, and they became very uneasy. In fact, the Commune increased the number of guards, and their distrust of everyone in the prison left Cléry with little means to obtain news from outside the prison walls.

Cléry had to be creative. Under pretext of getting his linen and other necessities brought to him, he obtained permission for his wife to come to the Temple once a week. She was always accompanied by a lady friend who pretended to be one of her relatives. Considering the steps Madame Cléry took and the risks she ran on various occasions, no one proved more attachment to the royal family than she. On their arrival, the two ladies were taken into the council chamber, but Cléry could only speak to them in the presence of the municipal officials. They were closely watched, and the first visits brought no results, but Cléry managed to make them understand that they needed to arrive precisely at 1 o'clock in the afternoon, the hour of the king's walk, during which time most of the municipal officers followed the royal family. Usually only one official was left in the council chamber, and if he was a kind man, he gave the guests some liberty without, however, losing them from his sight.

Getting thus a chance to speak to them without being overheard, Cléry obtained news about people in whom the royal family took an interest, and he heard about what was going on in the Convention. It was his wife who had also engaged the street crier who came near the walls of the Temple every day revealing the headlines from the daily newspapers.

To this information Cléry added whatever information that he could not only pick up from the municipal officers, but also from Turgy who served in the Temple kitchen. Out of devotion to the royal family, Turgy had dangerously contrived to get himself employed in the Temple with two of his comrades, Marchand and Chrétien. They brought the royal family's meals, which were prepared in the Temple kitchen, to the small tower. They were also in charge of provisions, and Turgy, who was thus able to leave the Temple two or three times a week, obtained information about all that was happening in Paris.

The difficulty, however, was to convey that information to Cléry. Turgy was forbidden to speak to him except about the service of the king's table, and he could only speak in the presence of the municipal officers. When Turgy wanted to tell Cléry something, he made a sign that they had agreed upon, and Cléry made different pretexts to approach him. Sometimes Cléry asked him to do his hair. Then, Madame Elisabeth, who knew of Cléry's schemes with Turgy, would speak to the municipals in order to give him time to exchange a few words unobserved. At other times, Cléry would find reasons for Turgy to enter his chamber, and Turgy seized the moment to hide the newspapers and other printed documents in his bed.

When the king or queen desired some particular information from the outside, and the visiting day of Cléry's wife's was far off, Cléry employed Turgy. If it was not his day for going out, Cléry would pretend to be in need of something for the royal family. "It must be for another day," he would answer. "Very good," Cléry would then say with an indifferent air, "the King can wait." By speaking in such a manner, Cléry expected to induce the municipals to give Turgy an order to leave the Temple for provisions. Often they did give the order, and he brought Cléry the details that the king had requested, either that same night or the next morning. Cléry and Turgy had agreed upon this system of communicating, but they had to be very careful not to employ the same means twice in front of the same commissioners.

Turgy's Secret Role

Turgy was under close scrutiny in his duties. Before any meal, the municipal guards had to be summoned to the kitchen where the dishes were prepared and tasted before them so they might see that nothing was concealed in them, or that there was anything suspicious about them. Turgy had to fill the wine and almond milk decanters and the coffee pots in front of them. The guards would also supervise tearing the pieces of paper that would cover the decanters.

Turgy, however, was often able inconspicuously to replace the paper stopper of a decanter with another one when he was in a passage or a corner of the staircase. The replacement would contain some warning or news that had been written with lemon juice. Such messages were invisible but could be read by the prisoners when held up close to a candle's light.

Sometimes Turgy would roll a note around a small pellet of lead, cover it with a stronger piece of paper, and drop it in a decanter of almond milk. With a sign upon which he and the prisoners had agreed, he would indicate that there was a note hidden in the bottom of the decanter. If there were no messages on the stoppers when the queen or the king's sister received them, they would prick pin holes in the paper in order to give Turgy orders or information to transmit to someone else.

Due to the close scrutiny and the need for the greatest caution, there were often delays in transmitting information. To be on the safe side, the queen and her sister-in-law devised ways of communicating directly with Turgy. Being imprisoned in the Temple, the royal family was aware of the possibility of being rescued by their English or Austrian allies. In fact, Marie-Antoinette's brother, Leopold II of Austria, who was also the Holy Roman Emperor, had declared his readiness to defend Louis XVI, but on the 20th of April, 1792, France declared war with Austria, and launched an offensive into the Austrian Netherlands (Belgium).

Furthermore, on the 27th of August, Leopold issued the famous *Declaration of Pillnitz* in conjunction with the King of Prussia. This proclamation enflamed the revolutionaries, stating that Austria and Prussia were ready to join other European rulers in an attempt to place the king of France back on the throne." In the meantime, they promised to prepare their troops for active service, and threatened to "destroy Paris" if any harm should come to the imprisoned royal family.

The Declaration was little more than an empty threat, but it appeared to the French people that the Louis and Marie-Antoinette were scheming with the foreign powers to restore the old regime at any cost. The idea of foreign rulers meddling in the affairs of the

French would in itself have been intolerable to such a proud people, or the revolutionaries.

Therefore, the family wanted to be kept informed of the progress of the foreign armies and any action taken by the French government. Over time the following signals were secretly devised between the family and Cléry, which were then communicated to Turgy:

- For the English, place a right thumb upon the right eye. If they are landing near Nantes, place it on the right ear, but if near Calais, on the left ear.

- If the Austrians are successful on the Belgian frontier, place the second finger of the right hand on the right eye. If they are entering the country by way of Lille or from the Mayence direction, use the third finger in the same way.

- For the troops of the King of Sardinia, use the fourth finger in the same way.

- Should the troops advance and be successful, touch the nose with one finger of the right hand, and use the whole hand when they are within fifteen leagues of Paris.

Turgy wrote in his mémoires that hardly a day passed that he did not deliver some message or other information while he was in the Temple, despite the vigilance of eight to ten guards or officers on duty at all times. Sometimes Turgy would put a message in a ball of thread or cotton, and hide it in a corner of a cupboard, or under a table, or in crevices of the stove, or even in the "basket that the sweepings were carried away in." A movement of his hand or his eyes indicated the spot where he had succeeded in hiding the note.

Turgy's responsibility of leaving the Temple several times a week to fetch provisions enabled him to deliver any messages from Their Majesties in Paris and to bring back any notes or news that he received outside the prison walls. He often visited Hüe, the king's former servant, in obscure parts of Paris or outside the city limits to get news for the king. Neither fear of persecution or imprisonment ever affected Hüe's devoted courage, and Turgy never feared for his own safety.

The queen and Madame Elisabeth corresponded most with Madame la Marquise de Sérent, a former governess to the king and his brothers. The noble lady had instructed her household to let Turgy in at any hour of the day or night because he was one of her business associates. The year 1792 was known as the year of exodus in France. Priests were required to take an oath to the new constitution or resign. Many rejected the oath, however, and the Assembly decreed that any so-called non-juror would be deported; the decree banished an estimated 30,000 priests.

The exodus of the nobility was not decreed, but as a protest against the revolution, the exodus gained steam. Many counter-revolutionaries flocked to *émigré* colonies on the border of France from Turin to Brussels for fear of their safety, and many of the elite gravitated to London to escape the "demoralized society." The property of the émigrés was confiscated; moreover, those who had departed after the 1st of July 1789, and had not returned before the 9th of May 1792, were banished forever. The aristocratic quarters of Versailles were thus deserted by 1792; several thousand nobles had left their places to escape the drama in Paris. As a result, according to the mayor, the town suffered financially.

One of Turgy's important tasks was to discover the fate of those nobles who had been so loyal to the royal family and had been forced to leave France because of their devotion. As the laws against the nobles became more and more severe, Madame Elisabeth became more concerned. In one of her notes to Madame de Sérent she wrote: "When the laws against the *émigrés* are quite completed, let us know, and go on giving us news on the subject." The princess was a pious woman, and Turgy and Cléry both remarked how often they would find her on her knees praying at her bedside.

Turgy was rarely searched when entering the Temple because he "always tried to supply the warders with everything they asked for when they visited the kitchens." However, as soon as he entered the tower or any room occupied with the royal family, all of his movements were observed. He was subjected to particular vigilance because of his contacts outside the prison walls.

The royal family was thus very cautious and increased their efforts not to draw any attention to him. On one occasion the king had given Turgy a knife with a broken handle to have it mended. The king remembered, however, that he had not shown the knife to the guards, and he at once asked Turgy to return the knife to him. He then handed it to the guards, saying: "You see, gentlemen, there is nothing inside." Afterwards, he returned the knife to Turgy asking him not to replace the handle with a new one, but only to repair it. He added, "I value it very much as it is, because it was given to me by my father."

When the royal family first entered the Temple, they were confronted by a very gruff municipal, François Toulan, who was a member of the Commune and also an administrator for the confiscated property of the nobles who had emigrated. Turgy noted, however, that in time the royal family's generosity and gentleness made an unexpected impression on the young man. Although he continued to speak and behave in an almost violent and harsh manner to keep up appearances in the Temple, he soon began to sympathize with the royals. Turgy had no idea how Toulan communicated his changed feelings to the family, but Madame Elisabeth assured Turgy that he could trust Toulan. Turgy had several meetings with Toulan, and they were able to talk about various projects of the queen and Madame Elisabeth. In fact, they referred to Toulan with a very distinguishing name, as revealed in a note from the princess:

> You will give this note to Toulan, who in the future we should call *Fidèle*. If you cannot deliver it at dinner time, go tomorrow, so as to be able to give him an answer to what we should receive from him today. Tell us the bad news as well as the good, when there is any.

Although some enemies of the royals who did not know them were moved to pity them because of their misfortunes, there were others who remained atrocious in their treatment of the family. One day the queen said, "Turgy, I have broken my comb; please buy me another."

When a guard, actually a poet who doomed the royals to the scaffold everyday in verses that he composed, heard the queen's request, he cried out: "Buy one of horn; wood is too good for her." However, the queen continued as if she had not heard the insult. Turgy replaced the comb with a similar one in tortoise shell. The queen was somewhat surprised when she saw the replacement.

"So you have disregarded the poet's order because he declared that wood would be too good for us?" the queen said quietly. "He who, but for the kindness of the king ..."

The queen paused, but Turgy ventured to say, "Madame, there were many who seemed to favor the royal family, but it was only because of the treasury."

The queen nodded and added, "You are quite right, Turgy."

Cléry Raises Suspicion

Many obstacles kept Cléry from informing the king what he had learned. He could only speak to the king in the evening when the Temple guards changed and when he went to bed. Sometimes he could say a word to him in the mornings when the guards were not settled in his room. Cléry would wait until they finished their toilet, letting them see, however, that the king was waiting for him. If they let Cléry enter, he immediately opened the curtains of the king's bed, and while he helped the king with his shoes and stockings, he was able to speak to him without being heard. More often, however, his plans miscarried, and the municipal officers made him wait until the end of their own toilet before they would let him attend to that of the king.

Several officials occasionally mistreated Cléry in a rude manner. Some ordered him to take away their own bedding in the morning and made him replace it in the evening; others constantly made insulting remarks to him. By being kind and compliant, however, Cléry was being more useful to the royal family. He ended up winning the guards' confidence without them noticing it, and, in turn, he was able to slyly retrieve information for the king.

Cléry dealt with the municipal officers with great skill ever since he entered the Temple, but a singular and unexpected event made him fear that he might be separated from the royal family forever. One day when Cléry was going down the stairs in the tower, a uniformed guardsman approached him and whispered, "How are you, Mr. Cléry?" Somewhat surprised, Cléry nodded slightly and motioned to pass around him. "I would like to speak to you for a few minutes," added the soldier.

"Sir, speak loudly," said Cléry. "It is not permitted to speak in a low voice here."

"I have heard that the king has been locked up in a cell for a few days, and that you were with him," said the soldier quickly.

"You can now see that is not so," replied Cléry.

Cléry made no haste in leaving the soldier, because every day it seemed that some indiscretion or other careless action compromised the safety of the royal family. One of the two guards nearby might have had heard the exchange, but the other appeared to far away to hear a word. Cléry tried to forget the encounter, but he also reminded himself to stay alert, fearing that someone might be trying to set a trap for him.

The following day two officers of the criminal tribunal, accompanied by six guards with swords in hand, entered the king's chamber as he was having supper with his family. The king, thinking that they had come for him, asked the officials what they wanted. The family all stood up from the table, fearing the worse.

Without any explanation to the king, the officers asked Cléry to step into the next room where they read a decree ordering him to appear in front of the tribunal court. Cléry asked for permission to inform his master of his arrest, but the officer replied, "No, it is useless; you are no longer permitted to speak to him."

A few minutes later, the king and his family were frantic when they heard the atrocious cries of the onlookers outside the Temple gate, calling for the head of the "friend of the king." Cléry was hardly in the street when the crowd swarmed around his carriage. If an officer had not informed the mob that the person in his charge had important secrets to reveal to the tribunal, Cléry might easily have lost his life that afternoon.

Palace of Justice from the courtyard

At the Palace of Justice, Cléry was kept in a cell until 8 o'clock in the evening. When he was brought in front of the tribunal, he saw a young man sitting on a bench that was reserved for the accused party. He was the same man with whom Cléry had exchanged words a few days earlier in the tower stairwell. One of the Temple guards was also present in the court room, and he was called forward to testify, swearing that he had heard the rustling of the paper that the soldier gave to the "tyrant's" servant.

Cléry denied the accusation, arguing that, if the officer had heard the rustling of paper, he should not have waited 24 hours to report the incident. "Why did he not search me on the spot?" asked Cléry. The other guardsman who had spoken to Cléry in the stairwell also denied any wrong doing, and due to the lack of further evidence, the two men were acquitted of any crime.

The president of the tribunal ordered the four officers present to drive Cléry back to the Temple, and he sentenced the guardsman to 24 hours in jail for conversing with a servant of the Temple. When Cléry finally returned to the Temple, it was almost midnight and the king had just retired to his chamber. Nevertheless, Cléry was permitted to inform his master of his return.

This frightening incident would have naturally raised suspicions among the royal family in the Temple. Due to the importance of the story, it has been verified by examining court records from the dates given in Cléry's memoires, and it appears that the young guardsman's name was Alexandre-François Breton, a 26-year old merchant living on the Rue de Bièvre in Paris. Curiously, the soldier had previously served as one of the queen's guards in her household at Versailles.

AFFAIRE BRETON

26 octobre 1792

160 17. — Procédure contre Alexandre-François Breton, négociant, prévenu d'avoir, étant de garde au Temple, le 5 octobre, devant la porte de la ci-devant Reine, enfreint la consigne et d'avoir cherché à nouer des intelligences avec Cléry, valet de chambre de Louis XVI — 1 dossier.

Breton Case, October 26, 1792. No. 16017—Process against Alexandre-François Breton, merchant, charged with, being the guard of the Temple on the 5th of October in front of the Queen's door, having breached his instructions and having sought to relay messages to Cléry, the valet de chambre of Louis XVI—1 file.

The municipal officer that brought the complaint against the guardsman and Cléry was Jean-Baptiste Fournet, a laborer that repaired carriages for a living. The following notice was found in the National Archives which documents Cléry's ordeal:

Princess Marie-Thérèse's version of this story differs substantially. She claimed in her mémoires that Cléry was actually brought before the Tribunal because he engaged in a handshake and a long conversation with one of the guards. She also revealed that Cléry sincerely apologized to the king and queen for his prior "indiscretions" when he returned from the tribunal. She added that he "changed his ways" due to the suffering he had caused the king and queen in the Temple, and that he was "faithful" from that time onward.

Her version implies that Cléry might have collaborated with the revolutionaries in exchange for being allowed to continue his service to the royal family in the Temple Prison. The tribunal records do indicate that Cléry was required to take an oath of allegiance to the new republic. It is therefore more likely that Cléry apologized for taking the oath, but it may have been necessary to do so in order for him to resume his duties in the Temple.

Moreover, other rumors were circulating in the prison; the municipal officer Verdier had even reported to the Assembly that the valet Hüe had been replaced by Cléry because Cléry had shown himself to be a "bon patriote" to the republic. Cléry denied this accusation much later, but Marie-Thérèse would never trust Cléry while she was in the Temple or later as revealed in her mémoires. She would also never speak of the subject out of respect and reverence for her father while in the Temple. What was the truth? Was Cléry really a "bon patriote" of the revolution, or was he wrongly accused?

Around this time the queen went to live in the apartment prepared for her in the same tower that the King occupied. That day seemed to promise Their Majesties some consolation, but Cléry reveals in his mémoires that the day was also marked, on the part of the municipal officers, with sudden animosity toward the queen. Since her arrival at the Temple, the officers and guards noted that she was devoting all of her time to the care of her son. She seemed to find some relief to her troubles in his affection and his caresses. On this treacherous day, however, they separated the young prince from his mother without any warning. Her distress and anguish was indescribable.

At the age of 7, it was customary for princes to be taken from their governesses and entrusted to a male tutor. With the young prince being placed with his father, Cléry thus had sole charge of his care. The queen tenderly begged Cléry to incessantly watch over her son with all his might.

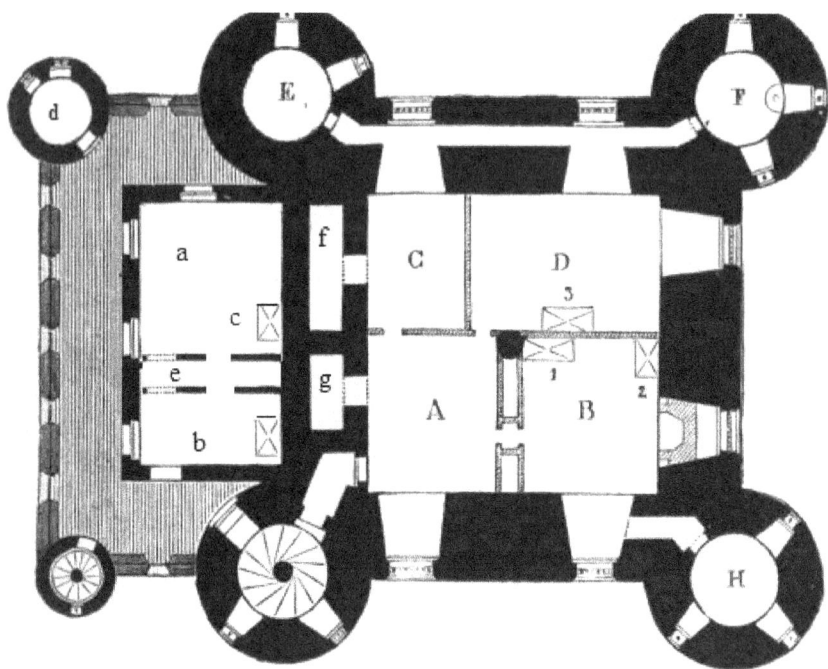

Small Tower (4th floor)   Great Tower (3rd floor)

Small Tower: *Occupied by King Louis from August 13 until September 29, 1792*

a - king's chamber; b - Madame Elisabeth's chamber; c - king's bed; d - king's reading room; e - valet's chamber; f - toilet cabinet; g - staircase

Great Tower: *Occupied by Louis from September 29, 1972 until January 21, 1793*

A - antechamber; B - king's chamber; 1 - king's bed; 2 - prince's bed; C - dining room; D - Cléry's chamber; 3 - Cléry's bed; E - wood cabinet; F - wardrobe; H - king's reading room

The great tower in which the queen was situated was about 150 feet high and had four stories, all vaulted and supported up the middle from base to roof by a huge shaft. The third and fourth floors were allotted to the king and queen; the floors were divided into four rooms with the king taking one room on the third floor and the queen taking one room on the fourth. The ground floor was used by the municipal officers, the floor above it was the guardroom, and the next floor was that of the king.

The first room of the king's floor was an antechamber (A) from which three doors led into the other three rooms. Opposite to the entrance was the king's bedroom (B), in which a bed was now placed for Prince Louis Charles. Cléry's room (D) was on the left, as well as the dining room (C) which was separated from the antechamber by a glass partition. In the king's room was a chimney, but a great stove in the antechamber heated the other rooms. Each of these rooms had a window, but thick iron bars and shutters on the outside prevented the air from circulating freely in the rooms.

The floors of the great tower were connected by a staircase placed in one of the smaller alcoves in the corner of it. From this staircase, each floor was entered through two doors, one of very thick oak and studded with nails and the other of iron. The other alcove of the tower which opened into the king's chamber was made into a reading room. On the floor above, the space was turned into a privy, and above that the firewood was stored. The bedding of the municipal officers who guarded the king at night was also stored there during the day.

The four rooms on the king's floor had canvas ceilings. The room partitions were covered with paper, and that of the antechamber represented the interior of a prison. On one of the panels hung, in very large type, "The Declaration of the Rights of Man" framed in a border of the three revolutionary colors. A washstand, a small bureau, four covered chairs, one armchair, four straw chairs, a mirror on the fireplace, and a bed of green damask furnished the rooms. This furniture was salvaged from the Tuileries after it was ransacked.

The queen's apartment was on the fourth floor with the distribution of the rooms being nearly the same as that of the king's. The bedroom of the queen and princess was directly above that of the king and prince. Madame Elisabeth occupied the room above Cléry's. The municipal officer sat in the antechamber all day and slept there as well. Tison and his wife lodged in the room above the dining room of the king's apartment.

The top floor was unoccupied, but a gallery ran around the inside of the battlements and was sometimes used as a promenade. Blinds had been placed between the battlements, however, to prevent the royal family from seeing or being seen.

After the reunion of the royal family in the great tower, there was little change in the hours of meals, readings, walks, or the time for king and queen's lessons to their children. Louis XVI was truly a religious man, and he read biblical works every morning, but this never caused him to neglect his other interests. He also read travel books, the works of Montesquieu, those of the Comte de Buffon, *The Spectacle of Nature* by Pluche, Hume's *History of England*, the *Imitation of Jesus Christ* in Latin, and Tasso in Italian, to name a few.

Madame Elisabeth of France

Madame Elisabeth and the queen asked for the same books of devotion as those of the king, so His Majesty ordered Cléry to obtain permission to buy them. Cléry remarked how often he had seen Madame Elisabeth on her knees at her bedside praying fervently. It was well known throughout France fact that the princess had always been a very pious and charitable woman.

At 9 o'clock in the morning, the queen and the king's sister came to fetch the king and his son for breakfast in the queen's room; Cléry always accompanied them. He then did the hair of the princesses and the queen, and on one occasion, by order of the queen, he showed the young princess how to dress her own hair. During this time, the king played chess or dominoes with the queen or with Madame Elisabeth.

After dinner the young prince and his sister played games in the antechamber. Madame Elisabeth was always present, sitting near a table with a book in her band. Cléry remained in the room, sometimes reading or assisting Madame Elisabeth. This dispersal of the royal family often made the municipal officers very uneasy. They were unwilling to leave the king and queen alone, but they were still more unwilling to separate from one another because they did not trust each other as well. This was the moment that Madame Elisabeth would ask Cléry questions or give him orders. He listened to her and answered without turning his eyes from the book which he held in his hand, so as not to be detected by the municipal officers. The prince and princess, in collusion with their aunt, facilitated these conversations with their noisy games and often warned her with certain signs whenever any officers were about to enter the room.

Cléry was most distrustful of the wretched Tison, who was suspected by the commissioners as well. Tison spread rumors that Cléry was "as much an agent of the revolution as he was himself." It was in vain that the king and queen treated Tison kindly, because nothing they did could ever soften his demeanor.

In the evening, the municipal officers placed their beds in the antechamber so as to barricade the room in which His Majesty slept. They then locked the door leading from Cléry's room into that of the king and took away the key. Cléry was therefore required to pass through the antechamber whenever the king called for him during the night, disturbing the commissioners who thus had to get up and let him pass.

On the 7th of October, at 6 o'clock in the evening, Cléry was ordered down to the council chamber, where he found some 20 of the municipal officers assembled. Manuel, a prosecutor for the

Commune of Paris who had risen to be a member of the National Convention, presided over the assembly, and his presence surprised Cléry and made him extremely nervous. They ordered Cléry immediately to take the king's medals with which he was still decorated, such as those of Saint-Louis and the Golden Fleece.

Cléry objected, saying that he could not obey because it was not his place to announce the decrees or orders of the council to the king. He then saw by the reaction of the municipal officers that they were acting this time without authorization from either the Commune or the Convention. The commissioners refused at first to go up to the king, but Manuel persuaded them to do so by offering to accompany them. The king was reading when Manuel interrupted him.

"How are you?" asked Manuel. "Do you have everything that you need?"

"I am content with what I have," replied His Majesty.

"You are no doubt aware of the victories of our armies, the taking of Spire, of Nice, and the conquest of Savoie?"

"I heard mention of the victories a few days ago by one of those *messieurs* who was reading an evening journal," answered the king.

"What! Do you not read the newspapers which are now so interesting?" Manuel asked abruptly.

"I receive none," answered the king calmly.

"*Messieurs*," said Manuel, addressing the municipal officers, "give all the newspapers to monsieur (pointing to the king); it is well that he should be informed of our successes." Then, addressing His Majesty again, he said: "Democratic principles are evolving. You know, of course, that the people have abolished royalty and adopted a republican government?"

"I have heard about it, and I hope that the French will find the happiness that I have always wished for them," answered the king.

"Do you also know that the National Assembly has forbidden all orders of knighthood? They ought to have told you to turn in all of your decorative medals to the authorities. Since you are now a citizen like all of the others, you must be treated in the same manner as they. As for anything else, just ask for what is necessary and they will hasten to procure it."

"I thank you," said the king. "I have no need of anything." He resumed his reading, irritating Manuel somewhat. He had hoped to provoke the king, but he found the king too reserved and too composed. The king was determined not to show any emotion.

Actually, Louis had not worn the order of the Holy Ghost ribbon for some time. The Assembly had suppressed the orders of chivalry and marks of distinction for nobility months earlier, allowing only the king and the dauphin to wear the decoration. The king had told Cléry that the distinction had no other value in his eyes other than the power of granting it to others, and that he would simply lay it aside.

As the deputies left the room, one of the municipal officers told Cléry to follow everyone to the council room, where he was again ordered to confiscate the king's decorations. Manuel added, "You would do well to send the crosses and ribbons to the authorities at once. I ought to warn you," he continued, "that Louis XVI may very well be imprisoned for a long period, and if you do not intend to remain here as a servant, you had better say so now."

Manuel continued sternly, "It is intended to reduce the number of persons employed here in the Tower, in order to make the surveillance easier. If you remain with this former King, you will be absolutely alone and your work will become even more difficult. Although wood and water will be brought to you every week, you will have to clean the apartments and do all other work yourself."

Cléry replied that he was determined not to leave the king, and he would submit to everything. The deputies then took him back to the king's apartment. "You heard what was ordered," said the king. "You will take my decorations away this evening."

The next day, when dressing the king, Cléry told him that he had locked up the crosses and medals, even though Manuel had told him that he should send them to the Convention. "You did right," said His Majesty.

On the 9th of October, the king received a newspaper describing the debates in the Convention, but a few days later, a municipal officer named Michel obtained an order that again prohibited delivering any public papers to the tower. Michel called Cléry into the council chamber and asked who had ordered the journals to be sent to Cléry's address. It was true that, without being informed how or why, four newspapers were brought daily to the tower, bearing this address: "To the personal servant of Louis XVI in the Tower of the Temple." Cléry could not name the persons who paid for these subscriptions when Michel ordered him to reveal those responsible. He even made Cléry write to the editors and publishers to get an explanation from them, but their replies, if they made any, were never communicated to him.

There were exceptions to the rule of not permitting newspapers to enter the tower, however, when they could be used to torment the royal family. If the newspapers contained insulting remarks or threats about the king or queen, some of the municipal officers would leave them on the mantel or the washstand in the king's room, in order that they would read them.

Caricature of Louis XVI

In one of the papers, the king once read that a soldier had demanded "the head of the tyrant, Louis XVI, so that he might load his cannon with it and fire it on the enemy." Another paper, speaking of Madame Elisabeth and wishing to destroy the admiration which her devotion to the king and queen inspired in the public mind, tried to destroy her virtue with the most absurd slander. A third said they ought to strangle the two little "wolf pups" in the tower, meaning thereby Prince Louis Charles and Princess Marie-Thérèse.

Cléry noted that the king never seemed too upset when he read such articles. Perhaps the king and his family believed that they were going to be liberated by their foreign allies, that loyal supporters were planning an escape, or that the National Assembly would free them and send them away in exile.

Although the king was not affected by such attacks, he would speak up when it concerned his subjects. "The French," he said, "are most unfortunate in letting themselves be so deceived."

Cléry always made an effort to hide those newspapers if he happened to be the first to see them, but they were often left in the king's sight when Cléry's duties took him out of the king's room. Sadly, most of these articles that were left out in the open for the purpose of outraging the royal family were indeed always read by the king.

The behavior of the municipal officers was becoming increasingly tortuous. One day after dinner, Cléry wrote an account of expenditures in the council chamber and locked it up in a desk to which they had given him the key. He had hardly left the room before Marino, a municipal officer, said to his colleagues that the desk must be opened and examined to prove whether or not Cléry was corresponding with the enemies of the people. "I know him well," Marino added, "and I know that he receives letters for the King."

Then accusing his colleagues of conspiring with Cléry, he insulted them and threatened to denounce them as accomplices. Out of fear, the others immediately drew up a written account of all the papers contained in Cléry's desk and sent it to the Commune.

Another day, the same officer declared that a backgammon board that Cléry had mended contained suspicious correspondence. Marino took it entirely apart and finding nothing he had it glued back together again in his presence.

One Thursday, Cléry's wife and her friend came to the Temple as they usually did on a weekly basis, and he talked with them in the council chamber. Walking in the garden, the royal family spotted them, and the queen and Madame Elisabeth gave them a little nod. That simple gesture, however, was noticed by Marino, and nothing more was needed to make him arrest Cléry's wife and her friend as soon as they left the council chamber. They were questioned separately. They asked Cléry's wife who the lady was that accompanied her. "My sister," she replied. The other, being asked the same question, said, however, that she was her cousin. This contradiction was the cause of long interrogations with Marino declaring that the lady was a disguised page of the queen. Finally, after three hours of the most painful and insulting questioning, they were set free.

They were allowed to continue to visit Cléry at the Temple, but they took extra precautions to avoid such compromising situations. Cléry often managed, in their short meetings, to give them notes which he secretly received from Madame Elisabeth. These notes usually related to information that the king and queen desired. Fortunately, Cléry had not given them any notes on that occasion. Had one of the secret notes been found, all three of them would have been in the greatest danger of mounting the scaffold.

Other municipal officers were just as suspicious as Marino. One broke up all the macaroons to see if they contained writings; another, for the same purpose, ordered that peaches be cut in two and their pits cracked. A third forced Cléry one day to drink some soap water with which the king shaved himself because he thought there might be poison in it. After each meal, Madame Elisabeth used to give Cléry a little knife with a gold blade to clean, and the municipal officers would often snatch it from his hands to see if a note had been slipped into its sheath.

Madame Elisabeth ordered Cléry one day to send the Duchesse de Sérent a book of devotions; however, the municipal officers cut off the margins of every page, fearing that she had written a secret message on them with invisible ink.

When Cléry received the linen from the wash, the officers made him unfold every piece and examine it in broad daylight. The washwoman's notes and all other papers were held to the fire to see if there was any secret writing on them. Even the linen from the royal beds was subjected to the same examination.

Some municipal officers, however, were not quite as harsh as some of their colleagues. However, if they were ever suspected by the Committee of Public Safety of assisting the royals in any way, they would die victims of their kindness, or they would languish in prison for a long time. A young man named Toulan, whom Cléry had always thought to be one of the worst enemies of the royal family, approached him one day and said mysteriously, "I cannot speak to the queen today on account of my comrades. Please tell her that the favor she asked is done, and that in a few days I will be on duty, and I will be able to bring her the answer."

Astonished to hear him speak in such a manner, and fearing that he was laying a trap, Cléry replied, "Monsieur, you are making a mistake by talking to me about such favors."

Toulan replied, "No, I am not mistaken," grasping Cléry's hand as he left. That afternoon Cléry mentioned the conversation to the queen.

"You can trust Toulan," she said. Little did they know that this young man would later be implicated in the queen's trial along with nine other municipal officers who were accused of wishing to see the queen escape from the Temple. Toulan was found guilty and sent to his death at the guillotine.

Chapter 10

The Damp Dungeon

I should like to take care of you myself, but you know how we are watched here. Have courage, and tomorrow I will send my doctor to visit you.

–Louis XVI to Cléry
Temple Prison, September 1792

The royal family shut up in the damp, dingy tower for three months had so far seen no one but the municipal officers. On the 1st of November, however, a delegation from the National Convention arrived at the Temple. The delegates asked the king how he was being treated, and whether the family had everything that they needed. "I cannot complain of anything," answered His Majesty. "I merely ask that the commissioners will remit to Cléry, my valet, the sum of two thousand francs for miscellaneous expenses. Also, I ask that we may receive linen and other clothing of which we are greatly in need." The deputies promised all this, but nothing was ever sent.

Some days later the king had a considerable amount of swelling on his face. Cléry requested that the municipal officers send for his dentist, Dr. Dubois. They considered it for three days but finally refused to allow the doctor to visit the Temple. When a fever set in, they finally permitted the king to consult his physician, Dr. Le Monnier. Cléry noticed how distressed the respectable family doctor was when he saw his old master in such a feeble condition.

The queen and her children almost never left the king's side during the day; they helped Cléry nurse him and often helped him make the king's bed. Cléry passed the nights alone beside him. The doctor came twice a day, accompanied by a large number of municipal officers, but he was always subjected to a body search beforehand, and he was not allowed to speak except in a loud voice so that the officers could hear everything that was being said.

One day when the king had taken his medicine, Le Monnier asked to be allowed to remain a few hours. He remained standing, but the municipal officers remained seated with their hats on—which was considered a disrespectful snub to both the doctor and the fallen king. To avoid any confrontation between the municipal officers and the doctor, the king asked the doctor to have a seat, but he refused out of respect for the king, which noticeably disturbed the municipals.

This was not Le Monnier's first confrontation with the revolutionaries. He had been Louis XVI's doctor since the death of Louis XV at Versailles, and he had followed the king to Paris after the March on Versailles on the 5th and 6th of October 1789. Unfortunately, he was also at the Tuileries Palace during the assault on the 10th of August 1792. One of his colleagues wrote that during the attack on the palace, he did not leave his room, and he had not changed into his professional clothing. National guardsmen, with hands and arms covered in blood, pounded loudly on his door; he opened it slowly and one of them asked: "What are you doing in there? You are acting awfully calm."

The old doctor answered, "I am at my post. I am the king's doctor."

"Are you not afraid?" the soldier asked.

"Of what?" he answered. "I have no arms. Do you harm people who are not armed?"

The soldier in charge shook his head, saying: "You should not be here, you old devil. Other soldiers might easily confuse you with the rebels. Where do you want to go?"

The old man answered, "To Luxembourg Palace."

Escorting him out of his room, the soldier added: "Come, follow us and do not worry." Surrounded by guards, the good doctor made his way through the palace, but he was heckled by angry onlookers with bayonets and pikes. As he left the palace, he was shocked to see the many dead bodies lying in the courtyard. He made it safely to his quarters at Luxembourg Palace, but he had not seen his master since those tumultuous days.

The king's illness lasted 10 days, but a few days later the young prince, who was sleeping in the king's room, also caught a fever. Because he was no longer allowed to stay in the queen's room, she became very upset about not being able to obtain permission to stay with him through the night in the king's apartment. Cléry noted that she did, however, give him the utmost care during the few hours that she sat with him.

Eventually, the same illness spread to the queen, her daughter, and her sister-in-law. Fortunately, Le Monnier had obtained permission to continue his visits to the Temple to care for the royal family until all the fevers subsided.

Cléry became ill as well. The room that he occupied was damp and had no chimney; the shutter of the window also blocked any fresh air to his chambers. He caught rheumatic fever with severe pains in his side, which forced him to stay in bed. The first day he did manage to get up to dress the king, but upon seeing Cléry's state, the king refused any services, and he ordered Cléry back to bed. The king took it upon himself to dress his son himself.

Curiously, during the first day of illness, the young prince hardly left Cléry's bedside. He even brought him something to drink. In the evening, the king took advantage of a moment, when he was not being watched, to enter the servant's room. He, too, gave Cléry a drink and said with a kindness that brought tears to Cléry's eyes: "I should like to take care of you myself, but you know how we are watched here. Have courage, and tomorrow I will send my doctor to visit you."

At supper time, the royal family came into Cléry's room, and Madame Elisabeth gave him, without the municipal officers observing it, a small bottle containing a cold remedy. This saintly woman, although she was terribly ill, deprived herself of the medication for Cléry's sake. He tried to refuse it, but she insisted. After supper, the queen undressed the prince herself and put him to bed for Cléry, and Madame Elisabeth rolled the king's hair for him.

Princess Marie-Thérèse was not very fond of Cléry, and there was no mention of her concern for the valet's health in her mémoires. Cléry does not mention her in his mémoires as well at this time. Others have alluded to the princess's mistrust of Cléry, and it is known that she did on one occasion mention that Cléry was "in the beginning" an agent of the revolutionaries. This stigma would haunt Cléry, and his descendants, to the very end of their days.

The next morning Le Monnier ordered Cléry to be bled, but the consent of the Commune had to be obtained to allow a surgeon to enter the tower. Instead, they talked about transferring Cléry to another area of the Temple. Fearing, however, that he might never get back into the tower to serve his king once he left it, Cléry pretended to feel much better. That evening new municipal officers arrived, and there was fortunately no further mention of transferring him.

Turgy, the kitchen attendant, asked to pass the night with Cléry, and the request was granted. His colleagues Chrétien and Marchand joined him, and they took turns watching over Cléry. He was bedridden for six days, and each day the royal family came to visit him. Madame Elisabeth often brought him some small token of her appreciation, and such kindness helped restore his strength. Who would not have been touched to see the royal family ignore its own misfortunes and busy itself with those of one of its servants?

It is also difficult to overlook here a trait of the young prince, which shows the kindness of his heart and his upbringing. One night, after putting the prince to bed, the convalescing Cléry retired to make way for the queen and the princesses, who always came to kiss the prince good night in his bed. Madame Elisabeth, who could not speak that day due to the close watchfulness of the municipal officers, took advantage of that moment to give the prince a little box of lozenges, telling him to give them to Cléry when he returned later. The princesses went up to their rooms, and the king retired to his cabinet. Cléry went to supper and then returned about 11 o'clock to prepare the king's bed. He was alone when the little prince called him quietly to his bedside. Much surprised at finding him awake and fearing that he might be ill, Cléry went to him immediately.

"My aunt gave me this little box for you," said the prince, "and I would not go to sleep without giving it to you. It was about time that you came, because I could hardly keep my eyes open." Cléry's eyes filled with tears. When the prince saw them, he hugged Cléry, and in two minutes he fell sound asleep. This encounter with the young prince affected Cléry immensely, and he later remarked that he was never able to forget the benevolence of such a young child, a child who would one day be king.

Cléry often noted that the young prince was naïve and playful in the Temple. The gaiety of his nature and his lightheartedness helped his parents forget about their cruel situation for the moment. Cléry thought that the prince himself felt it; although he was very young, he knew he was in a prison and being watched by enemies of the crown. In fact, his behavior and his talk acquired an instinctive reserve under the harsh and brutal circumstances. Never did Cléry hear him mention the Tuileries, or Versailles, or any other subject that might remind the king or queen of any painful memories. When he noticed any municipal officer kinder than the others on guard, he would always run to his mother and tell her about the occurrence with an expression of great satisfaction.

The prince was also very sensitive to the feelings of his parents. One day when a mason was making holes in a wall in order to bolt the door, the prince amused himself with the tools while the man ate his breakfast. The king took the hammer and chisels from his son's hands and showed him how to use them. The mason, touched at seeing the king work, said to His Majesty: "When you get out of here you can say that you worked in your own prison." "Ah!" said the king. "When and how shall I get out?" Upon hearing this, the little prince burst into tears; the king let the hammer and chisel fall to the ground, and he sadly returned to his room.

Dauphin Louis Charles

On the 2nd of December, the municipal government of the 10th of August was replaced by another; some of the former members were re-elected, but there now were many new faces in the Temple. At first, Cléry thought that the new group would be more congenial than the prior one, and he had hoped for some favorable changes in the prison. He was mistaken.

Until this time, only one municipal officer was constantly on guard over the king, and one over the queen. The new municipality now ordered two, and henceforth it was much more difficult for Cléry to speak with the king and the princesses. Even Turgy noticed the difference in the guards' disposition, and he relates an incident in his brief, but poignant, mémoires that shows the kind of men he and Cléry had to deal with on a daily basis.

The queen had been ill and had not eaten all day. She asked Turgy for some broth for supper, but as he was handing it to her, she discovered that Mrs. Tison had not been feeling well. She then ordered that her broth be taken to Mrs. Tison instead. After Turgy delivered the broth to the servant, he asked one of the officials to accompany him to the kitchen to fetch another bowl of broth for the queen. His request was denied, and the queen had to do without any supper that evening.

While Cléry personally witnessed the sorrows, and courage, of Louis XVI who was separated from the rest of the family, it was now Turgy who was confronted with the fears, the gleams of hope, and the anguish of the queen, the dauphin, and the two princesses, Marie-Thérèse and Madame Elisabeth. However, his presence with the royals was limited to meal times when he and his assistants delivered the meals from the kitchen.

On the 7th of December, a municipal officer read a decree to the king that ordered him to retrieve "knives, razors, scissors, penknives, and all other sharp instruments of which prisoners presumed criminal are deprived; and to make a most minute search of their persons and of their apartments."

The king emptied his pockets and showed the municipal officers a little red case from which he took out a small pair of scissors and a penknife. The municipal officers made the most careful search through the apartments, taking razors, a ruler for rolling hair, a toilet knife, small instruments for cleaning the teeth, and other articles in gold and silver. The same search was made in Cléry's room, and he was ordered to give up whatever was on his person.

The municipal officers then went up to the queen's apartment. They read the same decree to the queen and the princesses, and they took away even the smallest articles that were necessary for their needle work.

An hour later, Cléry was ordered to go down into the council chamber where the municipal officers asked him if he knew what articles remained in the little red case that the king had put back into his pocket. "I order you," said a municipal officer named Sermaize, "to take that case away from him tonight." Cléry replied, "It is not my place to execute the decrees of the Convention, or to search the king's pockets." Another municipal officer agreed, "Cléry is right, it was your place," he said, addressing Sermaize, "to make that search."

They then drew up an account of all the articles taken from the royal family and sorted them into small packets which they sealed up. They then ordered Cléry to sign his name at the bottom of a decree that ordered him to report to the council if he should discover any sharp instruments on the king or the princesses or in their apartments.

The registers of the Temple reveal that Cléry was often forced to sign decrees in which he did not approve either their purpose or their wording. He never signed anything, never said anything, and never did anything except by the special order of the king or the queen. Any exception on his part would have caused his immediate dismissal by Their Majesties. However, his signature on certain documents had no other meaning than to admit that those documents had simply been read to him.

Semaize took Cléry back to the king's apartment where the king was sitting near the fireplace with tongs in his hand. Sermaize asked him, in the name of the council, to show him what remained in the red case. The king drew it from his pocket and showed him a small screwdriver, a corkscrew, and a flint. Sermaize took possession of them. "Are not these tongs which I have in my hand sharp instruments?" said the king sarcastically, turning his back to him.

At dinner time, an argument arose among the commissioners. Some were opposed to the royal family's use of knives and forks; others consented to allow forks. Finally, it was decided to make no changes, but they decided to take away the knives and forks after each meal.

Confiscation of these small items was all the more trying to the queen and the princesses because they had to give up various kinds of handiwork like embroidery and darning, which until then had served to occupy their time and amuse them during those long days in prison. One day, when Madame Elisabeth was mending the king's tattered clothes, she broke off the thread with her teeth, having no scissors. "What a contrast!" said the king, looking at her tenderly. "You lacked for nothing in your pretty house at Montreuil."

"Oh brother, how can I have any regrets when I share your sorrow?" she replied with tears rolling down her cheeks.

Darker Days Ahead

Day after day, the deputies brought new decrees, each of which was increasingly cruel and oppressing. The officers' roughness and harshness towards Cléry was greater than ever. Even Turgy and his two comrades from the kitchen were forbidden to speak to him. These new developments made Cléry think that some new catastrophe was in the making. The queen and Madame Elisabeth asked him constantly for news from Turgy, which he was now unable now relay to them. Even though the royal family had breakfast together, the vigilance of the guards was so acute that they were unable to exchange a single word in private. The torture of this incessant supervision can only be imagined.

Fortunately, Cléry's wife and her friend arrived for a visit on the 6th of December. Cléry was taken down to the council chamber where his wife talked, as usual, in a loud voice in order to disarm any of the new guards' suspicions. While she was giving him details of some of their domestic affairs, her friend intermittently said to Cléry softly: "Next Tuesday, they will take the King to the Convention and his trial will begin. This is certain."

Cléry did not know how to announce this dreadful news to the king. He wanted to try to inform the queen or Madame Elisabeth of it first, but he was pressed for time, and the king had forbidden him to conceal anything from him. That night, as he undressed the king, he told him what he had heard.

Cléry also made him understand that they would certainly separate him from his family completely during the trial. They now had but four days to come up with some new methods of communication between the king and the queen. Cléry assured him that he was determined to do all that he could to help. The entrance of a municipal officer, however, did not allow him to say any more that evening, and it prevented His Majesty from replying to him.

The next day, when the king rose, Cléry could not find a chance to speak to him. When the king accompanied his son up to breakfast with the princess, Cléry followed him. After breakfast, the king talked some time with the queen, and Cléry saw by the sad look on her face that the king was telling her the bad news. Later in the day, Cléry found an opportunity to talk with Madame Elisabeth, and he explained to her how painful it was for him to inform the king of his upcoming trial and thus only add to his worries. She reassured him, saying that the king was touched by Cléry's concern. "What troubles him the most," she added, "is his fear of being separated from us. Try to get more information."

That evening the king told Cléry how glad he was to have heard in advance that he was to appear before the Convention. "Continue," he said, "to try to discover what they mean to do with me; do not fear to distress me. I have agreed with my family not to appear informed about the trial, in order not to compromise you."

The nearer the day of the trial approached, the more distrust was shown to Cléry; the municipal officers would not reply to any of his questions. He had already employed, in vain, various pretexts to go downstairs to the council chamber, where he might have overheard some new details to relate to the king. When the commission sent an official to audit the expenses of the royal family, the municipal officers were obliged to let Cléry go downstairs to give them information. He then heard from a well-intended municipal officer that the separation of the king from his family, though ordered by the Commune, was not yet decided in the National Assembly.

That same day Turgy brought Cléry a newspaper in which he found the decree, which ordered the king to be brought to trial before the Convention. Cléry had no other means of conveying the information to the king other than placing the documents under a piece of furniture in the privy, telling the king and the princesses that it was hidden there. Conveying information from outside the Temple became even more difficult; Turgy and his comrades, Chrétien and Marchand, were no longer allowed to leave the Temple.

On the 11th of December, at 5 o'clock in the morning, the inhabitants of the Temple all heard the drums beating throughout Paris, and cavalry and cannon were brought into the Temple courtyard. This uproar would have cruelly alarmed the royal family if they had not already known its cause. Nevertheless, they pretended not to know the cause, and even asked an explanation of the commissioners on duty, who naturally refused to reply.

At 9 o'clock the king and the dauphin went up to breakfast in the queen's apartment. They remained together for about an hour, always under the gaze of the municipal officers. The continued torture for the family of never being able to show any emotion was one of the most cruel acts of their tyrants and the one in which the tyrants took the most delight. The time came for them to separate. The king left the queen, Madame Elisabeth, and his daughter. The look on their faces expressed what they could not say. The dauphin went downstairs, as usual, with his father.

The little prince, who often persuaded his father to play a game of cards with him, was so insistent that day that the king, in spite of his situation, could not refuse him. The dauphin lost every game that they played. "Every time that I am about to win, I lose the game," he said with some vexation. The king made no reply.

At 11 o'clock, while the king was giving his son a reading lesson, two municipal officers entered and told the king that they had come to fetch young Louis and take him to his mother. The king wished to know the reason for his removal, but the commissioners replied that they were only executing the orders of the council of the Commune. The king kissed his son tenderly and charged Cléry to go with him. When Cléry returned to the king, he told him that he had left the young prince in his mother's arms, and that seemed to put the king at ease. One of the commissioners entered to inform the king that Chambon, the mayor of Paris, was in the council chamber and was coming up to see him. "What does he want of me?" asked the king.

"I do not know," replied the municipal officer bluntly.

The king paced hastily back and forth in his room for a short while. Then he seated himself in an armchair close to the head of his bed. The door was half closed, and the municipal officer dared not enter, presumably to avoid any questions from the king. Half an hour passed in deep silence, and the commissioner became uneasy at not hearing the king. He entered the king's room quietly, and found him with his head on one of his hands, apparently in deep thought. "What do you want?" asked the king in a loud voice.

"I feared you were ill," replied the municipal officer.

"I am obliged to you," said the king in a sorrowful tone, "but the manner in which my son has been taken from me is infinitely painful to me." The municipal said nothing in reply and withdrew.

The mayor did not appear for at least an hour. He was accompanied by Chaumette, the public prosecutor of the Commune, and Santerre, the commander of the National Guard. The mayor told the king that he had come to take him before the Convention according to the decree that read: "Louis Capet will be arraigned before the bar of the National Convention."

"Capet is not my name," said the king. "It is the name of one of my ancestors. I would have wished, monsieur," he added, "that the commissioners would have let my son remain by my side for the two hours I waited for you. This treatment is but a sequel of all that I have experienced here for the past four months. I shall now follow you, not to obey the Convention, but because my enemies have the power to force me." Cléry gave the king his overcoat and his hat as he followed the mayor out of the room. A large escort awaited the king at the gates of the Temple.

Left alone in the room with a municipal officer, Cléry learned from him that the king would never see his family again, but that the mayor was to consult with some of the deputies about the separation. Cléry asked the commissioner to take him to the dauphin, who was with the queen, which he did. He did not leave the little prince until 6 o'clock in the evening. The municipal officers had informed the queen of the king's departure for the Assembly, but they would not go into any details. The princesses and the dauphin went down as usual to dine in the king's room and returned to their own rooms immediately afterwards. Although they could not express their fears and anguish in front of the guards, Cléry could read the distress in their eyes that their lips could not utter.

After dinner, a single municipal officer remained in the queen's room. He was a young man in his mid-20s who normally worked in another section of the Temple. He was on guard at the tower for the first time and seemed to be less suspicious and more civil than most of his colleagues. The queen began a conversation with him, asking him about his profession and his parents. Madame Elisabeth seized the moment to pass into her own room and made Cléry a sign to follow her. Once there, he told her that the Commune had ordered the separation of the king from his family and that he feared it would take place that very evening.

"The Queen and I," answered Madame Elisabeth, "expect the worst. We are well aware of the fate they are preparing for the King. He will die a victim of his kindness and his love for his people, for whose happiness he has never ceased to work since he ascended the throne. How cruelly his people are deceived! But the King's religion and his great confidence in Providence will sustain him in this cruel adversity."

"And now, Cléry," added the virtuous princess with her eyes filling with tears and thinking she would never see him again, "you will be alone with my brother. Take extra care of him, and make sure news of him will reach us. However, do not expose yourself, for if you do we shall be left with no one in whom we can trust." Cléry assured Madame Elisabeth of his devotion to the king, and they then agreed upon a secret manner of keeping the lines of communication open.

Turgy alone was named as being worthy of being involved in the secret. It was settled that Cléry should, as before, stay in charge of the dauphin's clothes. Every other day, when sending up a change of clothing, Cléry would endeavor to send information as well. "If the King were to be indisposed, I wish particularly to hear of it," added Madame Elisabeth. "Take this handkerchief, and keep it as long as my brother is well. Should he become ill, send it to me with my nephew's linen. Take care to fold it in this way if the indisposition is slight, and in that manner if it is more serious."

"Have you heard the officers speak of the Queen," continued the princess. "Do you know what fate they reserve for her? Alas, what can they reproach her with?"

"Nothing, Madame," replied Cléry, "but with what can they reproach the King?"

"Oh, nothing, nothing; but perhaps they look upon the King as a victim necessary to their projects, or even to their safety. Whereas, the Queen and her children are no obstacle to their ambition." When Cléry expressed a hope that the King might only be banished, Madame Elisabeth replied sadly, "Oh, I keep no sort of hope."

This was the longest conversation that she had ever dared to have with Cléry, and the fear of the arrival of the officials soon brought it to a close, and not a moment too soon. Tison remarked about its length to Cléry, who put him off with some words about the probability of the dauphin now remaining with the queen.

The King's Sister

Who was this saintly woman who remained by her brother's side during the most horrid of circumstances? Where Louis XVI lacked firmness and royal assertion, Madame Elisabeth showed physical and moral courage to the end.

Elisabeth Philippine Marie Hélène de France, granddaughter of Louis XV, was born at Versailles on 3 May 1764. At her birth, she was so delicate that for months her health was a source of continual anxiety. Her father died the following year, and her mother in 1767. The little orphan was then given wholly to the care of the Comtesse de Marsan, then governess of the children of France.

Young Elisabeth was very different from her brothers and sisters. It was often necessary to reprimand her and guide her. Proud, inflexible, and passionate, she had, according to Madame de Marsan, "defects to be mastered which would have been regrettable in a lower rank; in a Princess of royal blood they were intolerable." The task of the princess's governess was a difficult one because the young princess was strong-willed and obstinate. Proud of her social standing, her governess said "She thought she had no need to learn and tire herself uselessly, and she would throw a tantrum if any of her servants did not immediately follow her orders."

Madame Elisabeth of France, sister of Louis XVI

On one occasion when Elisabeth became very ill, her sister Clotilde insisted on taking care of her. Clotilde taught her little sister the alphabet and how to spell and form words, she gave her tidbits of advice that tended to soften her character, and she instilled in her the first notions of religion. The two sisters became very closely attached to each other, and, little by little, Elisabeth learned to accept the wise and friendly suggestions from her family and governesses. The defects which retarded her progress soon disappeared.

Deprived of her parents, Elisabeth's heart turned to fraternal love. She cherished her three brothers, but she became especially attached to the dauphin, the future Louis XVI. She was also inspired by the Abbé de Montégut, who explained the Gospels to her and tutored her in her faith. Her governess, Madame de Marsan, also took her to Saint-Cyr on many occasions, a royal boarding school that emphasized religion and liturgy.

When her grandfather, Louis XV, died in 1774, Elisabeth was 10 years old, and the dauphin and his wife, Marie-Antoinette, became king and queen of France at the ages of 20 and 19, respectively. That year and the next, Elisabeth spent most of her time attending to her education, but she always accompanied the king and queen's court, whether at Versailles, Fontainebleau, Marly, Compiegne, or La Muette.

The following year, Elisabeth and Clotilde were separated by Clotilde's marriage to the future King of Sardinia. When the moment of separation came, Elisabeth clung to her sister with such force that they had to be torn apart. Queen Marie-Antoinette, writing a few days later to her mother, the Empress of Austria, said:

> My sister Elisabeth is a very charming child, who has intelligence, character, and much grace; she showed the greatest feeling, and much above her age, at the departure of her sister. The poor little girl was in despair, and as her health is very delicate, she was taken ill and had a very severe nervous attack. I own to my dear mamma that I fear I am getting too attached to her, feeling, from the example of my aunts, how essential it is for her happiness not to remain an old maid in this country.

After Clotilde's departure, the king decided to give Elisabeth her own household: He gave her the Comtesse Diane de Polignac as lady-of-honor and the Marquise de Sérent as her lady-in-waiting. From that moment, there was also the question of Elisabeth's marriage. It seemed that her hand was destined for the infant of Portugal, who was the same age as Elisabeth; such a proposal would have eventually brought her the title of queen. Although she understood the importance of this alliance, she dreaded the thought of leaving Versailles. Fortunately, the negotiations were later broken off. Shortly thereafter, however, two other princes sought the honor of obtaining her hand in marriage, but these negotiations failed as well. Although Elisabeth never married, she was still called "Madame Elisabeth," and not "Mademoiselle Elisabeth. The king's sisters were always referred to as "Madame" in the French court.

As time went on, Madame Elisabeth found companionship and happiness in her own little circle at the court of Versailles. She lived in perfect harmony with Louis and Marie-Antoinette. They met together for meals and only ate apart when their dinners were in public. Supper normally took place in the apartments of the Comtesse de Provence, and Elisabeth always took her place there as soon as she had finished her lessons. Such family intimacy, which was unknown to the court of Versailles, was the work of the queen, and she maintained it with perseverance. The interests and pleasures of such a young court, nevertheless, soon gave rise to intrigues that at times divided the members of the royal family.

Elisabeth's brother, Louis XVI, had always been a simple and frugal man. He enjoyed reading and studying, and he sought to forget the responsibility of the throne with hunting expeditions or even manual labor. He detested "women without virtue" and "men without conscience." He thus seemed a stranger in his own court, where high moral standards were lacking, to say the least. He preferred to spend his time making locks and amused himself in the royal locksmith workshop.

King Louis XVI in his workshop

The young king Louis was dutiful, and he regarded himself as the father of all Frenchmen, but his brother, the Comte de Provence, thought otherwise. He felt himself far superior to the king and thought that he should have been sitting on the throne in his place. On one occasion the king used an expression that was grammatically incorrect. "What a barbarism!" cried the Comte de Provence, "A Prince ought to know his own tongue."

"And you ought to hold yours!" replied the king sarcastically.

Like the Comte de Provence, the other princes and princesses of the blood seldom appeared at Louis XVI's court, finding the tastes and habits of the king's court too unsophisticated. Marie-Antoinette preferred the jolly company of younger, pleasure-loving youth to that of the elderly aunts of the king, who sought to rule her as they dominated him with stiff conventionalities. The Comte of Provence, however, was especially mischievous, because had Marie-Antoinette been childless, he would have been heir to the throne. One exception must be made, however, for the Princess de Lamballe, whose function as superintendent of the queen's household and her affection for the queen herself, always kept her at court.

Madame Elisabeth, at the age of 15, could have found herself surrounded by the splendors of fortune, and she could have enjoyed the circles of the noblest of ladies, yet she exercised the same control and watchfulness about her conduct that her governesses had taught her. "My education is not finished," she said. "I shall continue it under the same rules: I shall keep my masters, and the same hours will be given to religion, the study of languages, literature, instructive conversations, and to my walks and rides on horseback."

In 1781, the king acquired the property of the Princess de Guéménée at Montreuil after her family faced financial ruin and bankruptcy. He asked the queen to invite Elisabeth to go to Montreuil the next time that they took an excursion together and to take her into the house that belonged to her former governess. He knew that Elisabeth had very fond memories of her childhood there.

Delighted with the surprise she was about to give to the princess, the queen gave Elisabeth an invitation: "If you like," she said, "we will stop on our way at Montreuil, where you were so fond of going as a child."

Elisabeth replied, "It would be a great pleasure."

On arriving at the manor, and as soon as they had entered the salon, the queen said: "Sister, you are in your own house now. This is to be your Trianon. The king, who gives himself the pleasure of giving it to you, gives me the pleasure of telling you."

The brotherly generosity of Louis XVI was well received, and this gift became a source of infinite enjoyment. The princess was known to be timid, reserved, and at times embarrassed, not only in the queen's salons but also in her own when surrounded by all of her ladies. Now it was possible for the princess to escape the uncomfortable life at Versailles, when she was not required to attend according to court etiquette, and to enjoy the peaceful estate and rural surroundings of her new home.

The park and mansion of Montreuil were near the entrance to the town of Versailles on the road to Paris. The park itself was 12 acres, charmingly covered with willows and trees and shrubbery paths in all directions. Elisabeth devoted a large section of the property to a small herd of cows, and the rest she reserved to care for the sick and those in need. The milk of her dairy went to the children and the vegetables and fruit to the sick. She was often seen attending to the distribution herself. Furthermore, all this was not done without personal sacrifice: She only had a small pension which she received for being the king's sister.

"Yes, that is very pretty," she replied, when urged to buy jewels that she fancied, "but with that money I could set up two little homes for the needy." Moreover, Elisabeth herself frowned on taking any credit for doing good deeds. On one occasion, when a bishop praised her in a very admirable speech, she said, blushingly, that he judged her far too favorably. "Madame," he replied, "I am not even on the level of my subject."

"You are right," she said, with a certain little sarcasm that was all her own. "You are very much above it."

Elisabeth's religious fervor and zeal for charity is reflected in letters to her best friend, the Marquise de Bombelles. After visiting two poor families without her companion, she wrote the following lines:

> Perhaps you will think that rather vain-glorious, but I assure you, my heart [*mon coeur*], that I am very far from thinking that I can remain good; I feel I have very much to do to be good according to God. The world judges lightly; on a mere nothing it gives us good or a bad reputation. Not so with God; he judges us internally; and the more the outward imposes, the sterner he will be to the inward...

Elisabeth's relationship with Louis XVI was very different from that of her other brothers. Elisabeth and the king both seemed to be aware that she was, and would be, quite necessary to him in his court at Versailles. For example, the king knew that she enjoyed visiting her aunt Louise, the Carmelite nun at Saint-Denis, but the king became somewhat uneasy at the frequency of her visits. "I am very willing," he said to her one day, "that you should go and see your aunt, but only on condition that you will not imitate her. Elisabeth, *I need you.*" Her heart had probably told her that already, and the time was swiftly approaching when she would give up her life to him.

Such were the happy days of the young princess until the terrible winter of 1788–89, when the sufferings of the poor exhausted her financially, forcing her into debt to advance to the starved and frozen people what she called "their revenue." Her letters show that she already foresaw, and rightly, the public troubles that were soon to confront her family, and the king in particular. "I see a thousand things," she said, "which he does not even suspect, because his soul is so good that intrigue is foreign to it."

On the 5th of October 1789, the day when the Parisian mob of women marched to Versailles and compelled the king to take the fatal step of going to Paris, Madame Elisabeth was suddenly, without warning, hurried from her dear estate of Montreuil—never to see it again. From the terrace of her garden, she saw the first axe-yielding women, and, mounting her horse, she rode to the palace. The king was out hunting, but messengers had already gone for him, and when he returned, she urged him to stand firm against this vanguard of anarchy, saying that a "vigorous and immediate repression would avert great future evils." She also instinctly advised him that if the royal family left Versailles at all, it should be for a town at a distance from Paris, "where loyal men could rally to the King and enable him to break through the tyranny that the factions were beginning to exercise."

Madame Elisabeth at Montreuil

For a moment, he seemed to listen to her and to the counsels of Saint-Priest, his minister of the interior, whose opinions agreed entirely with those of the princess. However, his firmness soon gave way to the views of Necker, his finance minister, and he consented to negotiate with the rioters. Prompted by its leaders, the mob demanded that the king should immediately change his residence to Paris, and Lafayette sent message after message urging him to comply with the request. Elisabeth expressed her opinion: "It is not to Paris, Sire, that you should go. You still have devoted battalions and faithful guards to protect you. I implore you, my brother, not to go to Paris."

The king, pulled this way and that by conflicting opinions, hesitated too long; the moment for resistance was lost. The troops, resentful for being neglected, lost ardor, and the king finally deferred to the clamor of the multitude; he gave his promise to depart for Paris. As the miserable procession passed Montreuil, Madame Elisabeth bent forward in the carriage to look at the trees of her cherished domain. "Are you bowing to Montreuil, sister?" asked the king. "Sire," she answered softly, "I am bidding it farewell."

From this time forward, she shared the captivity of her brother and his family. Under house arrest at the Tuileries, a semblance of social life was maintained. The Princess de Lamballe tried to gather a society about her, and for a while the queen appeared at her gatherings. However, confidence and a sense of safety soon disappeared. This last effort by the princess to emulate the previous court at Versailles failed, and the royal family eventually took up a manner of living that they followed ever after, even in the Temple.

During the mornings, the queen and Madame Elisabeth supervised the lessons of Madame Royale and the dauphin, and they worked at large pieces of tapestry. Needlework became their sole distraction. Their minds were too preoccupied by the events of the day, the perils of the present, and the threats of the future to allow them to read books, as they did later in the awful silence and monotony of the tower.

During this time, Madame Elisabeth continued whenever the opportunity came to her to urge the king to assert himself and firmly maintain his power and the monarchy.

The queen shared the anxiety that the king's weakness inspired in Madame Elisabeth, but she had an idea which Madame Elisabeth did not share. She was convinced that the safety of the royal family and the French monarchy would be undertaken by her family in Austria, and that some help would come from that direction, without her making any appeal for it. She was wrong.

Madame Elisabeth judged the politics of the European powers with severity. Madame Elisabeth had been brought up, like all the princesses of the House of France, to distrust Austria. The same feelings could not be expected of the queen, the daughter of Maria Theresa. Although Marie-Antoinette never dreamed of sacrificing France to her native country, she did hope and believe, however, that the alliance with the House of Austria, on which her marriage had been based, would serve the interests of both nations and be a support to the French monarchy, now shaken to its foundations.

The day came at last when Louis XVI, provoked by his virtual captivity and the increasing monstrous insults of the street populace, attempted to recover the power that was rightfully his as king of France. He resolved to leave Paris and raise his banner elsewhere in France. On the 20th of June 1791, he followed the advice his sister had given him two years earlier when placed under house arrest in the Tuileries.

The royal family's escape from Paris and its capture in the village of Varennes was a tragic and humiliating experience for Madame Elisabeth, but she only makes a brief allusion to it in her letters. After their return to Paris, Lafayette, appointed governor of the Tuileries and keeper of the king and royal family, offered to allow Madame Elisabeth to leave the kingdom. Not wanting to leave her brother and his family, she refused to accept his offer, and that decision sealed her fate.

Nevertheless, she shuddered as she thought about the position of the king and queen, deprived of all military support, reduced to begging their friends to leave the court for their own safety, isolated on a throne without power, and held captive in a palace that was really a prison. In spite of the vast emigration of nobles and gentlemen who abandoned their country and their king from the time of the first revolutionary alarms in 1789, a few faithful men remained in Paris, resolved to save the king and his family if it were still possible. Their attempts failed, too.

On the 10th of August, when the king was persuaded, against the will of his wife and sister, to seek refuge in the National Assembly, his Swiss Guard fought to defend the Tuileries Palace. They were unaware, however, that the king had already left; believing that he was still in the palace, they fought to defend him to their death—only to be outnumbered and butchered by the revolutionaries.

Long before this day, Madame Elisabeth had abandoned hope; she no longer sought to arm the king with courage. The lines of her face, and the look in her eyes now revealed her resignation, and such was her demeanor from that day forward. The tower of the Temple, that historical purgatory of the royalty of France, was soon to be the last scene of the virtues of Madame Elisabeth. She had written earlier on the 8th of October 1789:

> My letter's date alone will tell you to what a point
> our misfortunes have come. We have left the cradle
> of our childhood—what am I saying? Left? No, we

were torn from it. What a journey! What sights! Never, never will they be effaced from my memory …What is certain is that we are prisoners here; my brother does not believe it, but time will prove it to him. Our friends are here; they think as I do that we are lost.

Although Elisabeth had given up all hope long before being imprisoned in the Temple, she continued to use any opportunity to get information about her brother, who was now being tried for treason. Cléry could still confide in Turgy, but he seldom had the opportunity to speak to him, and then only with precaution. The municipal officers had agreed that Turgy should continue to take care of the linen and clothes of the dauphin, and that every two days Cléry should send him what was necessary. This suggested to Madame Elisabeth the idea of giving Cléry one of her handkerchiefs. "Keep it," she said, "as long as my brother is well. If he should become ill, send it to me in my nephew's linen." Also, the manner in which the handkerchief was folded would indicate the kind of illness.

The king escorted to his trial at the Convention

Madame Elisabeth's grief when speaking to Cléry about the king, her indifference to her own personal situation, and the value she accorded to Cléry's service to the king affected Cléry deeply.

"Have you heard anything said of the Queen?" she asked in a frightened manner. "Alas! What charges could they possibly bring against her?"

"No, Madame," Cléry replied, "but what more charges can they possibly bring against the King?"

"Oh, nothing, nothing," she said, "but perhaps they regard the King as a necessary victim, a scapegoat. The Queen and her children, however, cannot be obstacles to their ambition."

Cléry took the liberty of remarking that the king might only be sentenced to exile. He had heard that Spain, being the only country that had not declared war against France, might be the location where the king and his family would be taken. "I have no hope," she added sadly, "that the King will be saved."

Cléry reminded her that the foreign powers were consulting as to the means of freeing the king from prison, and that all Europe was interested in preventing the death of the king. Therefore, the Convention would have to reflect very seriously before deciding his fate.

This conversation lasted an hour, and then Madame Elisabeth (to whom Cléry had never spoken at such length), fearing the entrance of the new municipal officers, left him to return to the queen's apartment. Tison, who watched Cléry incessantly, remarked that he had spent a long time with Madame Elisabeth, and he was certain that the guard on duty might have noticed it. Cléry told Tison that the princess had been talking to him about her nephew, Louis Charles, who would probably stay in his mother's apartment in the future.

At 6 o'clock, the commissioners sent for Cléry to come to the council room. They read him a decree of the Commune that ordered him to have no further communication with the princesses and the little prince, because he was to serve only the king. It was also decreed, in order to put the king into more solitary confinement, that Cléry should no longer sleep in the king's apartment, but in the small tower. He would only be escorted to the king at such times as he had need of him.

At half-past 6 o'clock, the king returned from the Convention. He seemed fatigued, and his first desire was to be taken to his family. The request was refused. He then insisted that the queen should at least be told of his return, and this was promised to him. He ordered Cléry to ask for his supper at half-past 8 o'clock, and in the meantime, he returned to his usual reading, surrounded by four municipal officers.

Louis XVI on trial

At half-past 8, Cléry went to inform the king that his supper was served. He asked the commissioners if his family were not coming down to eat, but they did not answer him. "But at least," said the king, "my son will spend the night with me, his bed and clothes being here." His reply met the same silence. After supper, the king again insisted on seeing his family. They answered that he must await the decision of the Convention; he waited in vain.

That evening, while Cléry was undressing the king, the king said sadly: "I was not expecting the questions that were put to me in the trial." He then went to bed tranquilly. The decree of the Commune relating to Cléry's removal during the night was not executed; it appears it would have been too troublesome for the municipal officers to have fetched him every time the king needed his services.

The next day on the 12th, the king no sooner saw the municipal officers when he asked if a decision had been made about his request to see his family. They told him they were still awaiting orders. The king commanded Cléry to have the young prince's bed taken up to the queen's room, where he had passed the previous night on one of her mattresses. In fact, the queen had given him her own bed, and she sat up all night so grief-stricken that her daughter and sister-in-law did not leave her.

Cléry begged the king, however, to wait for the decision of the Convention. "I do not expect any justice, any consideration," replied the king, "but I will wait."

The next morning, the queen pleaded with the municipal officers to see her husband. She was never to see him again except for one occasion—on the eve of his execution.

That same day, a delegation of the Convention brought the king a decree that authorized him to obtain legal counsel. The king chose Monsieur Target, and failing him, Monsieur Tronchet, or both of them if the National Convention would consent to it. The deputies made the king sign his request, and they signed it themselves in front of him. The king added that it would also be necessary to furnish him with paper, pens, and ink to prepare his defense.

The next morning, the same deputation returned and told the king that Target refused to be his counsel, but Tronchet had been sent for and would likely appear during the day. They also read to him one of several letters addressed to the Convention; it was from Lamoignon de Malesherbes:

> CITIZEN PRESIDENT,–I do not know whether the Convention will appoint Louis XVI counsel to defend him, or whether it will leave the selection up to him. In the latter case, I desire that Louis XVI should know that if he chooses me for that function I am ready to devote myself to it. I do not ask you to present my offer before the Convention, because I am far from thinking myself of enough importance to occupy its time; but I have twice been called to be his counsel who was once my master, in the days when everyone was ambitious for that function. I owe him the same service when that function is one which many persons would think dangerous. If I knew any possible means of letting him know my inclinations, I would not take the liberty of addressing you. I think that in the position you occupy, you will have better means than anyone to convey to him this suggestion. I am, with respect, [signed] L. de Malesherbes.

The king replied that he knew there were many individuals offering to sacrifice their lives to serve as his counsel, and he wanted to express his gratitude to all of them. However, he finally accepted Malesherbes' offer as his counsel, but he added that if Tronchet was unable to lend him his services as well, he would consult Malesherbes and then choose someone else to replace Tronchet.

Chapter 11
The King's Trial

I have learned how wicked and malevolent a man can be. I did not believe that there were such men.

–Louis XVI to Cléry,
Temple Prison, December 1792

On the 14th, Tronchet agreed to assist in representing the king. On the same day, Malesherbes was finally brought to the tower. The king ran forward to meet and embrace the respectable man. Recalling the past years of his reign and facing the virtuous king in the midst of his misfortunes, the former minister burst into tears on seeing him.

Malesherbes (1721–1794)

Since the king had permission to meet with his counsel in private, Cléry closed the door to the king's room, so that he might speak more freely with Malesherbes. A municipal officer chastised him, however, and ordered the door to be opened. He forbade Cléry to shut it again.

On the 15th, the king received the reply regarding his family, which stated that the queen and Madame Elisabeth could not communicate with the king during the course of his trial. His children might be allowed to visit him if he so desired, but only on the condition that they could not have any contact with their mother or their aunt until the trial was over. As soon as it was possible to speak to the king freely, Cléry asked for his orders. "You see," said the king, "the cruel alternative in which they place me. I cannot resolve to have my children with me. I feel it would cause too much grief for the queen." The king then ordered Cléry for the second time to have the dauphin's bed sent up to the queen's room, which he did immediately. He kept the prince's linen and his clothes, however, and every second day he sent up what was necessary as agreed upon with Madame Elisabeth.

On the 16th, at 4 o'clock in the afternoon, another delegation from the Convention arrived. They brought the king his arraignment, and certain documents on which the accusations were based. Reading of these documents, more than 100 in all, lasted until midnight. All were read and signed by the king, and copies of each were left in his hands. The king was seated at a large table with Tronchet beside him and the deputies opposite him. He interrupted the long session by asking the deputies if they would have supper. They accepted, and Cléry served them cold chicken and some fruit in the dining room. Tronchet declined, however, and remained alone with the king in his room.

One of the deputies asked Cléry several questions as to how the king was being treated. He was about to answer when a commissioner told the committee that it was forbidden to speak to Cléry, and that they would give him all the details he could require in the council chamber later. The deputy, fearing that he might compromise himself, said no more to Cléry.

Being separated from the king, the queen could not be comforted. She remained in a sort of mute despair, hardly speaking to her children. She incessantly tried to procure some information from the guards, who answered with great caution. Nevertheless, they did show her some compassion and encouraged her not to give up hope.

From the 14th to the 26th of December, the king saw his counsel on a regular basis. They came at 5 o'clock in the evening and retired by 9 o'clock. Every morning, Malesherbes brought the newspaper to the king with the printed opinions of the deputies relating to his trial. He prepared the work for the evening and remained with the king for one or two hours. The king would sometimes let Cléry read those opinions, and on one occasion the king asked Cléry: "What do you think of that man's opinion? I have learned how wicked and malevolent a man can be. I did not believe that there were such men."

King Louis XVI in the Temple

The king never went to bed without reading all the different papers, and, in order not to compromise Malesherbes, he took the precaution to burn them afterwards in the stove in his chambers.

By this time, Cléry had found a favorable moment to speak to Turgy and to send news to Madame Elisabeth about the king. The next day, Turgy told him that, when she had given him her napkin after dinner, she had slipped a little note in it using pinpricks that asked the king to write her a line himself. The day after, Cléry took the note to Turgy, who brought him the answer inside a ball of cotton, which he threw on Cléry's bed as he passed by it. The king was completely satisfied with the success of this means of communicating with his family.

The wax candles which the commissioners gave Cléry were tied in bundles with twine. As soon as he had enough twine he told the king that they could improve their communication by sending messages to Madame Elisabeth whose room was directly over his. With her window perpendicularly above that of a little corridor upon which his room opened, Cléry thought the princess could attach letters to the string and lower them down to the passage window during the night. The same means would serve to send answers to the princess as well as paper and ink of which she was deprived. "That is a good project," the king said to Cléry. "We will use it if the other means become impracticable."

As a matter of fact, they soon used this new method exclusively. Cléry always waited until 8 o'clock in the evening. Then he would shut the door of his room and that of the corridor, and he would go to talk to the commissioners or get them to play cards, which would divert their attention.

After the king was separated from his family, he refused to go into the garden, and when the municipal officers proposed that he take a walk, he replied: "I cannot resolve to go out alone; walking was only agreeable to me when I enjoyed it with my family." Nevertheless, in spite of being thus parted from those who were so dear to his heart, he never complained; in fact, he had already forgiven his oppressors.

The question arises: Why was the king so generous to forgive his oppressors? He and his family were subjected to the most inhumane treatment and surveillance in the Temple every day. Perhaps his daughter's memoires provides insight into his character:

> Such was the life of the King, my father, during a
> severe imprisonment. Piety, magnanimity, firmness,

gentleness, courage, kindness, patient endurance of the most horrible calumnies, whole-hearted forgiveness of his assassins, and the most profound love for God, his family, and his people—these and these only were the qualities he showed until he breathed his last, and went to receive his reward for them in the bosom of an almighty and pitiful God.

The king also treated Cléry as if he were more than his servant, and he treated the municipal officers that guarded him as if he had no reason to complain about them. He talked to them, as he formerly did with his own subjects, about matters relating to their family, their children, and the advantages and duties of their profession. Those who listened were astonished at the accuracy of his remarks, at the depth and variety of his knowledge, and the manner in which it was all stored away in his memory. However, it never appeared that his conversations were disguised to distract him from his worries. He always seemed genuine and reserved.

On the 19th of December, the king said to Cléry while dining: "Fourteen years ago you got up earlier than you did today." Cléry understood His Majesty at once. "That was the day my daughter was born," he continued tenderly, "and today, her birthday, I am deprived of seeing her!" A few tears rolled from his eyes, followed by a moment of respectful silence.

The day for his second appearance before the bar of the Convention was approaching. He had not been able to shave since they took away his razors, and he had to bathe his face in cold water several times a day. Not willing to speak to the municipal officers about it himself, he asked Cléry for scissors and a razor. Cléry took the liberty of remarking to him that if he appeared in his present condition before the Convention, the people would see with what barbarity the council of the Commune had treated him. "I ought not to try to interest persons in that way in my fate," replied the king. "I will address the commissioners." The following day the Commune decided to return the razors to the king, but for use only in the presence of two municipal officers.

During the three days before Christmas, the king wrote more than usual. There was discussion of making him stay at the Feuillants for two or three days in order that he might be tried continuously. They had even given Cléry orders to prepare to follow him and to get everything ready that he might need, but that plan was changed, too.

It was on Christmas Day that the king wrote his last will and testament. Cléry read it and copied it before it was handed over to the council of the Temple; the original was written entirely in the king's own handwriting with only a few erasures. The first paragraph portrayed not only the King's suffering but his claim of innocence as well.

> THE LAST WILL AND TESTAMENT OF LOUIS XVI, KING OF FRANCE. In the name of the Holy Trinity, Father, Son, and Holy Spirit, this day, twenty-fifth of December, one thousand seven hundred and ninety-two, I, Louis, sixteenth of the name, King of France, being for the last four months shut up with my family in the Tower of the Temple by those who were my subjects, and deprived of all communication whatsoever since the eleventh of the present month with my family; involved moreover in a trial of which it is impossible to foresee the issue, because of the passions of men, and for which no pretext or means can be found in existing laws; having God as the sole witness of my thoughts and the only being to whom I can address myself, I here declare in his presence my last will and sentiments.

In another passage, the king forgave his accusers but also asked forgiveness from his family and especially the queen, Marie-Antoinette. Despite the animosity of the public against the Austrian princess, the king insisted that she was in no way the cause of the royal family's misfortunes. Moreover, he did not want her to share the burden of any guilt.

> I beg my wife to forgive me for all the ills she has suffered for me, and the grief I may have caused her in the course of our union; just as she may be sure that I keep nothing against her should she think she has anything for which to blame herself.

Next the king addressed the plight of the young prince who would inherit the throne—should the French ever accept a monarchy again. The King considered it a misfortune if the young prince should ever sit on the throne of France. Undoubtedly from his own experience, he found that it was impossible to rule without full authority and respect from the people. Moreover, he asked the young prince to forgive, and forget, all those who had mistreated the royal family.

> I beg my son, if he has the misfortune to become King, to reflect that he owes himself wholly to the welfare of his co-citizens; that he ought to forget all hatred and all resentment, especially that which relates to the misfortunes and grief that I have borne; that he cannot make the happiness of the people except by reigning according to the laws; but, at the same time, that a King cannot make the laws respected and do the good which is in his heart to do unless he has the necessary authority; otherwise, being fettered in his operations and inspiring no respect, he is more harmful than useful.

He also advised the young prince to "take care" of all those and their families who had sacrificed their lives and their worldly goods for the monarchy.

> I recommend that my son take care of all the persons who have been attached to me, so far as the circumstances in which he may be placed will give him the ability; to remember that this is a sacred debt contracted by me towards the children and relatives of those who have perished for me, and towards those who are so unfortunate for my sake.

Cléry was perhaps not too surprised that the king would also recommend that the prince, if ever king, should remember the kindness and dedication of the royal servants that risked their lives to serve Their Majesties. The question thus arises if Cléry was aware that it would be in his best interest to see the young prince someday returned to the throne. The king also bequeathed some personal articles to Cléry.

> Nevertheless, I think I should calumniate the sentiments of the nation if I did not commend openly to my son MM. De Chamilly and Hüe, whose true attachment to me led them to shut themselves up in

this sad place, and who came so near being also the unfortunate victims of it. I likewise recommend to him Cléry, whose care I have every reason to praise since he has been with me; as it is he who will remain with me to the end, I beg the gentlemen of the Commune to give him my clothes, my books, my watch, my purse, and whatever little property has been deposited with the council of the Commune.

The king ended his last will and testament by once again pardoning all those who had mistreated him and his family, and by thanking those who were assisting him with legal counsel during his trial. His final words simply expressed his innocence of all charges against him.

Louis XVI cross-examined by the Convention at his trial

On the 26th of December, the king was taken for the second time before the bar of the Convention. Fearing that the noise of the drums and the movements of the troops would frighten the queen, Cléry had warned the queen beforehand. The king left at 10 o'clock in the morning and returned at 5 o'clock in the afternoon. The members of his counsel came that evening just as the king was finishing supper, and he asked them to have refreshments. Only one of them accepted the offer. The king also thanked them for the pains they had taken in making their speeches to the Convention.

On the 1st of January 1793, Cléry went to the king's bedside and asked him in a low voice to be allowed to offer his earnest wishes for the end of all his troubles. "I receive those wishes," the king said affectionately, holding out his hand which Cléry kissed with tears in his eyes. As soon as he rose, the king begged a municipal officer to go and inquire news about his family and give them his wishes for the new year. The municipal officers were very moved by the tone of his voice, so pitiful in view of the king's situation. The officer that had gone to see the queen returned and announced to the king that his family thanked him for his good wishes and they sent him their own. "What a New Year's Day!" exclaimed the king.

Turgot and Malesherbes also visited the king to offer their good wishes for the New Year, but the king would not allow them to remain with him, reminding them that they should not neglect their own families. "You especially, my dear Malesherbes, who has three generations behind you," the king cried. "I could not forgive myself if I took you away from them."

That same evening, Cléry took the liberty of telling His Majesty that he was almost certain that the Convention would give its consent if he would only ask to be permitted to see his family. "In a few days," the king replied, "they will not refuse me that consolation; I must wait."

As the day for the verdict approached, Cléry's fears and anguish increased. He asked the municipal officers hundreds of questions, and everything he heard only added to his terror. Madame Cléry came to see him every week, and she gave him an exact account of what was going on in Paris. Public opinion seemed still to be favorable to the king; it was shown in a startling way at the Théâtre Français and at the Vaudeville. At the Théâtre, they were playing "L'Ami des Lois," in which all the allusions to the trial of the king were portrayed—and applauded—vehemently. At the Vaudeville, one of the actors asked, "How can you be accusers and judges both?" The audience insisted on the repetition of that speech many times.

"Citizen" Laya wrote the play in response to the horrors of mob rule, asking for religious tolerance. Ten days after its opening, the play was condemned by the Convention, but Cléry managed to sneak a copy of "L'Ami des Lois" to the king. He often told him, and he himself almost came to believe it, that the members of the Convention, being opposed to one another, could only ask for the penalty of imprisonment or exile for the king.

L'AMI

DES LOIS,

COMÉDIE EN CINQ ACTES, EN VERS.

*Représentée par les Comédiens de la Nation, le 2
janvier 1793.*

PAR LE CITOYEN LAYA,

AUTEUR DES DANGERS DE L'OPINION ET ET DE JEAN CALAS.

> *Tùm pietate gravem ac meritis si forté virum quem
> Conspexére, silent, arrectisque auribus adstant :
> Ille regit dictis animos , et pectora mulcet.*

A PARIS,

Chez MARADAN , Libraire , rue du Cimitcère Saint-
André-des-Arcs , n°. 9.

Et chez LEPETIT , Commissionnaire en Librairie , quai des
Augustins , n°. 32.

1 7 9 3.

Laya's play prohibited by the Convention

"May they have that moderation for my family," said the king. "It is only for them that I fear."

Certain persons sent Cléry word through his wife that a considerable sum of money deposited with an editor of a daily tabloid was at the king's disposal. They requested that Cléry ask for the money to be paid to Malesherbes if the king so wished. "Thank those persons much for me," the king replied. "I cannot accept their generous offer; it might implicate them." The fact that Cléry begged him at least to mention the matter to Malesherbes reveals Cléry's utmost optimism for the king's fate, and the king promised to do so.

The secret correspondence between the king and queen also continued. The king, informed of his daughter's illness, was very uneasy for some days. The queen, after many requests, finally obtained permission for Dr. Brunier, her children's physician, to come to the Temple. The princess's body was covered with boils due to the lack of fresh air and the confinement. The fact that Brunier was summoned seemed to calm the king.

On the 16th of January, at 6 o'clock in the evening, four municipal officers entered the king's chamber and read to him a decree of the Commune. It stated that the king "was to be guarded night and day by four municipals; two of whom were to pass the night beside his bed." The king asked if his sentence had been pronounced. One of the municipal officers sitting in the king's armchair answered that he should not trouble himself about what went on in the Convention, but he had heard someone say they were still calling the votes.

A few moments later, Malesherbes arrived and told the king that the call of the votes had not yet ended. While he was there, however, a chimney in one of the rooms of the Temple had caught fire. A considerable crowd of people gathered in the courtyard. A commissioner entered the king's room to tell Malesherbes that he had to leave the premises immediately. Malesherbes withdrew after promising the king he would return to inform him of his sentence.

"Why are you so alarmed?" Cléry asked the commissioner.

"Royalists have set fire to the Temple," he said, "in order to rescue Capet in the tumult, but I have surrounded the walls with a strong guard." The fire was soon put out, but it was later shown to have been a mere accident.

On Thursday, the 17th of January, Malesherbes came at 9 o'clock in the morning, and Cléry went to meet him. "All is lost," he said; "the King has been condemned to death." Cléry was so overcome with emotion that he was unable to utter a single word as he escorted the king's old friend to his chambers upstairs.

The king, who saw him coming, rose to receive him. The minister threw himself sobbing at his feet, and it was some time before he could speak. The king raised him and embraced him with affection. When Malesherbes told him that he had been sentenced to death, the king made no movement that showed either surprise or emotion; he seemed to be affected only by the grief of his old friend, and he tried to comfort him.

Malesherbes gave an account to the king of the tribunal's voting. His denouncers, his relatives, personal enemies, ecclesiastics, laymen, and absent deputies—all had voted. Those who had voted for death either for political reasons or believing the king was guilty carried it by a majority of only seven votes. Even the king's cousin had voted for his execution.

Louis XVI notified of his trial, he faces the tribunal

The king obtained permission to see Malesherbes in private. He took him into his cabinet, shut the door, and was alone with him for about an hour. Malesherbes was overcome with grief. "My friend, do not weep," the king said. "We shall meet again in a better world. I am grieved to leave such a friend as you are." He then escorted him to the entrance door and asked him to come early that evening and not to abandon him in his last moments. "The sorrow of that good old man has deeply affected me," said the king as he returned to the room where Cléry was waiting for him.

From the moment that Malesherbes had given him the shocking news, Cléry could not keep from trembling. Nevertheless, he prepared what was necessary for the king to shave himself. The king put the soap on his face himself, while Cléry held the basin. Forced to control his grief, Cléry did not dare raise his eyes to look at his master. By chance, he looked at him and his tears flowed in spite of himself; his knees began to give way from under him. The king, who noticed that he might faint, took him by both hands, squeezed them hard, and said in a low voice, "Come, more courage."

The king remained in his chamber until dinner time. In the evening, Cléry watched him go towards his cabinet, and he followed his master under pretext that he might need his services. "Have you read the report of my sentence?" asked the king.

"Ah, Sire!" Cléry said, "Let us hope for a delay. Malesherbes thinks it cannot be refused."

"I am not hopeful," replied the king, "but I am much grieved that my cousin, the Duc d'Orléans, could have voted for my death. Read that list." He gave Cléry the list of the call of the House which he held in his hand.

"The public is protesting loudly," Cléry said to him. "Dumouriez is in Paris; they say his army is against the trial that has just taken place. The people are revolting against the infamous conduct of the Duc d'Orléans. There is a rumor that the ambassadors of the foreign powers are going to assemble and go before the Convention. They say that the members of the assembly fear a popular uprising."

"I should be very sorry if it took place," said the king. "There would only be more victims. I do not fear death," he added, "but I shudder at the cruel fate that I leave behind for my family, for the queen, for my unfortunate children, and for those faithful servants who never abandoned me."

Then after a short silence he continued: "Oh my God, is that the price I must receive for all my sacrifices? Did I not do all to procure the happiness of the French?" As he said those words, he warmly clasped Cléry's hand. The king's eyes filled with tears and, as they rolled down his cheeks, Cléry was obliged to leave him in such a pitiable condition.

The king waited vainly all that evening for Malesherbes to return. Much later, he asked Cléry if the confessor had made an appearance at the Temple gates. Cléry had asked the same question of the commissioners, and they had simply answered, "No."

On the 18th, the king had still heard nothing of Malesherbes, and he became very uneasy. That evening, Cléry took the liberty of telling him that he could not be deprived of his counsel, except by a decree of the Convention, and that the king ought to ask for them to be admitted to the tower as soon as possible. "I will wait until tomorrow," replied the king.

Saturday, the 19th, at 9 o'clock in the morning, a municipal officer named Gobeau entered with a document in his hand, and he was accompanied by the porter of the tower, who carried an inkstand. The officer told the king he had orders to make an inventory of all his property and effects. His Majesty left Cléry with him, and he retired to his reading room. Then, under pretence of the inventory, the municipal officer began to rummage through the king's items to be certain, he said, that no weapons or dangerous instruments had been hidden in the king's room.

Louis XVI on a silver coin (sol) dated 1791

Everything was searched except for a small desk where the king kept some papers. The king was required to return to his chamber and was obliged to open all the drawers and to unfold and show every document one at a time to the municipal officer. There were also three rolls of coins at the back of one drawer that they wished to examine. "That money," said the king, "is not mine; it belongs to Malesherbes which I was preparing to return to him." The three rolls contained 3,000 francs in gold; on the paper that wrapped each roll the king had written in his own hand handwriting, "Belonging to Monsieur de Malesherbes."

After the same search was made in his small reading room, the king returned to his chamber and wanted to warm himself. The porter was standing before the fire at that moment, holding his coattails up with his back to the fire. The king could not warm himself on either side of the man, and the insolent porter was not going to move. The king then told him in sharp tone to move over. The porter finally withdrew, and the municipal officers soon left, after having failed in their search.

That evening, the king told the commissioners to ask the Commune the reason why the members of his counsel were denied admission to the tower, and he added that he desired at least to consult with Malesherbes. They promised to relay his message, but one of them said they were forbidden to take any communication from the king to the council of the Commune unless it was written and signed in his own handwriting. "Then why," replied the king, "have I been left ignorant of that change for two days?"

He wrote the request and gave it to the municipal officers, but they did not take it to the Commune until the next day. The king asked to see his counsel in private and complained of the decree that ordered the municipal officers to keep him in sight day and night. "They ought to feel," he wrote to the Commune, "that in the position I am in, it is very painful not to have the tranquility necessary to enable me to collect myself."

Chapter 12
The King's Last Day

Here is a letter Mayor Pétion wrote me at the time of your entrance to the Temple. It may be useful to you for remaining here.

–Louis XVI to Cléry
Temple Prison, January 23, 1793

On Sunday, the 20th of January, the king inquired if the municipal officers had taken his request to the Commune in order to meet with his counsel, and they assured him that they had taken it immediately. Towards 10 o'clock Cléry entered the king's room, and the king asked quietly, "Malesherbes has not yet come?"

"Sire," Cléry replied, "I have just learned that he has been here several times, but his entrance to the tower has always been refused."

"I shall know the reason of that refusal," replied the king, "when the Commune decides upon my letter." He walked about his room, read some documents, and wrote a few notes to himself to occupy his time the entire morning.

Two o'clock had just struck when the door suddenly opened to admit the Executive Council. Some 15 persons came in at all at once, including Garat, the minister of justice, and Lebrun, the minister of foreign affairs. The king heard the group arrive; he rose and took a few steps forward. Garat, his hat remaining on his head as a sign of disrespect, spoke and said: "Louis, the National Convention has ordered the Provisional Executive Council to make known to you its decrees of the 15th to the 20th of January, 1973. The secretary of the Council will now read it to you." The secretary then unfolded the decree, and read it to the king in a weak and trembling voice:

ARTICLE I. The National Convention declares Louis Capet, last King of the French, guilty of conspiracy against the liberty of the Nation, and of criminal attempts against the general safety of the State.

ARTICLE II. The National Convention declares that Louis Capet shall suffer the penalty of death.

ARTICLE III. The National Convention declares null the act of Louis Capet brought to the bar of the Convention by his counsel, called an appeal to the nation from the judgment rendered against him by the Convention; it forbids all persons from taking it up, under pain of being tried and punished as guilty of criminal attempts against the safety of the Republic.

ARTICLE IV. The Provisional Executive council will notify the present decree in the course of this day to Louis Capet, and take the necessary police and safety measures to carry out the execution within twenty-four hours from the time of its notification, rendering an account of all to the National Convention immediately after the execution.

During the reading of the decree, not the slightest change appeared on the king's face. Cléry noticed only that in the first Article, when the word "conspiracy" was uttered, a smile of indignation came upon his lips. However, at the words "suffer the penalty of death," he cast a heavenly look on all those who surrounded him which told them that he did not fear death—he was innocent.

The king made a step toward the secretary, took the decree from his hand, folded it, drew his portfolio from his pocket, and put the document into it. Then, taking another paper from the same portfolio, he said to Garat: "Monsieur the Minister of Justice, I beg you to send this letter at once to the National Convention." Garat seemed to hesitate, so the king added, "I will read it to you," and he read:

I ask for a delay of three days so that I may prepare myself to appear before God. I demand for the same purpose to be able to see freely the person I shall name to the commissioners of the Commune, and that the said person shall be protected from all anxiety about the act of charity which he will do for me.

I ask to be delivered from the incessant watching which the council of the Commune established recently.

I ask to be able, during that interval, to see my family when I ask it, and without witnesses.

I much desire that the National Convention shall at once concern itself with the fate of my family, and that it will permit them to retire freely wherever they may wish to go.

I commend to the beneficence of the Nation all the persons who have been attached to me. Many have put their whole fortunes into their offices, and now, receiving no salaries, they must be in need; the same must also be the case with those who had only their salaries to support them; and among the pensioners, there are many old men, women, and children who have nothing but their pensions to live upon.

Done in the Tower of the Temple, January 20, one thousand seven hundred and ninety-three. [signed] LOUIS

Signature of Louis XVI

Garat took the king's letter and assured him that he would take it to the Convention. As he was leaving, the king drew another paper from his pocket and said: "Monsieur, if the Convention grants my request for the person I desire, here is his address." That address, in handwriting other than that of the king, was: "Monsieur Edgeworth de Firmont, 483 rue du Bac." Monsieur Firmont, originally Madame Elisabeth's priest, was recommended to the king by the princess during his impending trial.

The king then took a few steps backwards, and the minister and those who accompanied him immediately left the room. His Majesty paced up and down his room for a moment. Cléry stood leaning against the door as if in a state of shock. The king went to him and said, "Cléry, ask for my dinner." A few moments later, two municipal officers entered the dining room and read to Cléry the following order: "Louis is not to have knife or fork at his meals; a knife is to be given to his *valet de chambre* to cut his bread and meat in the presence of two commissioners, and the knife will then be removed." The two municipal officers told Cléry to inform the king, but he refused to do so.

On entering the dining room, the king saw the basket that contained the queen's dinner. He asked why they had made his family wait for an hour and added that the delay might have made them nervous. He sat down at the table and said, "I have no knife." The municipal officer informed the king of the order of the Commune. "Do they think me so cowardly as to take my own life?" said the king. "They impute to me crimes, but I am innocent and I can die without fear. I hope that my death will save the French from the evils that I foresee." A great silence fell upon the room. The king cut his beef with a spoon, and broke his bread. He ate very little, and his dinner lasted only a few minutes.

Cléry wrote that he was in his room, and he described his condition with the words *"affreuse douleur."* The king's servant was simply grief-stricken, and unable to further describe his distress when, about 6 o'clock in the evening, Garat returned to the tower. Cléry went to announce the arrival of the minister of justice to the king. Garat, advancing, told the king that he had taken his letter to the Convention, which ordered him to deliver the following answer:

> Louis is at liberty to call for any minister of worship that he thinks proper; and to see his family freely and without witnesses; the nation, always grand and always just, will concern itself with the fate of his

family; the creditors of his house will be granted just indemnities; as to the three days' respite, the National Convention passes to the order of the day.

The king listened to the reading of this reply without making any observation. He then returned to his room and said to Cléry: "I thought, from Santerre's air, that the delay might have been granted."

A young municipal officer named Boston, seeing the king speak to Cléry came nearer. "You seem to feel badly for what has happened to me," the king said to him. "Receive my thanks." The man was surprised and did not know how to answer. Cléry was himself amazed at the king's words because this young municipal officer with such a kind face had remarked a few moments earlier that he had only come to the Temple to delight in seeing the "horror on the king's face."

After reading the answer of the Convention, the commissioners who had accompanied the minister of justice addressed him, asking how the king was to see his family. "In private," replied Garat; "that is the intention of the Convention." It was then agreed that the king should receive his family in the dining room where he could be kept under surveillance through the glass partition. However, it was also agreed that the door should be shut so that the king could not be heard by the onlookers.

Louis XVI, King of France

The king then asked Garat if he had notified Monsieur de Firmont. Garat replied that he had brought him in his carriage, that he was waiting in the council room below, and that he would be escorted up immediately. The king then gave a municipal officer who was talking with Garat the sum of 3,000 francs in gold, requesting him to return it to Malesherbes, to whom it belonged. The municipal officer promised to do so, but he took the money to the council room; it was never returned to Malesherbes. Firmont appeared, and the king took him into his reading room and closed the door. After Garat had departed, no one remained in the king's apartment but the four municipal officers.

At 8 o'clock, the king came out of his cabinet and told the commissioners to take him to his family. They replied that it was impossible, but they could bring his family to him if he so desired. "Very well," said the king, "but I can, at least, see them alone in my room?"

One of them answered, "No, we have arranged with the Minister of Justice that you shall see them in the dining room."

"You have heard the decree of the Convention," said His Majesty, "which permits me to see them without witnesses."

"That is true," replied the commissioner, "you will be in private, and the door will be shut but we shall have our eyes upon you through the glass partition." Nodding, the king then asked them to bring his family down.

The king then went to the dining room. Cléry followed him and drew the table to one side, placing the chairs at the farther end of the room to make more space. "Bring some water and a glass," said the king. There was already a bottle of iced water on the table, so Cléry only brought one glass and placed it beside the water pitcher. "Bring water that is not iced," said the king. "If the Queen drank the other it might make her ill. Tell Monsieur de Firmont," he added, "not to leave my cabinet; I fear the sight of him would make my family too unhappy."

The commissioner who was sent to fetch the royal family was absent for almost a quarter of an hour; during that time the king went back to his cabinet, returning several times to the entrance and appearing very emotional.

At half past 8 the door opened. The queen appeared first, holding her son by the hand; Marie-Thérèse and Madame Elisabeth then appeared. They all ran into the arms of the king. A gloomy silence reigned for several minutes, interrupted only by sobs and whimpers. The queen made a movement to draw the king into his room. "No," he said, "let us go into the dining room. I can only see you there." They followed the king, and Cléry closed the glass door behind them. The king sat down, the queen on his left, Madame Elisabeth on his right, Marie-Thérèse nearly opposite to him, and the little prince between his knees. All were leaning toward him and held him half-embraced. This scene of sorrow lasted for more than an hour, during which time it was impossible to hear anything. It was easy, however, to judge from their emotions that the king himself was the first to tell them of his condemnation. Cléry and Firmont remained outside with the municipal officers to give the family some privacy.

Marie-Thérèse says in her mémoires that the king apologized to the queen for the actions of the vile men who had condemned him. He said that he would not consent to any attempt to save him, fearing that it might cause a frightful and violent disturbance all across France. The king also blessed the young dauphin, telling him that he must forgive all those who had caused so much distress and that he should never seek vengeance if he were ever to become king.

The king would not consent to the family's spending the night with him. At quarter past 10, the sad monarch rose first; they all followed him. Cléry opened the door, and the queen held the king by the right arm. Their Majesties each gave a hand to the dauphin. Princess Marie-Thérèse on the left clasped the king's body. Madame Elisabeth, on the same side but a little behind the rest, had caught the left arm of her brother. They all made a few steps towards the entrance, uttering the most sorrowful moans.

"I assure you," said the king, "that I will see you tomorrow morning at 8 o'clock."

"You promise us?" they all cried.

"Yes, I promise it," he replied solemnly.

"Why not at seven o'clock?" asked the queen in a trembling voice.

"Well, then, yes, at seven o'clock," said the king. "Adieu."

He uttered "adieu" in such an expressive manner that the crying in the room doubled. Marie-Thérèse fell fainting at the king's feet, which she clasped. Cléry raised her up and helped Madame Elisabeth to hold her. The king, wishing to put an end to this heartbreaking scene, gave them all a most tender embrace, and then finally had the strength to tear himself away from their arms. "Adieu, adieu," he said, and he returned to his chamber.

*Madame Elisabeth, the queen, the princess, the king, the dauphin,
and Cléry say farewell*

The princesses went up to their rooms. Cléry wished to go along to help the young princess, but the municipal officers stopped him on the second step of the stairs and forced him to go back. Though the two doors were shut, they continued to hear the sobs and moans of the princesses on the staircase. The king rejoined his confessor Firmont in his reading room.

Firmont was actually English by birth. As a boy he was brought up by the Jesuits, but he later journeyed to Paris to be trained for the priesthood. Although he originally was planning on becoming a missionary after his studies, he decided to remain in Paris where he devoted himself especially to the English Roman Catholics. Becoming friends with members of the royal court, he soon had the honor of becoming Madame Elisabeth's priest.

After supper, the king returned to his reading room, and Firmont came out an instant later and asked the commissioners to take him to the council room in order to obtain the sacerdotal robes and other things necessary to say mass the following morning. Firmont obtained permission for the items with great difficulty, but the officials eventually sent for the articles that he required for the religious service.

Returning from the council room, Firmont went back to the king. They both re-entered the reading room, where they remained until half past midnight. Then Cléry undressed the king, and as he was about to roll his hair, the king said to him, "It is not worthwhile." When the king closed the curtains after he was in bed, he said, "Cléry, wake me at five o'clock in the morning."

The king was hardly in bed before he fell into a deep sleep; in fact, he slept until 5 o'clock without waking. Firmont, whom the king had urged to take a little rest, threw himself on Cléry's bed, and Cléry spent the night on a chair in the king's room, praying God to preserve both his strength and his courage for the next day.

Cléry heard 5 o'clock strike on the city clocks, and he lit the fire in the king's room. At the noise he made, the king awoke, opened his curtain, and asked, "Is it five o'clock?" Cléry answered, "Sire, it has struck five on several of the city clocks, but not here."

After Cléry had the fire burning, he went to the king's bedside. "I have slept well," said the king. "I needed it, for yesterday tired me very much. Where is Monsieur de Firmont?"

"On my bed," answered Cléry.

"And you, where did you sleep?" asked the king.

"In this chair," he answered.

"I am sorry," said the king.

"Ah Sire!" Cléry exclaimed. "How could I think of myself at such a moment?"

The king held out his hand to Cléry and he held it with much affection. Cléry then dressed the king and arranged his hair. The king changed his shirt, put on a white waistcoat that he had worn the night before, and then Cléry helped him with his coat. The king took his portfolio, his eyeglass, his snuff box, and some other articles from his coat pockets. He then laid them down with his purse on the chimney mantle. He did all this in silence and in the presence of the municipal officers. His toilet completed, the king told Cléry to inform Firmont that he was ready. Cléry went to call him, but he was already up.

Cléry followed the king into his small reading room. He then placed a desk in the middle of the room and prepared it like an altar for the Mass. Fortunately, at 2 o'clock in the morning, all the necessary articles had been brought as requested. Cléry then took the priest's robe into his room; then, when everything was ready, he went to inform the king, who asked Cléry if he could perform the Mass. He said he would but added that he did not know all the responses by heart. The king had a book in his hand that he opened, turned to the pages of the Mass, and gave it to Cléry. He took another book for himself.

During this time, the priest robed himself. Cléry had placed an armchair before the altar and a large cushion on the floor for the king. The king made Cléry take it away, and he went himself into his cabinet to fetch another cushion which was smaller and covered with horsehair, the one which he used daily to say his prayers. As soon as the priest entered, the municipal officers retired into the antechamber, and Cléry closed the door halfway.

Mass began at 6 o'clock. During the impressive ceremony, a great silence prevailed. The king, always on his knees, listened to the Mass in deep thought, in a most noble manner. The king took the communion, and after Mass, before he went into his cabinet, he said to Firmont: "My God, how happy I am to have my principles! Without them, where would I be now? But with them, death seems so sweet to me! Yes, there exists an incorruptible judge above who knows how to render justice that is refused me here below."

The priest then went into Cléry's room to remove his sacramental garments, remembering in his mémoires that although the king was much calmer than he, the "blood was flowing like ice water" through his veins during the entire service.

Cléry assists with the Mass

Cléry seized that moment to enter the king's cabinet. The king took him by both hands and said in a touching voice: "Cléry, I am satisfied with your services." Throwing himself at his feet, Cléry cried, "Ah, Sire, why can I not die to satisfy your murderers and save a life so precious to the French!"

"Death does not alarm me," the king replied. "I am quite prepared, but you," he continued, "should not expose yourself. I shall ask that you be kept near my son. Give him all your care in this dreadful place. Remind him, and tell him often, how I have grieved for the misfortunes he must bear. Someday he may be able to reward your zeal."

"Ah! My master, my King, if my zeal and my care have been agreeable to you, the only reward I ask is to receive your blessing—do not refuse it to the last Frenchman who remains beside you."

Cléry was already at the king's feet, holding one of his hands. In that position, the king granted his prayer and gave him his blessing. Then he raised him with an embrace: "Give it also to all who are attached to me. Tell Turgy I am content with him. Now, go back," he added, "and give no cause for any complaint against yourself." Then, calling Cléry back and taking a document from the table, he said, "Here is a letter Pétion wrote me at the time of your entrance to the Temple. It may be useful to you for remaining here." Cléry caught his hand again and kissed it, and went out. "Adieu," he said to Cléry again. "Adieu."

L'abbé Edgeworth de Firmont, Confessor of Louis XVI

Cléry returned to his chamber, where he found Firmont praying on his knees beside his bed. "What a Prince!" he said to Cléry as he rose. "With what resignation, with what courage he looks at death! He was as tranquil as if he were hearing mass in his palace in the midst of his Court."

"I have just received the most sincere farewell," Cléry said to him. "He has promised me that he will ask to have me remain in the Tower to serve his son. Monsieur, I beg of you to remind him, for I shall not have the happiness to speak to him in private again." Firmont nodded as he turned to rejoin the king.

At 7 o'clock the king came out of his cabinet and called Cléry. He took him to the window and said: "You will give this seal to my son and this ring to the Queen; tell her that I part from it with pain and only at the last moment. This little packet contains the hair of all my family; you will give this to her as well. Say to the Queen, to my dear children, to my sister, that although I promised to see them this morning, I wish to spare them the pain of such a cruel separation. How much it costs me to go without receiving their last embraces!" He wiped away a few tears. Then he added in a most sorrowful manner, "I charge you to take them my farewell." He immediately returned to his room.

The municipal officers close at hand had heard the king's conversation, and had seen him give Cléry the different articles that he still held in his hands. They told him to turn them over to the officers, but one of the officials proposed that they leave them in Cléry's hands until a decision could be made by the council about them.

A quarter of an hour later the king came out of his room. "Ask," he said to Cléry, "if I can have scissors." When the king returned to his room, Cléry made the request to the commissioner, who answered, "Do you know what he wants to do with them?" Cléry said he did not know, so he knocked at the king's door. The king came out, and a municipal officer who followed Cléry said to him: "You have asked for scissors, but before we take your request to the council we must know what you wish to do with them." The king replied, "I wish Cléry to cut my hair."

The municipal officers retired. One of them went down to the council chamber, where, after half an hour's deliberation, they refused the king's request for scissors. The officers returned and announced the decision. "I should not have touched the scissors," said the king. "I should have requested Cléry to cut my hair in your presence; inquire again, monsieur; I beg you to take charge of my request." The municipal officer returned to the council, which persisted in its refusal.

It was then that Cléry was told to be ready to accompany the king and undress him on the scaffold. At this announcement he was seized with terror, but after collecting all his strength, he was prepared to render this last duty to his master; he knew that such a service performed by an executioner would have been most abominable. Then another municipal officer came to tell Cléry that he was not to going with the king after all. "The executioner will be plenty enough company for him," he added gruffly. Cléry, although prepared to accompany his master, was relieved. He would not have to witness the blood-curdling event.

Paris was under arms from 5 o'clock in the morning. Nothing was heard outside but the beating of the drums, the rattle of arms, the trample of horses, and the movement of cannon. The maniacs who guarded the Temple were shouting and applauding, and this all echoed throughout the tower.

At 9 o'clock the noise increased, and the Temple gates opened with a bellowing clang. Santerre, accompanied by seven or eight municipal officers, entered the tower at the head of 10 gendarmes that he had arranged in two lines. Hearing this disturbance, the king came out of his cabinet to meet the visitors.

"Have you come to fetch me?" he asked Santerre.

"Yes," he answered without any emotion.

"I ask you for one minute," said the king, and he entered his cabinet and came out again immediately with his confessor. He held his will in his hand, and to another priest who was standing nearby with Santerre, he said: "I beg you to give this paper to the Queen, to my wife."

"That is not my business," replied the priest, brutally refusing to take the document. "I am only here to escort you to the scaffold."

The king then addressed a municipal officer. "Give this paper, I beg you, to my wife. You can read it; it contains dispositions which I desire that the Commune should know." The officer took the document from the king without a word.

Cléry was behind the king, standing near the chimney. He turned to the king and offered him his overcoat. "Messieurs," said the king, addressing the municipal officers, "I desire that Cléry should remain near my son, who is accustomed to his care. I hope that the Commune will accept my request." Then, looking at Santerre, he said, "Let us go."

Antoine-Joseph Santerre

Those were the last words that the king spoke in his chambers. At the top of the staircase he met the porter of the tower, and said to him: "I was a little short with you day before yesterday; do not bear me any ill will." The porter made no answer, and he turned away when the king spoke to him.

Cléry remained alone in the room. The drums and the trumpets announced that the king had left the tower. In the queen's room, the young prince was crying in his mother's arms when he saw that the door to the apartment was left open. He broke away from his mother's arms and ran through the next room hoping to find the door to the hallway open. A municipal officer brusquely stopped him, and asked him where he was going. "I am going to speak to the people," he cried, "and beg them not to kill my father." The municipal officer ordered him to return immediately, but he could not resist showing a degree of admiration and tenderness on his part.

The king was then removed from the Temple in a green carriage with Firmont. He read prayers as the carriage proceeded slowly through the streets lined with shops that were half closed. The people were assembled along the route in a strict silence.

One hour later, artillery and cries of *Vive la nation! Vive la république!* were heard throughout Paris. Cléry wrote in his journal, "The best of Kings was no more!"

Cléry did not know, however, what had transpired at the scaffold. When the king's carriage arrived at the square, Place Louis

XV, the crowds yelled with joy as the carriage passed to the scaffold in the center of a large empty space surrounded with cannons. The king began to descend from his carriage only to be surrounded by three executioners that offered to help him down. He refused their assistance and stepped briskly out of the carriage. The executioners immediately began to remove his brown coat, but he pulled himself away and took it off himself. The chief executioner, Sanson, then approached him and tried to tie his hands.

"What are you trying to do?" asked the king, withdrawing his hands abruptly.

"Tie your hands," replied one of the executioners.

"Tie my hands!" replied the king in an indignant tone. "No, I will never consent; do what you are ordered to do, but I will not be tied." The executioners insisted, however, and were about to call for help in order to use force when Firmont said to the king with tears in his eyes, "Sire, in this new outrage I see only a final resemblance between Your Majesty and the Savior who is to reward you."

Hearing these words, the king lifted his eyes to heaven with a sorrowful look and said: "Do what you wish; I will drain the cup to the dregs." The scaffold steps were extremely steep, and the king, with his hands bound behind him, had to lean against Firmont for support. It appeared that midway up the steps his courage was beginning to falter. Upon arriving at the last step, however, he broke away from Firmont and crossed the length of the scaffold with his head held high. Bravely he stopped in front of the guillotine. His face was very red, and he distinctly pronounced these words: "I die innocent of all the crimes imputed to me. I pardon the authors of my death, and pray God that the blood you are about to shed will never fall upon France."

The last king of a royal line stretching 800 years wanted to continue speaking to the people, but Santerre, the brutal revolutionary on horseback, refused his very last request. In fact, he had the drum roll begin so that few could hear the king's very last words. Santerre cried, "Do your duty!" Later, this fierce Jacobin bragged in a café that "Louis Capet wished to appeal to the people for mercy, but I prevented it."

Four executioners seized him and flung him down roughly upon the long plank of the guillotine. As they strapped him to it, it is reported that the king gave out a terrible cry. His head was already in what the cruel onlookers called the "little window," and the wooden neck-piece was adjusted to keep it in place. Historians, including Thomas Paine of the American Revolution, have written that Cléry believed he heard the king screaming because "his head did not fall at the first stroke, his neck being so fat." There is evidence that Louis's neck might have been too fat to fit into the groove properly, but the authors are incorrect when they imply that Cléry witnessed the execution. Cléry was not permitted to escort his master to the scaffold; he remained in the Temple stricken with grief. Only the Abbé Firmont, Louis's confessor, accompanied the king from the Temple to the scaffold with the guards.

When the cord was pulled, the heavy blade dropped swiftly. The king's head fell into a basket of straw at 10 minutes after 10 o'clock in the morning.

Louis XVI refuses to have his hands bound

The ruthless Sanson seized the king's head out of the basket by the hair, and he showed it to the crowd in the midst of *"Vive la nation! Vive la république!"* Onlookers rushed to the scaffold to catch a few drops of the king's blood in their handkerchiefs or their gloves to preserve as mementos of the death of a tyrant, for others as relics of a martyr. Sanson, the executioner, later sold locks of the king's hair and fragments of the king's clothing for large sums of money.

Immediately after the execution, the body of Louis XVI was transported to the cemetery of the ancient Church of the Madeleine.

It was placed in a pit six feet square, close to the wall of the Rue d'Anjou, and it was dissolved instantly by a great quantity of quicklime with which the municipal officers took the utmost precaution to cover it.

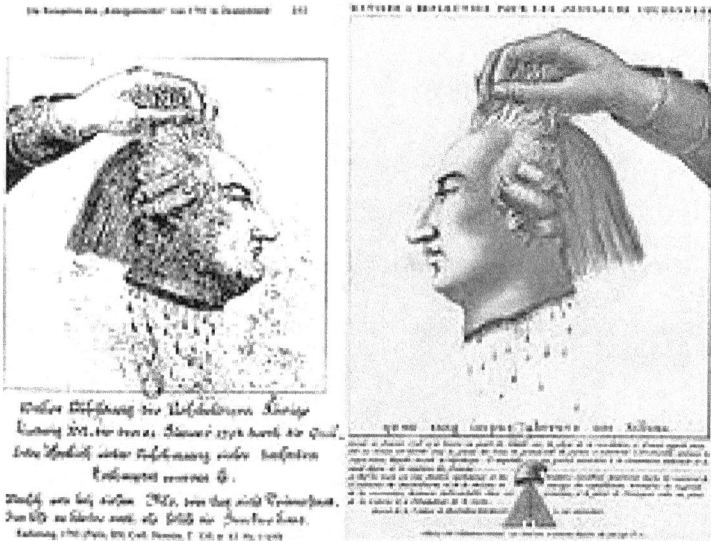

Pamphlets depicting Sanson showing the crowd the king's head

At 10 o'clock that morning in the Temple, the queen tried to persuade her children to have something to eat, but they refused. As soon as they heard the firearms celebrating Louis XVI's end, Madame Elisabeth raised her eyes to heaven and cried: "The monsters—now they are content!" The queen was speechless with grief, the young prince burst into tears, and Marie-Thérèse shrieked a piercing cry of despair.

The horrors did not end that day. Malesherbes, the loyal friend who had served as the king's counsel, was soon afterward arrested and guillotined for his royal ties. His daughter, his son-in-law, and his grandchildren were executed as well for their loyalty.

Although the queen had been known in earlier days to sneer at the king for his constant indecisiveness that might have led to his downfall, no wife could have been more sincerely attached or more protectively loving to her husband than was Marie-Antoinette to Louis XVI. But now she and the royal prisoners knelt in front of her 7-year-old son, their new King Louis XVII.

The Young Louis XVII

The young prince inherited the throne that morning in a gloomy room of the Temple, surrounded by the queen and two weeping princesses. The jeers of the Temple guards and the roar of his subjects in the streets rang in his ears. A week later, the Comte de Provence, his exiled uncle, proclaimed the accession of the child King of France to the world:

> We declare that the Dauphin Louis-Charles, born the twenty-seventh day of the month of March 1785, is KING OF FRANCE AND OF NAVARRE, under the name of Louis XVII, and that, by right of birth as well as the fundamental laws and customs of the Kingdom, we are and shall be Regent of France during the minority of the King, our nephew and seigneur.

The new king was recognized by most of the countries of Europe. The tragic death of his father had aroused nothing but horror all over the civilized world, a world that detested revolutionary France. In England, grief was so great that London's theatres closed, and the French ambassador was immediately dismissed from diplomatic circles. In other countries, feeling was much the same. The Russian Empress Catharine banished all French citizens in her territory that refused to formally swear allegiance to the new king. In short, Louis XVII was king everywhere except in France.

Opinion in the new United States of America was sharply divided, however, about the French Revolution and the execution of Louis XVI, the king who had wholeheartedly supported the American cause, morally and financially. On the one hand, some felt that Louis' death was necessary to remove the despotism to which the French people had been subjected for such a long time. On the other, however, many feared that the same chaos could happen in America if safeguards were ever stripped away in the name of liberty. Both sides were aware, however, that American needed to pursue a policy of neutrality with France and England always at war.

PART FOUR

CLÉRY REMOVED FROM THE TEMPLE

Chapter 13
Cléry's Plight

I do not fear death. I sacrificed my life when I entered the Temple to care for the King and his family. But to leave my wife and children without any income, that makes my last days very miserable.

–Cléry to his brother Hanet
La Force Prison, April 1794

Removed from his throne by rebels, insulted behind iron bars by unruly guards and insolent officials, and sent to the scaffold by his countrymen and relatives, the condemned Louis XVI's only concerns were for the fate of his family—and his servants. He left a last will and testament requesting that his *valet de chambre* Cléry remain in the service of the queen to care for his children. Cléry was refused the position, however, and he was detained in solitary confinement in the same space occupied by his royal master for another two months. Moreover, the municipal officers led him to fear that his confinement could possibly lead to life imprisonment or the guillotine for his loyalty to the unfortunate king, an act of treason in their eyes.

The queen and Madame Elisabeth asked to see Cléry before his departure from the Temple, but their request was also denied. Cléry succeeded in getting a message to the royal princesses asking them to help him regain his earlier service, but their pleas remained unanswered. Only the wife of Tison remained to serve the queen, and the queen had shown much kindness to this woman in the past. She even deprived herself of her own food to give it to the fragile servant when she was ill. In repayment, however, Madame Tison denounced those municipal officers that had shown any kindness to the royal family or had endeavored to soften the rigors of confinement in the Temple. They were guillotined soon afterwards.

At the time, there was discussion of deporting the survivors of the royal family to Spain. However, the officials notified Cléry that if he were liberated from prison, he would not be allowed to leave Paris to follow the royals in exile. Although there is no detailed information regarding Cléry's time in the Temple after the king's death, there is evidence that he was liberated two months after the king's execution, but the exact date is uncertain. Due to Madame Cléry's appeals, Minister of Justice Garat freed Cléry from the Temple in the first week of March, 1793. He also advised Cléry that he and his wife should leave Paris as soon as possible and return to the countryside. The minister added, however, that they would be kept under tight surveillance no matter where they travelled, and that they were absolutely forbidden to discuss the events that took place in the Temple with anyone.

Hanet, Cléry's brother, revealed in his mémoires that he was in Paris soon after Cléry's release from the Temple. He indicated that Cléry stayed in the prison until about the 12th of March, and upon release, the dedicated servant never abandoned his resolve to return to care for the young dauphin, the queen, and the princesses as he had promised the king.

Several days after his departure from the Temple, unknown benefactors offered Cléry safe passage to London where he could write about his experience in the Temple in peace and escape further prosecution. His supporters also offered to provide funds to care for his wife and children. It appears that Cléry might have been involved with a plot to help the queen escape. If not directly involved, he had at least unknowingly transmitted messages between Madame Elisabeth and an agent outside of the Temple. Cléry informed the concerned royalists, however, that he would not leave France as long as his young king, now the uncrowned Louis XVII, and his family were still imprisoned in the Temple. Distressed and overcome with worry, Cléry attempted to receive permission to return to the Temple, but he was denied any audience with the city officials.

Taking Garat's advice, Cléry returned to his mother's small cottage in Juvisy, southwest of Paris, with his wife and four children: Bénédicte, Charles, Hubertine, and Louis, ranging from 10 to 4 years old. Although the family would have been overjoyed to have their father home again, everyone was aware of Cléry's sworn duty to His Majesties. He would also, undoubtedly, been encouraged by his wife and mother who were ardent monarchists to continue his service for the royals, having both served the late king and his family at the court of Versailles.

Sophie Forest, the lady friend who often visited Cléry in the Temple with Madame Cléry, also joined the family in Juvisy. Although they all tried to keep a very low profile, they were constantly being questioned and even denounced for their previous royal ties.

The kitchen attendant, Turgy, was allowed to remain in the Temple after Cléry was released. However, he managed to visit Cléry secretly on various occasions to keep him informed of the royal prisoners' condition. On his first meeting, Cléry handed Turgy instructions that Louis XVI had given Cléry before he left the Temple for his execution:

> I charge you to tell Turgy how greatly I have been pleased with his faithful attachment to me, and with his zeal in fulfilling his duties. I give him my blessing, and beg him to continue caring, with equal devotion, for my family, to whom I commend him.

The king's wishes would never come true. Neither Cléry nor Turgy would ever have permission to remain with the survivors during their cruel imprisonment at the Temple. Although the king gave Cléry a letter that he had received from Mayor Pétion that praised the servant for his "bon" patriotism, it was in Cléry's best interest not to use the letter to be reinstated in the Temple—a letter which insinuated that Cléry had been a supporter of the revolution. Such a letter would only have incriminated him more in the eyes of the queen and the Princesses Marie-Thérèse and Elisabeth.

One might ask if Cléry had been an agent of the revolution or one of Mayor Pétion's pawns, why did not Pétion himself come to the servant's aid? More than likely, Pétion was actually out of the picture by this time since he was no longer mayor of Paris. In fact, he had voted for the king's execution and was now in the midst of a fierce political battle as a member of the Girondin party. Cléry's safety might have been the least of his worries at that time.

Cléry's brother, Hanet, was supplying munitions for the army at the northern front line when Cléry was released from the Temple. Because of the considerable amount of correspondence needed in his post, he requested that a secretary be hired. He recommended his younger brother, 17-year old Auguste, who was accepted for the post. In fact, Hanet had given him an excellent education.

One evening Hanet received orders to travel to the front. Leaving late at night and not knowing that the route was being repaired, his horse fell beneath him after running into a pile of stones. Hanet broke his leg, but Auguste was able to take his brother's place. The mission was still completed so perfectly that Auguste was promoted to inspector, and Hanet promoted to inspector general. Both were sent to join the Army of the Rhine.

Hanet had offered to help Cléry procure a passport and leave France, but Cléry still refused to leave the country. Unfortunately, at the end of September, Cléry was arrested during the night by a dozen gendarmes and taken to La Force Prison. Hanet learned about the arrest in a letter from his mother. It appears that Cléry's wife had left Juvisy for Paris in order to be near her husband in prison and to petition for his release. The brothers' mother was left in charge of Cléry's children at a time when bread was very scarce. She wrote, "We are all suffering; the tax on bread, which has now reached the villages, has threatened the means of our very existence."

Hanet remembered his promise to his dying father that he would care for the entire family in order that Cléry could remain in service with the royal family, and he immediately sent 2,000 francs to his mother in Juvisy and 1,000 francs to Cléry's wife in Paris. Hanet was terribly upset that he could not be with his family in person.

La Force Prison

As for Cléry, Hanet was well aware that any day could be Cléry's last day in La Force Prison. One morning when he looked at the morning Parisian newspaper in a café, he noticed the list of the "daily victims" that suffered the guillotine's horror. When he saw the name *Cléry*, he collapsed at his table and struck his head. Bleeding and unconscious, he was taken to his apartment.

When Hanet awoke, his friend was sitting at his bedside and asked him what had happened. When he explained that he had been informed of his brother's execution, his friend informed him that he was mistaken, that his brother was still alive. The man who was executed lived on the street *Cléry*, and his name was not Cléry.

Although the charges against Cléry were absurd, he was found guilty for relaying letters to the king from those members of the Girondin party who had been incarcerated by the Jacobins, the radical supporters of the revolution. Also, Cléry's service in the Temple, his steadfast loyalty to the king, and his name in the king's last will and testament were all considered inexcusable crimes in the eyes of the revolutionaries.

Cléry's wife had miscarried a week earlier, but she followed the coach that took Cléry to prison on foot. She also refused to leave Paris as long as her husband was imprisoned, leaving her children in the care of her mother-in-law. At night, she walked around the periphery of the prison constantly keeping an eye open for any prisoners that might be headed for the guillotine. She never left the prison until she was certain that Cléry was not among those condemned to death. In fact, Cléry was on the prison's fatal list 13 times in all, but he miraculously escaped the scaffold in the confusion that reigned in the prison. On several occasions, he simply did not respond to his name when called.

Cléry's brother, Hanet, returned to Paris in April after discovering that Malesherbes, the king's counsel, had also been imprisoned in La Force and had been executed—along with members of his family. Taking 10 days' leave, Hanet was determined to see Cléry in the event that he, too, should be escorted to the scaffold. When he visited Cléry's wife, she informed him that she and her friend, Madame de Beaumont, had befriended the wife of the prison's concierge. In fact, they had entered the prison on several occasions, disguised as cleaning ladies, to catch a glimpse of his brother.

Hanet soon made his way to the prison with the intention of delivering a small note to the wife of the concierge. He observed a merchant approach the woman and hand her a letter. She told him, "Return tomorrow and I will have a response for you." As he departed, Hanet approached him, saying, "Kind sir, could you do me a service?"

"Why not, that is all that I have ever done since I was born," answered the merchant. Hanet showed him the note along with a gold coin, and he pointed discreetly to the prison gate. "Keep your gold," he said, "I do not like to be paid in advance. To whom should I deliver this note?"

"Madame Lebeau, the concierge," answered Hanet. I do not know her, but I hope she will respond."

"Ah, I am sure she will," responded the merchant. "She is an excellent woman, and her husband the best of men." He then asked Hanet to wait on him while he went to the gate. When he returned, he told Hanet, "Go to the gate, and ask to speak with Madame Lebeau, your cousin!"

Hanet wasted no time in presenting himself at the prison gate and requesting to see "Citizen Lebeau." One of the guards escorted him to his so-called cousin, who cried out, "Oh, my cousin Philippe, it is about time that you arrived!"

As soon as they were alone, Madame Lebeau asked him to have a seat while she went to make his presence known to Cléry. Hanet later wrote that he needed to have a seat, because his legs were about to give away beneath him, being so moved by the experience.

Cléry arrived, but he had so changed that Hanet hardly recognized him. Cléry embraced his brother, and they both were in tears. "My dear Hanet, I saw Monsieur de Malesherbes taken to the scaffold in a carriage, along with a number of our unfortunate companions."

"Yet, I am still alive," continued Cléry. "I am indebted to the good concierge and his wife for their generosity. You perhaps think that I am only trying to escape death, but I do not fear death. I sacrificed my life when I entered the Temple to care for the king and his family. But to leave my wife and children without any income, that makes my last days
very miserable."

Hanet tried to console his brother, but Cléry added, "You, yourself, Hanet, how will you ever regain your fortune? You continue to provide for my family, as you always have in the past."

"Be courageous, dear brother," responded Hanet. "Your heroic conduct has impressed the most royal supporters. They have the utmost admiration for your loyalty." Handing Cléry a wallet with cash and a roll of gold coins, Hanet said, "Take this, it could be useful."

"No, dear Hanet, the gold could be dangerous in this establishment; I will hold on to the cash, however." It was time for Hanet to depart, and the concierge appeared with a sad look on her face. She escorted Cléry back to his cell, and she returned to Hanet who wanted to tell her how indebted he was to her, but he knew that she had read his thoughts. "No, Monsieur," she said, "save your money. We know how important it is for your brother's family. We cannot forget that you have supported them; they have often talked about his good brother. We, too, love him as if he were one of our own, and we will do our very best to save him."

Her husband, who arrived at that very moment, also showed his concern and then escorted Hanet to the gate. Shaking Hanet's hand, he said in a loud voice, "Adieu, cousin Philippe. Do not wait such a long time before paying us another visit."

When Hanet returned home after a long absence, he told his family and friends that he had never met such an admirable and brave couple, saying, "Monsieur and Madame Lebeau were the most humane and generous beings ever." He did not stay long because he had to return to his post in Colmar on the northeast border of France, but he parted knowing that he left his family less anxious and worried about Cléry.

As soon as Hanet arrived in Colmar, he received a letter from Madame Cléry that someone had stolen the wallet with the cash that he had given his brother. He hurried to replace the funds, and his sister-in-law sent such a tender and gracious response for his generosity that he kept the note on his person from that day forward.

Cléry's wife remained in Paris with her companion, Madame de Beaumont, in order to petition those in charge time and time again to secure her husband's release. Finally, on one occasion, one of the prison authorities promised to free her husband if she would play any of the songs that she used to play for the queen when she was the court musician. She was reluctant to play such songs for those who had at one time called for the imprisonment of the queen, but she finally acquiesced and played her harp so well that the group of officials applauded her with a standing ovation. Moreover, one of them was so moved that he surprisingly wrote an order for the release of Cléry from La Force.

Cléry was released but not without a damning statement, however, from the General Council:

Considering that there is no reason to keep citizen Cléry in the Temple prison any longer, considering that he was only arrested as a measure of national security, considering that there is no further evidence against him, and considering that he has fulfilled his duty to Louis Capet with scrupulous fidelity to the republic, the Committee of Public Safety decrees that citizen Cléry be granted his freedom.

This statement would be stigmatic for Cléry. He would not only be seen as a revolutionary in the eyes of the royalists, but he would be discredited in the eyes of the republicans for his guilt by association, having spent years of service in the royal household.

Chapter 14
Cléry's Year in La Force Prison

No, nothing can hurt me now.

–Queen Marie-Antoinette to her prison guard
October 1793

Madame Cléry's persistence was well-rewarded; her husband was freed from La Force on the 10th of August 1794. He had been imprisoned for one year with the constant fear for his life. During that time, however, the events in the tower had been just as distressing for the royal survivors. The queen had remained in mourning after the execution of the king in January 1793. In fact, she was so distraught that she would never venture down into the Temple courtyard for her daily walk; she could not bear to pass the door to the king's chambers.

On the death of his father, the 7-year old prince, the uncrowned Louis XVII, suffered from stomach pains and fevers. He had also bruised one of his testicles while playing, but he was only given the slightest medical attention. Being fond of the child, Mrs. Tison worried about him as well. However, her past conduct so troubled her that she became increasingly neurotic to the point of even talking to herself. Feeling herself responsible for the misfortunes of the royal family, she was finally removed from the Tower and placed in an asylum.

On the 3rd of July, at 10 o'clock in the evening, a delegation arrived with a decree stating that the young king was to be taken away from his mother. The child flew into his mother's arms, and she, overwhelmed with grief, flatly refused to give him up. "You shall kill me," cried the queen, "sooner than snatch my child from me."

Threatening to use violence and even kill her son, the officers finally coerced the queen into giving him up after an hour of anguish. Madame Elisabeth and Marie-Thérèse took the boy and dressed him because the queen was utterly worn out by the ordeal. Before they left, she asked the officers to request the Council to give her permission to see her son if it were only at meal times; they consented, but the request was not granted, and she never saw her son again except now and then for a few moments at a distance.

Prince Louis Charles being taken from his mother to stay in the king's room

The queen thought that he would be in the hands of honest and educated mentors, but later found that the cruel Simon was assigned to be in charge of the very unhappy child.

Although the child's mother, sister, and aunt did not know where he was being kept in the Temple, they did know that Simon was mistreating the child harshly because they could often hear him screaming and whimpering, followed by a period of silence. The queen and the princesses would then stand by the child's empty bed weeping inconsolably. The queen would also stand by her window for hours on end just for a moment's glimpse of her child when he was allowed to take a walk outside. She shuddered on the days when she could not see her fragile little king playing in the courtyard.

When she did see him playing with soldiers that kept watch over him, she saw that he wore the red cap of the revolutionaries. She would tremble when she thought about how the child had been taken so violently from her. Their separation was a needless act of cruelty, because the revolutionaries had already overthrown the monarchy.

Almost a week after the prince was taken from the queen, the commissioners paid her a visit because of the public cries for the young king's safety, believing he was kidnapped. They ransacked her chamber, looking in every corner and carefully examining every object that could be found. Finally, the official in charge spoke up: "We've come to see if there is anything you need or if there is anything of which you have too much."

Prince Louis Charles tormented by his caretaker Simon

"I miss my son," said the queen. "It is extremely cruel to keep me separated from him for such a long time."

"Your son is not being neglected…he has a patriotic tutor," snapped the official. You can no more complain of the way he is treated than of the way you are treated here yourself."

The queen took a deep breath and said, "I only complain about one thing, sir. It is the absence of a child that has never been out of my sight. It has been five days since he was taken away from me, and I have not been able to see him once since then. Because his is still ill, he needs my care."

Holding back her tears, she continued, "It is difficult to believe that the Convention cannot understand the legitimacy of my grievance."

The officials ignored her appeal for mercy, and left the room without a word. When they arrived at the Convention, they assured their colleagues that the public had nothing to fear, and that the son of Capet was found playing checkers with his tutor.

One of the officials said, "We went to the ladies' rooms, and we found Marie-Antoinette, her daughter, and her sister all in good health."

Another official added, "Although they wished that the foreign powers should find out that they were being mistreated, we were certain that they lacked nothing and are not being neglected."

Turgy, the kitchen attendant, did notice that the Temple environment had become somewhat calmer for the queen and princesses. The officers who had so harshly tormented Louis XVI and his family came more rarely to the Temple. The women in the Temple were watched less closely, and thus were able to talk more freely with each other and could give Turgy orders more openly. Except for the plight of the young prince in confinement, the queen and the royal princesses seemed to enjoy a semblance of liberty.

It was during this period that Toulan, the gruff official who in time began to sympathize with the royals, enlisted Turgy to join him in his plan to help the young, uncrowned Louis XVII and the royal princesses to escape from the Temple.

Turgy was to carry the young king in a basket covered with napkins and linens. The queen, disguised as a municipal officer, was to come to the door on the staircase to ensure that Turgy would be able to pass. Then she was to leave a few minutes afterwards. Princess Marie-Thérèse, dressed like the lamplighter's son, was to leave at the same time as Madame Elisabeth, who was to be dressed as a commissioner. Little is known of Toulan's plan after the prisoners were able escape from the Temple, but it was never executed in the first place. It is believed that those who were involved—not Toulan—had perhaps hesitated at the last moment, because an additional guard was on duty at the time.

Now that the guards had become somewhat more lenient, the princesses often reminisced about the various services that their loyal friends and servants had rendered them during the horrible drama of the revolution. On one occasion, Turgy was present as the queen recalled the very first occasion that the queen and king had recognized the degree of Turgy's faithfulness; it was on that unhappy morning of the 6th of October, 1789, when the royal family was forcibly escorted from Versailles Palace to Paris.

Turgy had saved the queen's life that day by opening the secret door for her between the private apartments and the room called the *Oeil de Boeuf*, through which she ran to take refuge with king, while being chased by revolutionaries. The door was locked from inside for the safety of the king and his children, but Turgy recognized the queen's voice. He quickly opened the door; then he slammed the door shut in the face of the murderers who were pursuing her.

Turgy later recalled how remarkable it was that the queen never reminisced about those who had treated her or her family so cruelly. While she always instructed her children to remember only the good actions of others, she set a good example in front of them by forgetting the injuries.

Soon after Cléry was released from the Temple, unfavorable reports about Toulan and his colleagues reached the General Council, and the municipal officers and guards on duty became even more suspicious than before. Turgy and the princesses were obliged to resort to notes once again. Madame Elisabeth reminded Turgy of the importance of keeping the manner of communicating secret:

> M's words gave us much pleasure (M refers to Monsieur, the King's brother, who had declared himself the Regent of the young imprisoned King; being a minor, the child could not rule himself). As it is most important that our secret should be known by no one, do not speak of our method of correspondence.

Various accusations, notably those brought by the servants, or rather spies, Tison and his wife against the queen, the princesses, and many others, were the reason that Toulan's name and those of some other officers were erased from the list of those permitted to serve in the Temple. The men who replaced them received stringent orders, and were, moreover, so devoted to the enemies of the royal family that correspondence again became quite difficult between Turgy and the prisoners.

During June, the woman Tison began to have signs of mental derangement. She had always been a sad creature, and she was always sighing as if she were suffering from remorse. Old man Tison, who was a brutal man, for some reason made her bring fresh charges against the queen and Madame Elisabeth; she accused them of carrying on a daily correspondence with Turgy. To prove her

~ 219 ~

accusations, she took a candlestick that she had taken from Madame Elisabeth's room down to the Council Room of the Temple to show it to the commissioners. It appears that a drop of wax had fallen on the base of the candle holder. It was true that the princess that morning had given Turgy a sealed note for the Abbé Edgeworth de Firmont, and Turgy had wasted no time in taking it to Madame la Duchesse de Sérent, who would relay the message. Also, the princess never sealed her notes with wax, except those she sent to this priest.

When the Tison woman returned and entered the princess's room, she became dreadfully agitated upon seeing the queen. She completely disregarded the presence of the commissioners. Flinging herself at her queen's feet, she cried: "Madame, I entreat your Majesty to forgive me. I am a miserable woman. I am responsible for your death and for Madame Elisabeth's."

The princesses kindly raised her from the floor and tried to calm her. A moment later Turgy and his two assistants entered the room with dinner for the royal family, accompanied by four commissioners on duty. The woman then threw herself on her knees in front of Turgy, crying: "Monsieur Turgy, I ask your forgiveness. I am a miserable woman, and I have been the cause of the Queen's death and yours."

Madame Elisabeth raised her up, and said: "Turgy, forgive her." He replied, "The woman Tison has done nothing to offend me. Even if she had, I would forgive her with all my heart." The woman then fell into fretful convulsions and was carried into another part of the tower, taking eight men to hold her. Two days later she was taken to a mental asylum at the Hôtel-Dieu, and she never appeared in the Temple again.

The official to whom the Tison woman made her statement told Turgy about the accusations she brought forth against him and the queen. The official also advised Turgy not to be seen with the princesses too much, so as not to confirm the suspicions of the other guards and commissioners. That evening, he succeeded in persuading his colleagues, however, that Madame Tison's accusation and the scene that had taken place earlier were both the effect of the poor woman's madness. The official then threw her depositions into the fire.

Turgy was most afraid of being arrested on that day, not only for his sake but for that of the royals as well. Without him, they would have had no means for any correspondence with the outside world—the only solace to help soften their horrible imprisonment. On several occasions, the commissioners detected the signals and glances that were exchanged between the princesses and Turgy, but they could not guess what they meant. This only caused more anxiety in the Temple.

View of the towers of the Temple

One day the old man Tison made off with the paper stopper in a bottle. He examined it carefully and held it up to the light. Finding nothing on it, he put it in his pocket and departed. The princesses turned pale from the fear of their secret being revealed. Either Tison lost the paper, or he did not know how to make the writing visible, so it was a false alarm. Fortunately, not one of the secret notes was ever discovered, but the ladies trembled with fright at the thought of being caught and implicating Turgy.

After the close call, the princesses and Turgy became increasingly more cautious in the days that were to come. Two days after the incident with Madame Tison, however, the Princess Elisabeth managed to slip a piece of paper into Turgy's hand when she returned her napkin to him. It was a touching note in which the queen asked the following questions:

> What are they shouting under our windows? Perhaps
> my sister will ask for some almond milk (to get an

answer on the paper stopper). Has the Commune been reinstituted? Is the woman Tison as mad as they say? Do they mean to replace her here? Is she well cared for?

It was at this time that Turgy informed the queen of his intentions to be confined to the Temple in order to devote himself entirely to the personal service of the princesses to "spare them many very irksome cares." Her Majesty answered:

What you suggest would give us great pleasure, but it is through you that all our information comes, and if you were shut up, we should be completely in the dark in the future. If anyone should come to take us away, and you are unable to accompany us, come and join us wherever we may be, with your wife, your son and your whole family.

In this message from the queen, the princesses' trust in Turgy is clearly established. It should be remembered that Cléry spent most of his time serving the king and the young prince. For this reason, it can be argued that after the revolution, Turgy's place in society would outshine Cléry's since only one princess would survive such tumultuous times. Furthermore, this princess had never trusted Cléry.

The circumstances related to Madame Tison's insanity greatly affected her husband. The kindness shown by the queen and the princesses to this woman who had given them so many reasons to complain touched the old jailer to such an extent that he told Turgy that he wanted forgiveness for his past conduct and he wanted to give some proof of his remorse. This he did on the first opportunity.

When the young uncrowned king, Louis Charles, came to the dinner table, he was always given a higher seat than the others, a seat with a cushion on it. This was a practice that the royal family instituted on the day that his father, Louis XVI, was executed. In other words, the young prince was actually treated as a king. One day, the child was seated on an ordinary seat so low that he could hardly reach the food on his plate, because one of the commissioners, named Bernard, had taken the child's seat. However, no one dared to disturb Bernard, who was known for his rudeness and vulgarity.

When Tison came into the room, Turgy made a sign to him about the chair, and Tison understood it. He brought forth another chair and asked Bernard if he would give the child the seat that he normally used. Bernard roughly refused, saying, "I never saw a table or chair ever given to prisoners; straw is good enough for them."

Although Tison was appearing more congenial to the prisoners, the princesses were hesitant about confiding in him. When Tison offered to give Turgy information and provide him with newspapers, Madame Elisabeth discovered it, and she wrote:

> Be very cautious in regard to Tison's suggestion, and do not let your zeal lead you into any course of action that might be dangerous to you. If you agree, let it be only after making him promise the most absolute secrecy. Have you not been forbidden to speak to Tison? Think that over, too.

Madame Elisabeth was also becoming increasingly concerned for the welfare of the queen and the princess, but she also never forgot to show Turgy how grateful they were:

> Try to find out whether the movements of the enemy are to be directed against my companion (the Queen), and if they are not going to remove her property (there was some question of taking the child and Madame Royale to the Choisy-le-Roi Chateau) to some greater distance than two leagues. This is not urgent. The way you serve us is our one comfort.

Other notes that the princess wrote give an indication of how the royal prisoners lived from day to day. The following note reveals their concern for the young king who had been separated from the women and placed in solitary confinement:

> Give Fidèle (Toulan) this note from us. Tell him— and my sister wishes you to know—that we see the child (Louis Charles had been taken to another room in the Temple) every day from the staircase window, but that need not prevent you from giving us news about him.

The following note gives an indication of the prisoners' indebtedness to the servants as well as the servants' creativity in relaying messages:

Tell Fidèle how much his last note touched us. We did not need his assurance to make us trust him completely and forever. His signals are good (Toulan had taken a room in a house near the Temple where he played on a horn different tunes that conveyed the ideas to be signaled).

One day the city councilors came to the Temple to notify the princesses that since the principle of equality from the *Declaration of the Rights of Man and of the Citizen* (1789) ought to prevail everywhere, in prisons as elsewhere, they would no longer be allowed to choose their menus. Soon afterwards, the councilors drew up an order by which the prisoners were limited to only one kind of food at each meal.

When Turgy served their dinner that day, he was also not allowed to set the table. He was required to give each prisoner a plate, in which he put some soup and a slice of beef with a coarse piece of bread beside it. He gave them a tin spoon, an iron fork, and a knife with a black wooden handle. A bottle of wine was brought from the tavern.

The guards then began to eat the dinner that had originally been prepared for the royal prisoners. This is an example of how the guards and officials on duty began to carry out their orders; this is also an example of how the princesses were to be treated throughout the rest of their imprisonment. In his memoires, which have survived to this day, Turgy was able to document the prisoners' daily struggles, and this has helped to fill the gap of information that existed since Cléry's removal from the Temple.

The Queen's Nightmare Begins

On the 2nd of August, at 2 o'clock in the morning, the queen was awakened and told that she was to be taken to the Conciergerie, a medieval place turned prison, to await trial. "She heard the decree read," Princess Marie-Thérèse revealed, "without emotion, and without saying a word." The princess begged the officers to be allowed to accompany her mother, but her request was denied. The queen gathered her things in a small bundle, and she was forced to dress herself in front of the officials. She kissed her daughter many times, pleading for her to take care of herself. She also asked her to treat Madame Elisabeth as her second mother in her absence, but the princess was so grief-stricken that she could not answer her. At last, Madame Elisabeth embraced her sister-in-law and whispered some words in her ear. Then the queen left room, not looking back at her daughter—fearing that her strength would fail her.

As the queen departed down the stairs, she accidentally struck her head against the top of the portal, not knowing that it was so low. When an official asked about her condition, she replied, "Nothing can hurt me now." Stunned by her grief and the strangeness of her fate, she stepped into a hired carriage with a municipal officer and two police officers.

The princess and her aunt, now alone in the tower, spent the night weeping inconsolably. The princess later wrote in her mémoires that she knew it would be the last time that she would ever see her mother. The queen was even refused permission to visit her son before she left the Temple. Regrettably, she would never see her children again.

Despite the pleas of Marie-Thérèse and Madame Elisabeth to the municipal officers for news about the queen, they were kept in the dark about her misfortunes. Furthermore, for many months they heard very little about the young uncrowned king, who was kept secluded elsewhere in the tower; they were also unaware of the extent of the child's mistreatment, which eventually caused him to become very ill. Simon, his new caretaker, forced him to eat disgusting food and drink enormous quantities of wine and brandy to get him intoxicated. He also taught him to curse and to sing vulgar revolutionary songs.

Although the princesses had no word of the queen's condition from the municipal officers while she was imprisoned in the Conciergerie, they did receive limited news that Turgy was able to acquire from her former servant, Hüe. On the 13th of October, however, Turgy received orders that he was to leave the Temple immediately with his comrades, Chrétien and Marchand. Turgy wrote in his journal that they left the Temple with "very sad hearts, because they were worried about the future of their royal masters." Turgy left Paris and joined his family in Tournan-en-Brie, saying that he suffered a great deal of persecution for his royal ties at first, but, little by little, it ceased, and he was finally allowed to live in peace.

Marie-Antoinette awaits execution in the Conciergerie

As for Cléry, he had already been imprisoned in La Force for a month when the queen was removed from the Temple to be tried. He was likely aware of her arrest, but he would not have known about the details of her final days in the Conciergerie Prison without the help of Hüe and Bault, one of the jailers of the Conciergerie, and his wife. Information that came out in the queen's trial, as well as the mémoires of Hüe, Bault, and the prison's maid, Rosalie, reveal horrendous details of her captivity.

It was 3 o'clock in the morning when the queen, dressed in a black robe, arrived at her new prison. She was taken to a damp, cold cell on the main floor. The only light in the room came from a small window with iron bars and no curtains that looked out upon the prison courtyard. The only furniture in the room consisted of a bed, two chairs, and a small table. The torn mattress was stuffed with rotting straw; the only cover was a dirty used woolen blanket with holes. Even the guards that slept on similar beds complained that they were too hard. In fact, her bed had been rejected by the guards on duty because they had found it too uncomfortable. A small basket was kept under the table to hold sewing materials, and a small wooden box was placed on the table for powder.

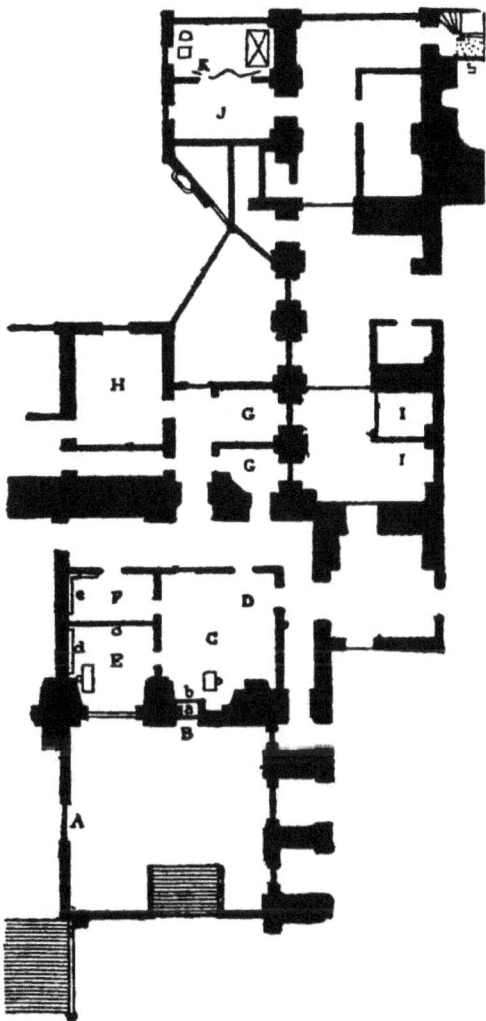

The Conciergerie

(A) Guard house door; (B) Entrance to the prison; (C) Room used by the jailer Richard; (D) Area where condemned prisoners' hair was cut and sold; (E) Registrar's office; (F) Back office; (G) Rooms where the keeper of the keys slept; (H) Council room, the queen's first room; (I) Small rooms where women condemned to death slept the night; (J) Room of the officers guarding the queen; (K) The queen's second cell.

The queen could not help but notice the bare, cold walls when she entered her cell. She first removed her watch and let it hang from a nail that she saw on the wall. She then she lay on her bed. A young woman who worked as a maid in the prison, Rosalie, whom the queen hardly acknowledged the first day, was also stationed in the cell. She wrote, "I observed that the Queen had brought no clothes or personal effects when she arrived from the Temple in the middle of the night."

Until the queen was moved to another cell, Rosalie only went there to carry in the queen's breakfast at 9 o'clock and her dinner at 2 o'clock. The guards, in the beginning, did not give her any solitude. They remained in the room night and day to keep watch over her, and the staff arranged their beds in the cell in order never to lose sight of the royal prisoner. The queen would ask for some linen, but Madame Richard, the wife of the concierge, did not dare to lend her any, fearing to compromise herself.

Marie-Antoinette in prison

Marie-Antoinette was still a queen, however, even in the depths of this dingy, little cell. In time, she was able to befriend

Madame Richard and her husband, the concierge of the prison. When Madame Richard revealed the queen's request to a municipal officer, Michonis, he went to the Temple and arranged for a packet to be delivered to the queen. When it arrived, she opened it at once to find an array of pocket handkerchiefs, scarves, stockings, and some ribbons. One of the items was a white robe, a robe she would wear on the day of her execution. She cried as she looked through the linen, and turning to Madame Richard and Michonis, she said, "By the care taken of these things I recognize the hand of my poor sister Elisabeth."

She spent her days praying, meditating, watching the guards play cards, or perhaps thinking about her sad past. She sometimes read a book that the guards lent her on days when they would feel compassion for a fellow human being. One of the friendlier guards lent her *Captain Cook's Voyages*. Her eyesight, however, was failing and the prison maid, Rosalie, managed to secretly give her an eyeglass.

The queen was refused needles for needlework because they feared that she would create secret messages or that she would commit suicide. Although the queen did not drink wine and could not drink the water from the Seine, she was fortunately allowed special waters from Ville-d'Avray during her first weeks in the prison.

After some time, the guards became somewhat lax in their surveillance of the queen. One of the guards even stopped smoking his pipe because he noticed that the smoke kept the queen from sleeping well at night. Another guard, noticing the queen's love of flowers, would sometimes bring her some carnations. In general, access to the tortured lady was easier at the Conciergerie than at the Temple. Her past servant, Hüe, was actually able to win the concierge Richard and his wife over to the queen's cause. He was able to gain entrance to the prison and get news to the queen about her children and Madame Elisabeth, thus consoling her that her loved ones were doing well in the Temple. It was actually easier for one to enter the Conciergerie and have access to Marie-Antoinette than it was at the Temple.

According to Hüe, the queen had once mentioned to Madame Richard that she was craving melon. This woman, doing her best to soften the harsh reality of prison for the queen, ran to a market near the prison. "I need a superb melon," she said to a woman selling vegetables that she knew. "I can only guess," she replied, "that the melon is for our unfortunate Queen; choose the finest melon that you can find." She then picked the one that she thought was the best, and gave it to Madame Richard who wanted to pay for it. "Keep your money," replied the woman, "and tell the Queen that there are many of us who fret for her." She wanted to talk more, but the concierge left quickly. She took the melon to the queen and told her what had happened, and the queen was deeply touched by the story.

Life in the prison, however, remained agonizing for the queen. The noise was unbearable. The rusty hinges screeched loudly, the locks and chains clanked and jangled, the iron cell doors were ferociously slammed shut, bulldogs barked constantly at the slightest noise, prisoners moaned and whined waiting for the executioner, and the prostitutes laughed and squealed all through the night.

Despite the exasperating nuisances in the Conciergerie, there was still a glimmer of hope that the queen would be saved. In his mémoires Hüe described in detail the courageous efforts of those supporters willing to help the queen escape from the prison. One plot was named the "Carnation Affair." On the 28th of August, two visitors to the prison, Rougeville and Michonis, arrived at the Conciergerie to find the queen dressed in black. Her hair, now white from the grief, had been cut short in the front and back, and she was so thin that Rougeville could hardly recognize her. She was also so weak that she could barely stand up when the gentlemen arrived.

"Oh, it is you, Monsieur Michonis!" she said. Approaching him, she asked if he had any news of her children. When she saw Rougeville, however, she was so overcome that she had to sit down again with tears rolling down her emaciated cheeks. Rougeville was a friend of the royal family, and he had spent time with her husband before his execution.

After consoling her and telling her that she would be rescued, Rougeville motioned for her to accept a carnation in which he had hidden a note that said, "I have men and money at your disposal." The queen was so moved, however, at seeing the king's dear friend that she did not understand what was going on. Rougeville dropped the flowers behind a small stove in her cell, and then he left with Michonis.

Moments later the guards called for the two gentlemen to return to the queen, at her request. While Michonis distracted the guards, the queen begged Rougeville not to get involved in such a dangerous plot to rescue her. He replied that he had arms and money, and that the queen should be courageous. Fearing that their conversation would raise eyebrows, Michonis then motioned for Rougeville to leave with him. Before leaving, however, Rougeville had made the queen aware of the flowers on the ground that he had brought her.

While the guards were playing cards, she picked up the flower and secretly read the hidden note in a corner of the room. She tore the note into hundreds of pieces. Without a pen she could not reply except by poking small holes in a small strip of paper. As soon as she had finished, however, a guard entered the cell, discovered what the queen was doing, and seized the note immediately. Rosalie indicated that a woman by the name of Harel had seen everything, and she had reported the entire episode to the prosecutor, Fouquier-Tinville. The plan was thus foiled, and the government, believing that there was a wide-spread plot to help the queen escape, immediately issued orders that were more severe regarding her imprisonment.

Rougeville was able to escape, but Michonis was arrested along with Madame Richard and her son. Fortunately, they were later able to escape the scaffold for their efforts to save the queen. Michonis, however, was later guillotined for another prison conspiracy, but not for the "Carnation Affair."

A new concierge was thus solicited for the Conciergerie. Madame Bault, the wife of the jailer at La Force Prison, had heard talk that a horrible man by the name of Simon was being considered as a replacement for Richard. Working at La Force Prison, jailer Bault would have been acquainted with Jean-Baptiste Cléry. In fact, when the jailer Bault heard about the idea, he shuddered and was determined, on the spot, to propose that he become the queen's jailer. Madame Bault wrote in her mémoires that she and her husband had the honor of knowing Cléry, and they thus informed him about their plan. She remarked that Cléry heartily encouraged them to proceed, and the Baults were eventually installed in the Conciergerie on the 11th of September 1793.

Security thereafter became much tighter. The guards searched the queen's cell and removed all articles that were not bare necessities. The queen's watch, jewels, and rings were all confiscated as well. She was later moved to a more secure cell with no female guard. Two guards remained in the room day and night behind a divider, and two guards were also placed outside her window in the courtyard.

The queen was not allowed any handiwork; she only read and prayed. The bad air and the lack of exercise took their toll on the queen; she also suffered at this time from constant uterine hemorrhaging, which undoubtedly contributed to her ghostly appearance. Although the food was carefully prepared for the queen, she had no appetite and often did not eat at all. The autumn was cold and damp, and the queen had no fire in her new cell. There was no light in the evenings for reading.

Any compassion shown on the part of her guards or prison attendants was considered treasonable acts and punishable by death. The incarceration of the queen was an example of the cruelty that was associated with this almost godless and inhumane period of time. She suffered severely from the cold and had to use her meager pillow to keep her feet warm. The concierge, Madame Bault, touched by the courteous dignity and sad sufferings of the captive, approached Fouquier-Tinville, the public prosecutor, for more coverings for the queen's bed, or rather for the bed of the Widow Capet, but the heartless wretch replied, "How dare you ask for such a thing? You yourself deserve to be sent to the guillotine for doing so."

Marie-Antoinette contemplates cutting her hair

Despite the stricter prison rules precipitated by the "Carnation Affair," Madame Bault was able to attend to some matters. Her daughter mended the queen's linen and other garments that had worn out completely. Also, the young girl was allowed to dress the queen's hair, a simple *coiffure* every day. To keep from compromising himself and his family, the jailer Bault feigned harshness against the queen in the presence of the municipal officer and other officers. The Bault family put their lives at risk to show kindness to the unfortunate prisoner.

Chapter 15
The Queen's Trial

If I have not answered, it was because nature itself rejects such an accusation made against a mother. I appeal from it to every mother who hears me.

–Marie-Antoinette's response to accusations of incest
October 1793

After two months in the Conciergerie, the queen was finally arraigned. The prosecutor, Fouquier-Tinville, arrived at the Conciergerie Prison on the 13th of October to inform Marie-Antoinette of the accusations. The maid, Rosalie, said that she warily stood while the long indictment of her legendary crimes was read. In a nutshell, her crime was to have been a queen, the wife and mother of a king, and to have abhorred the revolution that wrestled the crown from her husband, her children, and her life. She did not utter a word. Later, she chose two counselors, Lagarde and Ducoudray, to defend her, but she had no hope of being found innocent.

The next day, she dressed herself as neatly as her poverty permitted, not wishing to inspire pity either in her friends or her enemies. As she slipped off her dress in order to change her under linen for the last time, an officer came from behind the screen to watch her. "In the name of decency, monsieur, let me change my linen without being watched," she said gently. "It is impossible for me to allow it," he answered roughly; "my orders are to keep my eye on you, whatever you are doing." Rosalie wrote that she was much disturbed by the officer's brutality.

The queen then made her way, amid a battalion of gendarmes, to the tribunal of her judges: Hermann, Foucaud, Tellier, Coffinhal, Lelliege, Ragmey Maire, Denizot, and Masson. Most of these names were obscure for a long period of time; history had been indulgent enough to bury them in oblivion. She looked around the court with such an assured and serene glance that a woman nearby exclaimed, "See how proud she is."

The people gathered in the room gazed with mute curiosity on the woman who was recorded to sit with an imposing, but admirable stature.

"Accused," demanded President Hermann, "what is your name!"

"Marie-Antoinette de Lorraine of Austria," she answered stoically.

"Your condition?" he asked coldly.

"Widow of Louis, formerly King of the French," she said.

"Your age?" snapped the president immediately.

"Thirty-seven years," answered the queen without any emotion.

Then Hermann read the act of accusation. Besides the supposed crimes of foreign birth, of despotism, of conspiracy, and of hatred for the French people, there also existed the vilest pamphlets which defamed the character of the queen and her conduct as a woman. Every despicable rumor that circulated was submitted as evidence, yet the queen let this torrent of scornful contempt pass without showing any outward sign of resentment or bitterness.

During the interrogation of the witnesses, the sickly woman replied and questioned with an aura of simplicity, refuting her accusers for the record while endeavoring not to compromise those who were helping with her defense. Only Hébert succeeded in arousing any anger in her, yet inspiring one of the most eloquent expressions ever recorded in history. Hébert, in recounting the events in the Temple, dared to assert that the queen had sought to corrupt her own son "in order to enervate at once his body and his soul, and to reign in his name upon the ruins of his intelligence."

In other words, this cynical madman was accusing the queen of incest. He had the audacity to accuse this mother of having depraved her son, in order "to enervate his body, weaken his mind, and thus secure herself the prospect of reigning in his stead." Marie-Antoinette kept silent after hearing the contemptuous accusation. The most hardened sans-culottes, the poorest of the revolutionaries, who were present in the room gasped with horror.

As for the queen, the horror conquered her steadfastness. She rose to reply, but fearing to compromise her innocence, she stopped short of speaking and sat back down. After a delay of half an hour, one of the jurors asked the queen why she had remained silent upon hearing Hebert's allegations. "If I have not answered," she said at last with the dignity of innocence and the indignation of modesty, "it was because Nature itself rejects such an accusation made against a mother!"

Trial of Marie-Antoinette

Then turning, perhaps more majestically and more worthy of admiration on this bench than on the throne of France, toward the women in the audience she exclaimed in a voice which penetrated all of their hearts, "I appeal to every mother present!" A long silence followed, and Hébert recoiled under the weight of his shame. There was a rumbling of applause throughout the chamber, and Hebert remained dumbstruck by the crowd's disdain.

Robespierre, one of the most influential figures of the French Revolution who dominated the political scene after the fall of the monarchy, chastised Hébert's overzealous and clumsy approach: "It was not enough then for the villain to have made her a Messalina, he must also make her an Agrippina as well?" In other words, by exaggerating his charges against the queen, Hébert was actually helping her cause.

The condemned queen courageously defended the memory of her husband, but the decree had already been decided. Hermann coldly resumed the accusation and declared that Marie-Antoinette had been condemned by the people. Her counsel, Lagarde and Ducoudray, defended her, but to deaf ears. Then the jury that had been well paid by the prosecutor pretended to deliberate and pronounced the penalty of death, amid the cruel applause of the audience. The queen returned to listen to her sentence, without uttering a word or making a gesture. "Have you any observation to make?" asked Hermann. She shook her head and rose of herself, it is said, as if to walk straight to her execution.

The queen had defended herself with honor and without compromising others. Tortured with 15 hours of questioning and debate, the queen was overcome with fatigue and thirst. She had only been allowed one drink of water. When she returned to her cell, she could hardly walk. A guard, Busne, offered her his arm as she stepped down into her cell. The following morning he was arrested and imprisoned for his humanity that was considered counter-revolutionary. He was later executed.

The Final Hours

It was 4 o'clock in the morning, and the first rays of dawn were shedding shadows of light in the dungeons of the Conciergerie. Conducted to the funeral cell where the condemned prisoners awaited execution, the queen obtained pen, ink, and paper from the concierge, and she wrote to her sister-in-law, Madame Elisabeth, a touching letter that could be regarded as her last will and testament.

ce 16 8bre à 4 h ½ du matin

c'est à vous, ma sœur, que j'écris pour la dernière fois. je viens d'être condamnée, non pas à une mort honteuse, elle ne l'est que pour les criminels, mais à aller rejoindre votre frère; comme lui innocente, j'espère montrer la même fermeté que lui dans ces derniers moments. je suis calme comme on l'est, quand la conscience ne reproche rien; j'ai un profond regret d'abandonner mes pauvres enfants; vous savez que je n'existois que pour eux, et vous, ma bonne et tendre sœur; vous qui avez par votre amitié tout sacrifié pour être avec nous; dans quelle position je vous laisse! j'ai appris par le plaidoyer même du procès que ma fille étoit séparée de vous. hélas! la pauvre enfant, je n'ose pas lui écrire, elle ne recevroit pas ma lettre, je ne sais même pas si celle-ci vous parviendra. recevez pour eux deux ici ma bénédiction. j'espère qu'un jour, lorsqu'ils seront plus grands, ils pourront se réunir avec vous, et jouir en entier de vos tendres soins. qu'ils pensent tous deux à ce que je n'ai cessé de leur inspirer; que les principes, et l'exécution exacte de ses devoirs sont la première base de la vie; que leur amitié et leur confiance mutuelle, en feront le bonheur; que ma fille sente qu'à l'âge qu'elle a, elle doit toujours aider son frère par les conseils que son expérience qu'elle aura de plus que lui et son amitié pourront lui inspirer; que mon fils à son tour, rende à sa sœur tous les soins, les services, que l'amitié peut inspirer; qu'ils sentent enfin tous deux que, dans quelque position où ils pourront se trouver; ils ne seront vraiment heureux que par leur union. qu'ils prennent exemple de nous. combien dans nos malheurs, notre amitié nous a donné de consolations, et dans le bonheur on jouit doublement quand on peut le partager avec un ami; et où en trouver de plus tendre, de plus cher que dans sa propre famille? que mon fils n'oublie jamais les derniers mots de son père que je lui répète expressément; qu'il ne cherche jamais à venger notre mort. j'ai à vous parler d'une chose bien pénible à mon cœur. je sais combien cet enfant doit vous avoir fait de la peine; pardonnez-lui, ma chère sœur; pensez à l'âge qu'il a, et combien il est facile

It is to you, my sister, that I am writing for the last time. I have been sentenced to death but not a death that is shameful, for it is only shameful for criminals, but to be reunited with your brother. Like him, innocent, I hope to display the same firmness as he did in his last moments. I am as calm as one is when one's conscience holds no reproach. I deeply regret having to leave behind my poor children. You know that I lived only for them and for you, my dear good sister. In what a situation I leave you, who out of your affection has sacrificed everything to be with us! All that is left is for me to confide in you my last thoughts. I should have liked to have written them down before the start of the trial but quite apart from the fact that I was not allowed to write, events took place so rapidly that I really did not have the time. I die in the Catholic, Apostolic and Roman faith, that of my fathers, in which I was brought up and which I have always acknowledged. Having no hope of spiritual consolation and not even knowing if there are still any priests of my faith here and if so, whether the place at which I am would endanger them too much, I simply ask God for forgiveness for all my trespasses. I hope that He in His love will hear my prayers kindly and will receive my soul mercifully. I ask all those whom I know, especially you, my sister, to forgive me for any unhappiness I may unwittingly have caused them. I forgive all my enemies the wrongs they have done to me. I now say farewell to my aunts, brothers and sisters. I used to have friends; the thought of being separated from them forever, and their unhappiness, will pain me even in my death; let them know at least that I thought of them until the last moment. Adieu, my dear and good sister. I hope this letter will reach you. Think of me always. I embrace you from the bottom of my heart and also my dear poor children. My God, it breaks my heart having to leave them forever. Goodbye, goodbye. Now I must devote myself only to my spiritual duties. Since I am not able to act freely they will perhaps send me a constitutional priest; however, I declare here and now that I shall have nothing to say to him and shall treat him as a complete stranger.

After having finished her letter, the queen covered it with kisses, as if her children would find them there along with her tears.

Then, she entrusted it to Madame Bault, who was to send it to Fouquier-Tinville. However, this letter blotted with tears never reached her dear friend, the Princess Elisabeth.

The sound of drums had echoed through the city since 5 o'clock in the morning. At 8 o'clock a priest arrived to see if she wanted him to accompany her to the scaffold. She answered coldly, "As you please."

At 10 o'clock, Sanson, the executioner, arrived at the queen's cell. He tied her hands behind her back. Curiously, he held his hat under his arm as he escorted his prisoner out of the cell. Was this a sign of respect for the woman that he was about to behead?

Marie-Antoinette taken to the guillotine

Some 30,000 soldiers were placed along the route from the Conciergerie to the scaffold at the *Place de la Revolution*. The tumbril, a farmer's cart that was normally used to carry manure, carried the queen slowly through the streets of Paris amid cries of scorn; many had even been paid by the revolutionaries to insult her.

A drawing by the artist David from his balcony depicted the queen's expression as one of profound indifference, with her hands tied behind her back but her head held high. Only when a small child in the arms of its mother waved did the queen show any emotion; her eyes filled with tears. She had been in rags during most of the time of her imprisonment, but her dress on this day was neat and clean. She wore a white muslin cap tied with a piece of black ribbon and a white gown and kerchief. Her white hair was cut short round her cap. Her face, pale except for the spots on her fevered cheeks, and her bloodshot eyes witnessed her agony.

Sketch by Jacque Louis David

The King had been garbed in court dress, and he rode to the guillotine in a closed carriage. David's sketch on the other hand symbolized the fact that the there would never be another queen in France. Described as an "aged hag" in the newspapers, she was sketched not simply as the king's wife but as a notorious, dangerous, and powerful public woman of France who was blamed for the moral decline of society.

When the queen finally arrived and ascended the steps to the scaffold, she accidentally stepped on the executioner's foot. "Je vous demande pardon," she apologized. When all was ready, she said to him, "Make haste." In a sense, death was life to her.

Four minutes later the executioner pulled the infamous string as the queen kneeled with her throat in the wooden *lunette*, and the blade of the guillotine dropped to the cries of *"Vive la République!"*

According to the queen's daughter, the execution was not known in the Temple, but Cléry, in La Force Prison, would have been informed by the jailer Bault or Hüe. If not, he would certainly have known that it had taken place by the noise and chaos in the streets.

Execution of Marie-Antoinette

Although Cléry was locked away in his cell in a different prison some distance from the Conciergerie, the former valet de chambre of the dauphin would have been deeply saddened by his queen's trial and execution. Cléry had been in the service of the royal family for almost 10 years, beginning in 1784 as the king's barber. He became valet de chambre of the Prince Louis Joseph a later when he was born. Moreover, Cléry could never forget that it was the queen who had ensured his marriage to the 17-year old Mademoiselle Duverger, a court musician who had taught the Queen how to play the harp at the court of Versailles.

When the royal family had been sent to the Temple Prison, Cléry remembered the day well when the queen expressed her joy and amazement when she discovered that Cléry had been permitted to enter the Temple and resume his service as *valet de chambre* to the dauphin. He was presented to the family as they were having dinner, and it was difficult, Cléry wrote, for him to describe the impression that the "sight of that majestic, but unfortunate, family" made upon him. The queen spoke to him first, and after a few words of kindness, she added: "You will serve my son, and you will arrange with M. Hüe all other matters that concern us." Cléry wrote that he was so overcome with feelings that he could scarcely answer her without succumbing to tears.

Cléry's veneration and respect for the queen can best be exemplified on the horrendous day of the 3rd of September. The queen had not slept well because of the drums rolling continually through the night. As she was sitting down to backgammon with the king at 3 o'clock in the afternoon, a great clamor was heard in the streets. Cléry at this moment entered, and the queen asked him why he was not having his dinner. He replied that he was indisposed. In fact, he had just sat down to dinner with Tison and his wife, when something was held up in the window which he knew at a glance to be the head of the Princess de Lamballe which was perched atop a pike. He ran immediately to prevent the queen from seeing it, if possible.

Meantime, curses of the queen were heard without; and one of the guards told her that the people wanted her to see her friend's head, that she might see how tyrants were to be served; and that if she did not go to the window, the people would bring the princess's head to her.

The queen dropped in a fainting fit; and the brute left the room. The Princess Elizabeth and Cléry lifted the queen into an armchair and frantically tried to revive their heartbroken queen.

Cléry could never have forgotten the queen's good nature. In his service to the royal household, he often saw that the queen was always ready to reward her servants generously for their zeal. The queen was also well aware of the value of her servants, and Cléry wrote that she always made sure that they were never overburdened in their work.

Chapter 16
One Royal Survivor

Marie-Thérèse is the unhappiest creature in the world. She can obtain no news of her mother; nor be reunited with her, though she has asked a thousand times.

–Words scratched on the walls of the princess's prison room, *1793*

On the 8th of October, a week before the queen was executed, Princess Marie-Thérèse had been escorted downstairs to be interrogated. On the way, she had the brief opportunity to see her brother; she kissed him affectionately until Simon forcibly dragged him away from her and took him to another room. Unknowingly, this was the last time that she would ever see her young brother.

The minister Chaumette told the princess to sit down, and he began his interrogation. "Your name?" he asked.

"Marie-Thérèse," she replied.

"You are being truthful?" he continued.

"Yes, monsieur," she answered. "Does this concern my mother?"

"No," he answered coldly.

The questioning continued about friends and loyal subjects of the royal family. More disturbing, the princess was asked if she had any information about the reported incestuous relations between the queen and the young prince. The princess denied any wrongdoing on her mother's part. This despicable accusation originated from Simon, who had caught the prince pleasuring himself one day. In his report to the authorities, Simon said that the prince blamed his mother and aunt for learning such practices. Simon also blamed them for the prince's bruised testicle, caused by the incestuous acts. It is documented, however, that the child had once injured himself while playing.

When the three-hour interrogation was over, the princess asked to join her mother in the Conciergerie. Chaumette replied: "That is not possible; retire, and say nothing to your aunt, for whom we are also going to send." And, under the escort of three municipals, the trembling young girl returned to her chamber. She later wrote:

> I was struck dumb with horror, and was so indignant that, notwithstanding all my terror, I could not refrain from saying that it was so infamous. Notwithstanding my tears they persisted very long; there were things that I could not well understand, but what I could comprehend was so horrible that I wept with indignation.

Still frozen with terror, the princess scarcely had time to throw herself into the arms of her loving aunt when she was torn from her, and obliged to depart, without knowing what was going to happen. She was interrogated in turn, and the same incredible accusations were made against the queen before her. Madame Elizabeth replied, as her niece had done, to all the horrific accusations with most noble frankness.

When the impromptu trial was over, she returned to her room in tears. "Oh, my child!" exclaimed Madame Elizabeth, extending her arms to her niece. Silence alone could express the confusion and the embarrassment of both after being confronted with the most humiliating accusations. For a moment they held each other in their arms, and then, falling on their knees, they began to pray.

Madame Elisabeth, the king's sister, is taken from the Temple Prison

These royal prisoners of the Temple were never aware of the results of the Chaumette's interrogations, nor the queen's trial and her treatment in the Conciergerie prison. For two years the princess Marie-Thérèse did not even know of the tragic fate of her mother.

Tragic Fate of the Pious Madame Elisabeth

On the evening of the 9th of May, an order was received from the Committee of Public Safety that Madame Elisabeth was to be executed the following day. The committee sent for Henriot, the commander of the Guard, to see if there was any danger to fear from the people. He replied that there was nothing to fear, and the committee ordered the sentence to be carried out. However, finding a soldier who was willing to find the princess, arrest her, and escort her to the Conciergerie prison was a difficult task.

One crass soldier, Saralier, readily accepted the charge and went directly to the Temple, accompanied by two officers. When he arrived, he went upstairs and entered the room where Madame Elisabeth was reading to Princess Marie-Thérèse. He interrupted them, acknowledging that he had come to take Madame Elisabeth to the Conciergerie.

Madame Elisabeth received the order of arrest with the greatest courage, according to the mémoires of her niece Princess Marie-Thérèse. "Prepare yourself, my dear, for you may soon follow me," said Madame Elisabeth. She wanted to hug her niece but Saralier refused her request. When the wife and daughters of the Temple guard began to cry, Saralier began to pull Madame Elisabeth away from her niece, fearing that his officers might not obey his orders. Not wanting to abandon her niece in the Temple, however, she resisted him. This only angered Saralier more, and he grabbed her by the hair and fiercely pulled her out of the room. Shocked by the brutal treatment of the officer, Madame Elisabeth left without a word.

She spent the night praying at the Conciergerie prison. The next morning she was readied to be taken before the judge at 11 o'clock. When Madame Elisabeth, called the "sister of Louis Capet, the last tyrant," was brought to trial, the jury, when they heard the name, without waiting for further information, cried out, "We've had enough. Death! Death!" She was then, of course, condemned to death, along with more than 20 other companions. They all were sentenced to death by the guillotine's blade.

Madame Elisabeth soon found herself seated in the same cart as two ladies, Madame Sénozan and Madame Crussol-d'Amboise. They spoke to each other along the route from the Conciergerie to the Revolution Square, and the princess consoled the frightened prisoners. Upon arrival at the square, she descended from the cart first. The executioner offered her his hand to help her, but she looked the other way. All the prisoners were then escorted to a long bank at the foot of the scaffold to await their turns.

None waivered. Encouraged by the presence of the sister of Louis XVI, each of the condemned women promised to stand up bravely when her name was called. The first name called was that of Madame Crussol. She stood up and bowed in front of Madame Elisabeth, showing the respect and love that the princess inspired in her. She asked permission to embrace the princess. "Gladly, with all of my heart," replied the princess, who then kissed her goodbye. All the other women followed her and received the same token of affection. The men also paid their respect to the princess by bowing the heads that a minute later would fall under the blade. During this entire time, the saintly woman prayed for those who met their destiny.

The princess's rendezvous with the blade was reserved until the last. When the executioner finally called her name, she majestically, but humbly, climbed the steps to the scaffold and looked up to the heavens as she presented herself to the executioner. As she was being fastened to the fatal plank, her *fichu*, a large kerchief worn by women in the 18th century to fill in the low neckline of their bodice, fell off and exposed a silver medal of the Blessed Virgin. The executioner's assistant, instead of replacing the *fichu* on her bosom, attempted to remove the pious emblem. "Cover my bosom, sir, in the name of your mother!" cried the princess, and these were her last words.

Her head fell, but this time the crowd did not give way to its habitual fury. The cries of "Long live the Republic!" were not heard. Her biographers recorded that as her head fell into the basket a perfume of roses was carried in the breeze over the square. They also recorded that Madame Elisabeth met her death with courage. She was in no way dangerous to the republic or to the revolution, and was, indeed, a most innocent victim. Cléry wrote in his mémoires that she was a gentle, tender, pious, modest, and benevolent woman. Her death was believed to be one of the greatest crimes of the revolution; in fact, the very same evening, the printers and journalists of Paris received an order from the government prohibiting them from revealing the details of her execution.

A member of the National Guard, who had witnessed the execution of Louis XVI, recorded that the people did not seem to be too moved. In fact, the crowd was so small that women and children found plenty of room to see the show comfortably. He wrote, "In general, the great events of the Revolution did not attract very large crowds." The very same guardsman was standing on the route to the scaffold when Madame Elisabeth passed in her tumbril, a cart used to carry condemned prisoners to their death, and he wrote, "There was hardly anyone there."

Since the time her aunt had been taken from her, Marie-Thérèse was unaware that this saint-like woman had been subjected to the same punishment as her mother. Madame Elisabeth was guillotined on the 10th of May 1974.

Cléry's Sorrow

Cléry, after being imprisoned for eight months in La Force Prison, would have been devastated by the news of the execution of this saintly woman. Madame Elisabeth had only shown him the kindest affection. On one occasion when Cléry was bedridden with fever, Madame Elisabeth risked her safety by giving him, without the municipal officers observing it, a small bottle containing a cold remedy. Moreover, this saintly woman, although she was terribly ill, deprived herself of the medication for her servant's sake. He tried to refuse it, but she insisted. She also took over Cléry's duties such as rolling the king's hair and dressing the dauphin for him.

On the 6th of December 1792, Cléry had heard that the king's trial was about to take place and that the king would be separated from the queen and the rest of the family during the course of the trial. After dinner one evening, Cléry risked his safety by contriving to follow Madame Elisabeth to warn her that during the trial the king would not be allowed to see his family. Noticing the princess's despair, he tried to encourage her to hope that the king would be sent into exile. She replied, "I now have no hope that the King will be saved, but his religion will sustain him in this last adversity."

Showing her confidence in the king's faithful servant and thinking that she was speaking to him for the last time since he was also forbidden to leave the king's side, she said: "You will be alone with my brother; double your attention to him, if it be possible, do not neglect to send us news of him. But for any other reason, do not expose yourself to any peril, for then we should have no one in whom we could confide."

Cléry would also have remembered that although the princess was not beautiful, not having the queen's grace or dignity, she had a beautiful smile and "sweet, blue eyes." While the family was in the Temple, and before they were separated from the king, she often sat up to mend her brother's garments and stockings, and those of the dauphin, since they only possessed one suit of clothes in the prison. In fact, for Madame Elisabeth, religion was the framework for her life, and Cléry observed, "How often have I seen Madame Elisabeth on her knees at her bedside, praying fervently for her family."

At the time of Madame Elisabeth's execution, the young Prince Louis Charles had been named King Louis XVII, although uncrowned, by the royal family in exile. The boy's uncle, Charles, the *Comte d'Artois*, had left France three days after the fall of the Bastille in 1789. His other uncle, Louis-Stanislas, the *Comte de Provence*, and his wife fled to the Austrian Netherlands at the time of the royal family's failed flight to Varennes in June 1791.

Despite the new king's status, he was barricaded like a wild animal in a small, dark room in the Temple. His meals were passed through iron bars on the door, and he was not allowed to leave his room, a room with a horrific stench due to the accumulated human waste and lack of fresh air. He was allowed no candle or light at night. He was subjected to solitary confinement for six months.

For the year of the dauphin's life that followed his separation from his mother, there is no continuous and reliable narrative such as Cléry's journal of the family's sufferings in the Temple. The heart-rending account of Cléry's former charge and his inhumane treatment must be documented by piecing together all the fragments of reliable information available. It is undoubtedly the most tragic story of the revolution.

The Uncrowned King

The rooms which King Louis XVI had occupied on the second floor of the tower were allotted to the wretched Simon, and it was there that the dauphin was escorted on the 3rd of July when he was snatched from his mother's arms. The child had not seen his father's rooms for at least six months since the time of the king's execution. Marie-Thérèse related in her *mémoires* that the dauphin cried for two whole days when he was first guarded by Simon. Other than these notes from his sister, there is little information about the first days during Simon's new guardianship.

Madame Simon arrived sometime soon afterwards and the couple was allotted 9,000 *livres* a year, a good income if it had been paid regularly, which it was not. There were rumors that the little prince had been removed from the Temple to be restored on the throne. The Council, therefore, sent a delegation of four of its members to the Temple to be sure that the prince was still incarcerated there.

In their report, they stated that they found the child playing checkers with Simon. They took the prince down into the garden so that the guards could see him, and they were no doubt taken aback when he began to ask for his mother and demand that he should be shown the decree that ordered him to be separated from her. Of Simon's behavior they said nothing, but the fact that he was playing checkers with the child cannot be taken as proof that he did not ever mistreat his young charge.

Naturally, the dauphin's request to see his mother was never granted, and after the 3rd of July, he never saw or spoke to her again. She, however, occasionally had a glimpse of her son from a distance. "Her sole pleasures," wrote Marie-Thérèse, "was to see him from afar through a little window; she would stay there for hours at a time to watch for this dearly-beloved child." The dauphin, however, did not know that she was ever looking at him, and he did not know that she had been removed from the Temple. To the very end he believed her to be in the room above him.

In some respects, it is clear that at this time the dauphin was not ill-treated; he was well fed and decently clothed, the doctor's orders were carried out, and Madame Simon kept him clean and tidy. It is also known that Simon would play billiards with the child on a table that was placed or found in one of the rooms of the Temple. Even the daughter of one of the laundresses was allowed to come to the Temple to play with him.

There is, however, a darker side to the picture. Simon forced the child to wear a liberty cap and "*sansculottes*" or knee-breeches that were the dress of the people. He wanted the child to see that there was no difference between a prince and other people. This must have been a bitter humiliation for the prince who had been treated with respect since his infancy as the king's son and future heir to the throne of France.

Moreover, Simon taught him to swear and use obscene language as well as sing blasphemous and filthy songs. In fact, one of the officials, Leboeuf, brought this to Simon's attention, but he was later reprimanded for doing so. There is obvious evidence that Simon had in fact affected the child's mind; one of the officials, Daujeon, recorded that one day when he was on duty and watching the prince playing, there was a loud noise in the room overhead where the two princesses were kept. The dauphin exclaimed, "Are not those damned b-----s guillotined yet!"

Perhaps the most damning evidence of abuse was recorded when Dr. Naudin was summoned to attend to Madame Simon when she was ill. He reported that Simon wanted the dauphin to sing some indecent verses, but when he refused and burst out crying, Simon seized him by the hair and shouted, "You wretched viper! I will smash your head against the wall."

The doctor rescued the child from Simon's grasp, crying: "You scoundrel. What are you doing?" An officer nearby spoke up: "Doctor, it's just a joke."

When the doctor returned the next day to the Temple, the dauphin offered him two pears, saying: "Yesterday you proved to me that you take an interest in me, and I thank you for it. I only have these to show you my gratitude; you will do me a pleasure by accepting them."

There are other stories that were written later about Simon's brutality, but they are not first-hand stories. Authors later wrote that Simon starved the child, played tricks on him, and made him get up in the middle of the night only to get splashed with cold water or struck with an iron bar. Although these stories cannot be relied upon, there is sufficient evidence that Simon was low-minded, often drunken, and definitely capable of being physically abusive to the prince.

The prince mistreated by Simon

But why did Simon bully and browbeat the unfortunate child? Was he carrying out a cold-blooded and premeditated plan of action? Was he following orders from the revolutionary government? Despite the reason, a man who can behave as Simon did to a defenseless child can only be called a monster—despite whether his actions were dictated or not.

The extent to which Simon deliberately debased the dauphin's mind is witnessed by the declaration that the child signed on the 6th of October in the presence of the mayor of Paris, Hébert, and other officers. The queen's enemies had been seeking evidence against her, and the diabolical idea occurred to make her little son a witness against his mother.

Simon reported that he and his wife had learned certain facts from the child's mouth that he wished for an opportunity to make a declaration. On the 6th of October, he was given the opportunity, and a declaration was brought against the child's mother and aunt of charges so disgusting that most authors thereafter found it impossible to repeat them.

This declaration of incest was signed Louis Charles Capet and witnessed by the mayor of Paris. The signature still exists, but so shaky and so irregular is the dauphin's signature, so unlike the neat, regular handwriting in which he wrote his exercises for his father during the early days in the Temple, that it is possible that he had been made drunk or someone guided his hand:

Signature of Louis Charles Capet (uncrowned Louis XVII)

It is inconceivable that the charges brought against his mother and aunt were true. It is also inconceivable that the dauphin was capable of fabricating them himself. But there can be no doubt that Simon cajoled or bullied his charge into making them. In fact, the next day Marie-Thérèse was brought down to be examined, and her little brother was in the room when she arrived. She embraced him tenderly, but the child was immediately grabbed and taken into another room. The officers were obviously trying to get her to support her brother's statements, but she wept with indignation about the disgraceful charges. The child later could only repeat what he had declared the day before, but one of the officers, Daujeon, could only come to the conclusion that "he was only repeating what he had been taught to say."

At her trial Marie-Antoinette had heard her son's accusation read, and she at first maintained her silence. On being pressed for an answer, she said: "If I have not answered," she said at last with the dignity of innocence and the indignation of modesty, "it was because Nature itself rejects such an accusation made against a mother!"

Also, in her last letter that she wrote to Madame Elisabeth, speaking of the dauphin she said, "I have to speak to you of a thing very painful to my heart; I know how much pain this child must have caused you. Pardon him, my dear sister, think of his age, and how easy it is to make a child say what one wishes—even what he does not understand."

From Clery's journal and Marie-Thérèse's mémoires, it is apparent that Marie-Antoinette's little boy was not a paragon of virtue; he was petulant and self-willed, and she often had to restrain him. He had bad habits that she and his servants tried to correct, but he was utterly incapable of having invented these slanders he had uttered against his mother and aunt.

Although the dauphin's lot was cruel while under Simon's guardianship, there was some alleviation, and not everyone with whom he came into contact was unkind. Gagnié, the chief cook, for example, often softened the boy's existence in the Temple. One day the officers were playing billiards, and in the excitement, started throwing the child from one to another and puffing smoke in his face. When one of them scratched his face with his beard, he screamed: "You are hurting me! Your beard pricks me."

He escaped and ran to Gagnié who said, "I am sorry to see you in this state Monsieur Charles." The cook was one of those who dared not address him with his royal title, but he also did not want to only call him "Capet" as Simon did.

After some teasing by Gagnié, the young prince burst out laughing. Thus, he could still laugh and play with those who were kind to him. However, this was not proof that Simon had not mistreated the boy with harshness and cruelty. The boy was kept in the dark about his mother; he did not know that his mother was dead, but rather that she was still in the room above his. He was forced to wear the *sansculottes,* and he was forced to clean Simon's shoes and wait on him at meals. Moreover, he was forced to be in constant attendance by his guardian.

The lot of a jailer is not a wholly enviable one if he must share the rigorous confinement of a room with his prisoner. Although Simon's wages were also not paid regularly, there was plenty of food. However, he soon tired of his job, and he left the Temple on the 19th of January 1974. On the same day, the dauphin's sister upstairs wrote: "It was Simon who had gone away ... and they had had the cruelty to leave the child alone."

The Months of Loneliness

On the 19th of January, four officers visited the Temple to relieve Simon of his duties. One, Lorinet, was a doctor who wrote that they found the "said prisoner Capet in good health." After Simon's departure, the dauphin was kept a prisoner in one room, apparently the one formerly occupied by Cléry, and no one was appointed to act as his guardian. The window was shuttered, and the entrance secured by an iron door containing a sort of hatch through which food and a jar of water was passed to him. Each night the officers on duty would go to his door to be sure that he was there, and if he was asleep they would awake him. After he had come to the door and they had a look at him, they would tell him, "Back to bed, young wolf!"

Except for this nightly visit, he saw no one and spoke to no one. During the day, his shuttered room was half dark, and at night he was not allowed a candle or lamp. The room was infested with rats, and to avoid them, the young prince would put some food in his cap and place it on the table for them to eat.

His health was deteriorating; he had three tumors on different parts of his body and an open sore on his neck that oozed when he scratched it. His legs and thighs were growing disproportionately long in comparison with the rest of his body.

It is no wonder that under such circumstances a little nine-year old boy neglected to wash himself or change his clothes; he neglected even the commonest decencies of life and "vegetated in a state of disgusting filth." It is a wonder that he managed to survive six months in such squalor.

The Dauphin Louis Charles

There were writers who thought that perhaps the child imprisoned on the second floor could not have been the dauphin because he would have shouted and thrown a tantrum in the dark room. However, considering that the child had just spent the last six months under the care of the rogue Simon, his spirit may already have been broken. It is said that the prince had stopped speaking after the horrific deposition that he was forced to make against his mother, but one could well imagine that the child had surely become afraid of the sound of his own voice in the lonely, dark, and terrifying room.

On the 28th of July, the day after the fall of Robespierre, Barras—the new dictator, as he may be called—paid the child a visit. Although he was known to be an unscrupulous scoundrel, he was a man of noble descent and courtly manners. The little prince who shrank in terror from the rough municipal offers obviously felt no fear of Barras and answered his questions. Barras found the prince lying on a small cot in the middle of the room; he was drowsy and woke with difficulty.

"How are you, and why are you not lying down on the big bed?" asked Barras.

"My knees are swollen and make me suffer from time to time when I am standing up," answered the child. "The little bed suits me better."

Barras looked at his knees and they were indeed very swollen, as well as his ankles and his hands. His face was puffy and pale. After asking the prince if he had everything that he needed, he persuaded him to walk around the room. Barras also asked if he would like a horse, a dog, some birds, playthings, or even one or more companions of his own age. The official later wrote:

> In vain did I repeat everything that I could think of as agreeable to his age. I received not one word in reply, not even a sign or gesture, although his head was turned toward me, and he was looking at me with a strange fixedness in his eyes which expressed the utmost indifference.

Barras later told the Committee of Public Safety that "the young Prince was dangerously ill, and that doctors ought to be called in to examine him." The immediate result of Barras' visit was the appointment of a guardian to care for the dauphin and his sister, who since the execution of her aunt had been alone. She had not, however, been as ill-treated as the dauphin, and being six years older had contrived to look after herself and keep her room and her person clean.

The guardian was Christophe Laurent, a young Creole who was selected by Barras. The princess later praised him for his behavior but admitted that he took better care of her than her brother. Laurent found the prince in a deplorable condition, however; he had lost his appetite and was very weak. Despite Laurent's complaints, for more than a month, no steps were taken to clean his room and disinfect it. Another guard also complained about the foul smell coming from the room, and that the filthy condition had taken away the child's appetite. Still no action was taken.

A few days later, there was a gunpowder explosion nearby, and a rumor circulated that there was a royalist plot. The committee sent a delegation to the Temple to make sure that the two royal children were still imprisoned. The delegation then ordered Laurent to have the room cleaned and the vermin caused by the filth to be exterminated.

The Dauphin Louis Charles

The next day, the cook Gagnié entered the room to find the pale, thin prince lying on his bed, and his dinner on the table untouched. "Monsieur Charles!" exclaimed the cook. "Why do you not eat? You ought to eat."

"No, my friend, no; I wish to die!" answered the child.

Laurent proceeded with the cleaning. He also had the prince's hair and nails cut. The child's filthy and verminous undergarments were removed, and he was given a bath. His wooden bed infested with bugs was removed and replaced with an iron one. Also, the iron door was removed and replaced with the original wooden door.

Although the dauphin's sufferings were alleviated a little, his sister later wrote that Laurent only paid him three short visits every day. He did not dare to do more for the boy for fear of compromising himself since he was always being watched by the guards. However, the child was still not allowed to have a lamp or candle at night, and he seemed to have grown more and more apathetic. The long torture he had undergone had simply crushed his spirit.

One may question why Laurent hesitated to help the prince or even let anyone see him. The answer is that Barras and his colleagues did not want anyone to know of the child's condition after six months of solitary confinement. The bright and healthy child that he had been a year ago might have been a useful pawn in the political game as future king, but the almost imbecile boy now could be of no use to anyone. It was thus important to keep the child concealed from public view.

At this time, Cléry, after being released from La Force Prison a month earlier, had moved across the street from the Temple Prison with the former servant Hüe to keep surveillance over the last two prisoners. An attempt, it is written, was made to bribe Laurent to help the dauphin escape the Temple, and money had been paid to people in higher positions by an unknown party in England.

If the government was aware of this plot, it is not surprising that Laurent kept the dauphin jealously guarded. However, Laurent was becoming increasingly discontent with the continual confinement in the Temple and his attempts to get a second guard appointed were finally successful. On the 8th of November, Jean Baptiste Gomin, a tried and true republican, was appointed.

Gomin

Although he was a revolutionary, Princess Marie-Thérèse wrote that the new guard took the greatest possible care of the dauphin and even obtained permission to allow the dauphin a light in his room after dark. She wrote that the child became attached to the new guard, but it must be noted that she was only repeating what Gomin had told her.

Although Gomin was afraid of compromising himself, he did show the prince some consideration whenever he had the opportunity. Laurent was now often absent from the Temple, and Gomin could spend a few hours each day with the child. There was a report that there was a stove in an adjoining room which had an opening in the wall, and that Gomin was "not to leave the fire at the child's discretion." These details indicate that the dauphin was now occupying his father's old room and not the one in which he had been confined after Simon's departure.

Despite the added care, the dauphin was gradually growing weaker. He was still left alone at night, locked in, not only in his room but on also all alone on the entire floor because Laurent and Gomin slept on the floor below. Gomin tried to get the child's food improved, but the kitchen staff had its orders and dared not disobey them.

This has been speculation that the dauphin may not have been completely alone on his floor in the tower. Coco, the spaniel, may have been allowed to stay with the child upstairs. His older sister, Marie-Thérèse, wrote later in her mémoires that the child had been very fond of Coco which was "a gift from Gomin." There was also question whether the dog was presented to the dauphin or to the princess as a gift. It is unlikely, however, that the dog accompanied the child in his confinement. First, he would not have been tormented by rats and other creatures if he had Coco by his side. Second, we know that the dauphin had always been afraid of loud noises such as a dog's bark. Finally, when the child was in need of medical attention, a visiting official asked if he would like "toys, a dog, or a bird." The prince never responded, and there is no mention of it again in the records. Perhaps even the child knew that it was too late.

One night in March when Gomin was alone with the dauphin, the child got up out of his bed and went to the locked door, looking at Gomin with a sad, questioning expression on his emaciated face.

"You know it cannot be," said Gomin, who guessed what the boy wanted.

"I just wanted to see her once more," exclaimed the dauphin. "Let me see her before I die, please."

Gomin, who understood that the child was asking for his mother, whom he still believed to be on the floor above, led him back to his bed, where he lay for some time motionless and apparently unconscious. The child finally opened his eyes, and Gomin, who was very distressed by the little boy's bitter disappointment, said to him: "It is not my fault if I cause you so such pain, but my duty forbids me to do it. It is not my fault—pray tell that you forgive me!"

The prince burst out crying, and Gomin said, "Do not cry like that, Monsieur Charles, less someone hears you."

When the child grew calmer, he added: "You know well that the door is locked, and even supposing it were open, you would not wish to go out with the knowledge that by doing so you would condemn me to death." Despite any of his shortcomings, Gomin cared for the dauphin, and dared not tell him that his mother had met her end at the blade of the guillotine many months before.

Lasne

At the end of March, Laurent resigned his post, and his place was taken by Etienne Lasne, a kind-hearted man who was not as timid as Gomin. However, it appears that Gomin and Laurent had not been so careful about cleanliness, and the dauphin's bed had to be purged again of fleas and mites on the day after Lasne's arrival. Lasne blamed Laurent and not Gomin, however, for neglecting the child in such an inhumane manner.

Lasne took the lead almost from the moment of his arrival in caring for the dauphin, whereas Gomin chiefly attended to the Princess Marie-Thérèse. Although the boy appeared to be afraid of Lasne at first, he soon became as attached to him as he was to Gomin. Apparently Lasne showed more attention to the prince; he washed and dressed him with great care everyday. He also arranged to have the locks and bolts greased on the doors to the dauphin's room to make less noise for the child, knowing that the child was always easily alarmed by any loud noise.

The child rarely spoke, however, and it was not until three weeks after Lasne's arrival that he finally said a word. Meanwhile, the boy was growing weaker, and on the 4th of May, Lasne and

Gomin made an entry in the Temple register that "the little Capet is unwell." The following day, they wrote that "the little Capet is dangerously ill." The next day they wrote, "His life is in danger."

A doctor was sent to examine the prince, and he reported that the child's condition was very serious—he had tumors on his right knee and left arm. He also suffered from tuberculosis, malnutrition, and numerous infections. He suggested that the child be removed to the country for rest, but the request was denied. As ill as he was, no woman nurse was sent to wait upon him, and neither Lasne nor Gomin was allowed to stay with him at night.

On the morning of the 8th of June, Lasne made the dauphin get up as usual and dressed him, but the boy was so ill that he soon had to put him back in bed. Doctors paid him a visit but said that his condition was hopeless. At 2 o'clock, the dauphin expired in Lasne's arms. Lasne and Gomin were deeply affected by the loss of their little charge and wept bitterly.

So ended the long martyrdom of the little prince, Louis Charles Capet. In his life of 10 years, he had suffered more in mind and body than most men do in their entire lives. Although his death may not have been due to the ill treatment that he had received, it does seem to have affected his mind to such an extent that his sister related that there was reason to fear that had he recovered, he would have become an imbecile. The surviving princess was not informed that her brother had died until months later.

Cléry would have found it difficult to realize the full cruelty of the prince's inhumane treatment, but it was consistent with the temper of the times, and with the terror and reckless tyranny of the Commune. There was no mystery in the treatment of the young king or in his abandonment. Had he been old enough for the guillotine, he would have perished in that manner, but he was left to die by a slow death by disease and decay. He was of slight political value because royalism was for the time being crushed.

The fragile, sometimes disobedient but always thoughtful, young prince had been in Cléry's charge ever since his birth. The child was known to have been very fond of Cléry: He would visit his valet when he was bedridden with fever, he would beg his valet to play ball with him in the prison courtyard, and he would present him with small gifts from time to time. It was not uncommon for valets to take on a paternal relationship with their charges, and it was evident that the dauphin and Cléry's relationship had remained very close until Cléry's last days in the Temple.

On the death of her young brother, Marie-Thérèse was now the final survivor of the Temple. For two years, the princess did not know of the tragic fate of her mother. Since the time her aunt had been taken from her, she was also unaware that this saint-like woman had been subjected to the same tragic punishment when she was guillotined on the 10th of May 1974.

PART FIVE

CLÉRY'S FINAL YEARS OF SERVICE

Chapter 17
Cléry's *Journal Du Temple*

*I served the King and his august family for five
months in the Tower of the Temple; and in spite of
the close watching of the municipal officers who were
the keepers of it, I was able, either in writing or by
other means, to take certain notes on the principal
events which took place in the interior of that prison.
As sole and continual witness of the injurious
treatment that the King and his family were made to
endure, I alone can write it down and affirm the exact
truth.*

–Jean-Baptiste Cléry
Introduction to his mémoires, 1798

Without any means to support his family and unable to find
work in Paris at the beginning of 1795, Cléry was finally forced to
sell his property in Juvisy, leaving half of the funds to his family. He
then rented a room with Hüe in Paris near the Temple to be near
Marie-Thérèse.

After the pitiable death of the young uncrowned King Louis
XVII in June, the Princess Marie-Thérèse was the sole prisoner in the
Temple. Gradually she was allowed visitors, and she had the freedom
to stroll in the Temple courtyard with her spaniel, Coco. The princess
could also now afford to be patient because her release in the near
future was almost certain. Her visitors informed her that her
prolonged imprisonment by the republic was an embarrassment to
the French government and that plans were being made to escort her
to the border for a diplomatic trade of prisoners.

The preparations for the journey were carried out in secrecy
and entrusted to Minister Bénézech. "Madame Royale wishes you
and Turgy to follow her to Vienna," said the Minister to Hüe, "but
Turgy is ill at present, and it is not possible for him to go."

Although the princess's day of liberation was drawing near,
the minister of the interior still had to make arrangements with

Marie-Thérèse and her keepers, as to the exact manner and the time of her departure. He wrote the following letter to the latter:

> I give you notice, citizens, that I shall come this evening, at five o'clock, for the purpose of seeing the prisoner in the Temple, and beg you will let her know it beforehand; but I also wish to have some conversation with yourselves before I visit her apartment.

Her uncle, the exiled King Louis XVIII (on the death of the young uncrowned King Louis XVII) had plans in Verona for her to marry her cousin, the Duc d'Angoulême. Naturally, her mother's Austrian relatives had other plans. Strained relations, therefore, were to be expected between the courts of Vienna and Verona when the princess was released.

The Release

On the 27th of November, the Directory gave the final order for the princess to be released from prison. Public opinion was focused on the imprisoned princess, and the government did not want her story to be told. Sparing no expense, a superb trousseau was ordered for the last survivor of the Temple, and she was also allowed to select a servant to accompany her to the frontier. She chose Gomin, her attendant who had also helped take care of the dauphin until Lasne arrived. She also was allowed to take Coco, the spaniel.

The princess herself made the preparations for the long journey. She picked out the clothes and linen that she wished to take with her (very little of either), and she left the rest to be distributed among the persons employed in the Temple. She then put on the dress which she had been accustomed to wearing on festival days, and, going into the garden, saluted the persons who had so often shown their sympathy for her from the neighborhood windows.

On the 18th of December 1795, at eleven o'clock, Minister Bénézech left his hotel in a carriage, directing the coachman to drive to a spot near the Temple. There he stepped down from his carriage, and, accompanied only by a confidential servant, made his way to the Temple. At the door he tapped twice, and with this signal the door was opened by Lasne who was expecting him and who recognized the minister. Bénézech then took a document out of his pocket, which he gave to Lasne, saying: "This is to end your responsibility to the princess."

> In execution of the decree of the Executive Directory, of which the above is a copy, the minister of the interior declares that citizens Gomin and Lasne have delivered into his hands Marie-Thérèse-Charlotte, daughter of the last King, in perfect health; which transfer was made at eleven o'clock, P.m., this day; and he further declares that the said commissaries are duly discharged from the custody of the said Marie-Thérèse-Charlotte.

The outer gate then opened. The night was dark, and the neighborhood of the Temple silent. Minister Bénézech offered his arm to the Princess with Gomin and the minister's valet following, carrying a carpetbag and a parcel. Marie-Thérése turned her head, and fixed a long sad look upon the Temple, and her eyes filled with tears. Bénézech tried to say a few words of comforting kindness, but could not.

"I feel your consideration and attention to me very much," said the princess to him, "but at the same hour when I regain my liberty by your assistance, how can I help thinking of those who have crossed that threshold before me? It is now three years, four months, and five days, since these gates closed upon my family and myself, and today I have passed through them once more—the last and the most unfortunate of all!"

They reached the spot where the minister's carriage was waiting. Madame accepted his offer to assist her, and the minister took his place followed by Gomin. The vehicle soon reached the Opera House, where the traveling berline was stationed. The princess thanked Bénézech warmly for the kindness he had shown her, and she took her place in the carriage. Madame de Soucy sat beside her, on the back seat, and Gomin sat in the front. To the latter the minister now gave his warrant stating that Gomin was to accompany the princess as far as Basle.

A last word was heard from the berline, addressed to the minister: "Farewell, Sir!" and the carriage drove off. Bénézech looked pleased by the good work he had just completed. Getting back into his coach, he looked at his watch—it was midnight. It was the princess's birthday. She was 17 years old.

Coco, Marie-Thérèse's last companion in the Temple

Evidence now suggests that Coco was actually Marie-Thérèse's dog. The servant Hüe, who was allowed to accompany the princess, mentioned that the dog had been by the princess's side "for the entire four years of her imprisonment" in the Temple. In fact, special precautions were taken the night that she left the Temple, because they were afraid that Coco would start barking and arouse suspicion as they departed. It was a dangerous task to secretly conduct the remaining member of the royal family across the border into Austria. The officials therefore arranged to have another carriage take the dog separately, accompanied by Hüe and the princess's lady-in-waiting.

Marie-Thérèse had entered the Temple as a young princess on a warm summer's evening accompanied by her father, mother, aunt, and brother. She left the dismal prison as a woman, alone, orphaned, and on a freezing winter's night.

Cléry's Strained Relations with the Princess

Cléry had received word that Marie-Thérèse was going to be released and exiled to Austria. He tried to gain access to the princess in the Temple many times but was unsuccessful. However, he did manage to send word to the princess asking for permission to join her in Vienna. She was hesitant, being concerned about the expense of such a long voyage. She finally agreed when she was informed that Cléry had sold his small home in the country. From the tone of her message, it appeared that although she was grateful for his service, she was not enthusiastic about Cléry's offer.

With the remaining funds from the sale of his property, Cléry set off for Strasbourg on the 5th of October 1795 to stay with his brother Hanet who was working there. He planned to stay until the princess arrived there on her way to Austria. Because it was almost impossible to travel in France, or change residence, except for government affairs, Hanet helped Cléry procure an administrative position in Strasbourg. Although he remained there for three months, he had no experience for his job, and he was forced to end his temporary work soon after being hired. Fortunately, he used this spare time wisely.

Early one morning Cléry brought a bag into his brother's room, saying: "I have a bundle of notes that were hurriedly scribbled in ink and pen. I have kept them hidden, because they document everything that happened in the Temple." Hanet looked bewildered when he saw the bag filled with scraps of papers. "I would like to organize them," Cléry continued, "because they could make an interesting journal. But I cannot do it all on my own, and I do not know if I can trust anyone."

Hanet soon found a gentleman that could help Cléry, and while everyone thought Cléry was working at his new position in Strasbourg, he was actually writing his mémoires of the Temple Prison. Hanet, knowing that there were those who questioned Cléry's authorship, later wrote, "I want to let everyone know that Cléry wrote his journal in Strasbourg, and that he had no help except for the person that I had found for him, the person that did nothing but hold a pen."

Soon afterwards Cléry learned from his wife that Princess Marie-Thérèse had finally been liberated from the Temple Prison and that she would be in Huningue on the 24th of December. His brother Hanet understood that Cléry's only ambition was to join the princess and hopefully continue his career with the exiled royal family. Hanet succeeded in helping him secure a passport, and he arranged for his carriage to Huningue. Hanet had not idea that this would be the last time he would ever see his older brother.

Marie-Thérèse being released from the Temple by Minister Bénézech

Cléry traveled day and night but did not meet the Princess Marie-Thérèse in Huningue; however, she had left a message for him to travel to Wels where he finally was allowed an audience with the princess, but little is known about their brief meeting. Although Cléry professed his loyalty to the princess, it is known that she had never thought highly of him. When she was imprisoned with her unfortunate family in the Temple, she had even mentioned to her aunt Elisabeth that she believed him to be an agent of the revolution. After all, he was the only family servant allowed to remain in the Temple, alongside the other revolutionary guards, commissioners, and the ruthless spies, the Tison couple. The old man Tison had even accused him of revolutionary ideals.

On one occasion, the princess also remarked that Cléry had apologized to the royal family for his indiscretions after being called before a revolutionary tribunal. Her version indicated that Cléry engaged in a mysterious handshake and conversation with a guard. Cléry's version, however, denied any wrongdoing. The accusation was never substantiated, but the fact remains that Cléry did apologize for conduct that was deemed indiscreet. However, it could be concluded that Cléry apologized for being forced to take an oath of allegiance to the republic. If he had not agreed, he would not have been allowed to resume his service in the Temple.

Hotel du Corbeau in Huningue

The princess added that, due to the king and queen's insufferable circumstances, Cléry "changed" and was "faithful" to his master from that time forward. This only added fuel to the fire that Cléry had perhaps collaborated with the revolutionaries when he first entered the Temple. Had he always been faithful, or was he wrongly accused?

At their meeting in Wels, she refused Cléry's request for a position in her household; rather, she asked him to assist the exiled Louis XVIII, the brother of the executed Louis XVI, in Verona. The fact that she did not keep him in her service in Austria raised eyebrows. However, Cléry's new master welcomed him warmly in Italy for his service to his brother in the Temple. Having completed several important missions for Louis XVIII in Germany and Italy, Cléry was rewarded with a position in the exiled king's household in Verona—not Marie-Thérèse's in Vienna.

In his service to the new king, Cléry did not reveal the horrific experiences in the Temple to any other interested parties. The king's counsel, Malesherbes, and his priest, Firmont, had already reported on the late King Louis XVI's last moments in their own mémoires. Cléry, however, had edited his *Journal du Temple* for the new king's eyes only, and he presented it to him personally.

Many of Cléry's critiques have wondered if he was the true author of the *Journal du Temple*. After its publication, his authorship was often contested. However, it has since been established that the journal describing the servant's service to the king and the royal family in the Temple Prison was written entirely by Cléry, and by

Cléry alone. Granted, there were discrepancies between different editions, but they were minor. For example, Cléry's first edition pointed out an exclamation by the king's sister, Madame Elisabeth, while Louis XVI and the queen were playing chess. The queen observed that Louis had not captured the king, and Madame Elisabeth cried out, "My brother is too good to do that!" This exclamation was omitted from a later edition in 1861.

Princess Marie-Thérèse of France

As soon as Cléry secured permission from the exiled Louis XVIII to publish the *Journal du Temple*, he left for Vienna. However, the Austrian government prohibited the mémoire from being published in Austria or any of its other possessions. The recent signing of the Campo Formio Treaty in 1797 seemed to be the government's motivation. This peace settlement between France and Austria followed Austria's defeat in Napoleon's first Italian campaign, and Austria feared angering Napoleon with any pro-royalist sentiment that Cléry's journal might encourage.

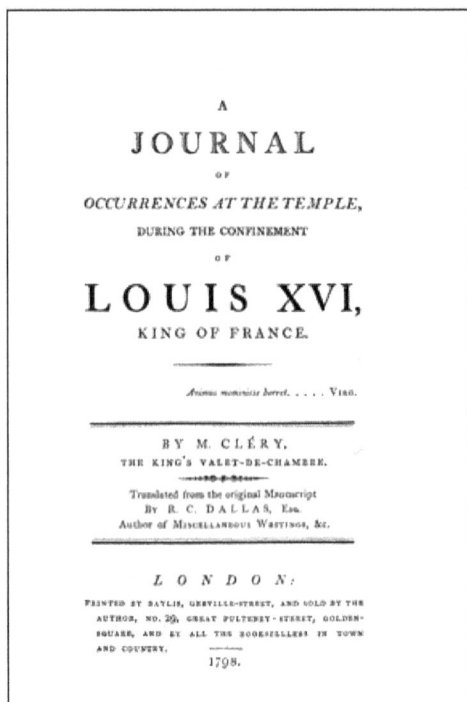

Cléry's Journal published in London in 1798

Cléry left immediately for London where the *Journal de Temple* soon appeared simultaneously in English and in French, and it was such a success that it was published in other European languages as well. It was difficult to find copies in France, however, until it was secretly printed in 1798, and again secretly in 1807, during the reign of Napoleon, a dictator who did not appreciate such royalist sentiments.

The exiled Louis XVIII, however, was ecstatic about Cléry's *Journal* depicting the cruel treatment of the royal family in the Temple. In fact, he decorated Cléry with the Order of Saint-Louis, a medal for his bravery. However, the government of France recreated a false edition of Cléry's journal, *Mémoires de Monsieur de Cléry sur la détention de Louis XVI,* which attempted to discredit the monarchy. Cléry protested vehemently in periodicals printed in Hamburg, despite the difficulty in communicating during these turbulent times, about this untrue depiction of the royal family in the Temple, but they were never published in France. In 1801, the *Spectateur du Nord* printed a notable letter that was written by Cléry; the following is a brief excerpt:

I have just read the libelous publication printed in my name entitled *Mémoires de Monsieur de Cléry sur la détention de Louis XVI* and it is inconceivable that someone could be so cruel to defame the name of a most faithful and virtuous servant. He will not succeed, my master, my King, my generous Queen, angelic Elisabeth! Your names will remain hallowed with respect.

It should be noted that the captivity of Louis XVI and his family was only published from the royalists' point of view in this fictitious version of Cléry's *Journal du Temple*. Also, the members of the anti-royalist factions had all been executed at the guillotine and thus had no opportunity to write from their perspective. The sham version depicted a lavish and luxurious lifestyle of the monstrous royal family.

There is no reason not to believe, however, that the royal family was cruelly mistreated as described by Cléry, but the curious fact remains that the royal family was adequately cared for at meal times during its cruel imprisonment. Dinner normally consisted of four entrées, two roasts, three side dishes and a decanter of Bordeaux wine.

Interestingly, the prison guards complained of the royals' demeanor. They found the queen at times to be demanding and condescending. The young princess, who was tight-lipped and refused to speak to guards, appeared haughty and snobbish. Historians have suggested that she was prone to pouting because the queen often kept the princess sitting indoors in royal dresses and donning a powdered wig while her brother was allowed to play outside in the gardens.

The guards also could not understand how a family faced with so much tragedy and terrorized on a daily basis could remain so calm and even play games. The king often slept peacefully in the afternoons, snoring to the point that the children would wake him by not being able to control their laughing. The surviving princess did mention, however, that playing games allowed the prisoners to speak freely among themselves without being overheard by the guards.

Historians, however, have documented that the family members appeared calm because they actually believed that they were eventually going to be saved. They had received news that the queen's family in Austria was in concert with other royal families of Europe to invade France and free the family. There were also several plots to free the family. Even the king and queen were confident to the very end that they would never climb the steps of the scaffold.

Chapter 18
Accusations Abound

Cléry is at least as eligible to be an agent of the republic as my colleague...

–Servant Tison to Marie-Antoinette
Temple Prison, September 1792

Jealous of the confidence which Marie-Antoinette seemed to have shown in Cléry at times, Tison remarked that Cléry could very well be as much an agent of the revolutionaries as his colleague Manuel. Such a compromising declaration needed to be taken very seriously. Not only did Tison make Cléry even more suspect, but he was also implying that he himself was not an agent or spy by excluding himself in the statement. It has been well-established that Tison was placed in the Temple by the revolutionaries to keep an eye on the royal prisoners as well as the other guards.

The question remains: How can we attempt to explain Cléry's behavior in such dangerous circumstances? Why did he ultimately choose to regain his position with the royal family in the heat of the revolution? Was he still honoring the oath he made to serve his king, an oath he had made 20 years earlier as a young farm boy on his father's estate at Jardy?

As a rule, people make those choices that maximize benefits relative to costs, and it is certain that the ultimate cost to Cléry was his own life, because fidelity to the king, at that time, was considered nothing less than high treason—any gratitude shown to the king was a rendezvous with the guillotine. Even the titles of royalty were forbidden, and to use them was a deadly mistake.

Cléry barely escaped death when the royal family was ousted from the Tuileries on the 10th of August 1792 and eventually escorted to the Temple Prison. Despite the fact that other royal supporters and servants were imprisoned, and often executed on the spot, for their loyalty, Cléry still remained steadfast in his decision to partake in the captivity of the royal family in the Temple under the cruelest circumstances. We know, however, that he did fear for his life quite often. In his *Journal*, he tells us that he trembled whenever the Temple guards threatened him, and he was always afraid that he might compromise himself if he were ever caught speaking to the royal family or passing notes among them.

Another question also arises whether Cléry might have harbored any revolutionary thoughts such as the pursuit of liberty, personal freedom, or outright rebellion. A pamphlet, *Avis à la livrée par un homme qui la porte,* published in 1789, attempted to sum up the grievances of male servants at that time:

> The confidant of the master at all hours, and an accomplice to his vices and his weaknesses, the servant no longer sees his master as a man, but rather a doll that he must dress, put to bed, drive, and pamper like a three-year old. He is humiliated and weary of his functions: running in the rain or the hot sun to fetch chickens every morning, jumping on and off the carriage in the mud, and remaining through dinner until the dessert before finally resigning to scraps in the pantry.

There is no evidence that Cléry had ever read this pamphlet, but it appears that very few servants would have fervently joined the revolutionary cause. They may, like many supporters of the revolution, have wanted a constitutional monarchy with the king at the helm, but they also faced the prospect of losing their livelihoods due to the emigration, or death, of their wealthy masters. In fact, most of the loyal servants of noble families followed their masters in exile abroad.

Cléry, on the other hand, decided to stay with his master, a very dangerous decision considering the daily persecution and threats of the guillotine for any allegiance with royalty. One may thus be puzzled by the risky situations in which Cléry often found himself. For example, he allowed his wife to visit him in the Temple to illegally exchange information; she and her friend were even arrested on one occasion, although they were acquitted. He conspired with Turgy, the king's cook who was allowed to leave the Temple, to pass messages from outside the prison walls to the royal family. Cléry even helped the king and Madame Elisabeth pass messages tied to strings from one floor to another at night—a very risky maneuver considering that the Temple was always heavily guarded around the clock.

One could understandably surmise that Cléry might have believed his livelihood, as well as his survival, was guaranteed by remaining in the Temple with his royal master. Did the servant fear for his life when his master was condemned to death, or was he perhaps relieved to discover that the king, beforehand, had requested that Cléry remain in the Temple to serve the young prince after his execution? Furthermore, in the king's last will and testament, the king asked his son, if he were ever to become king, to remember and reward the servants for their dedication and loyalty to the royal family. Could Cléry have believed that the benefits of his loyalty to the next king of France would someday outweigh the risk that he was then taking?

Cléry secretly took notes during his stay in the Temple, knowing that writing mémoires was very fashionable in 18th-century France. Was Cléry's desire to enter the Temple perhaps based on financial necessity? Did he plan on writing and publishing a journal describing the captivity of Louis XVI and his family for personal gain?

Another cost that Cléry had to consider was the estrangement he experienced with his wife and children. He was confined to the Tuileries and the Temple for four years, he was imprisoned in La Force an additional year, and he was then forced to sell his home in order to follow the surviving Princess Marie-Thérèse to exile in Austria. Finally, due to his attachment to the Bourbon dynasty and the final publication of his *Journal du Temple*, he was forced to remain in exile for the rest of his days except for one very brief, incognito excursion to Paris to visit his wife and children.

If Cléry was expecting to be rewarded for his service to the royal family, his hopes were certainly crushed when he discovered the tragic death of the young prince, actually the uncrowned Louis XVII. The only surviving member of the royal family in the Temple was now Marie-Thérèse, and Cléry and Hüe both had moved to the neighborhood near the Temple in order to hopefully gain access to the princess, the royal child of France who only "tolerated" Cléry. There was never mention of any conversation or interaction between Cléry and the princess in his *Journal du Temple*. Even the princess's own mémoires curiously avoided discussing Cléry in any detail.

Although permitted to remain in Vienna if he wished, Cléry had only been admitted in the princess's presence as a favor. In fact, the princess wrote a letter to her uncle, King Louis XVIII in exile, that she actually had no use for Cléry: "I have seen Hüe and Cléry; but now that they have nothing more to say to me, it is not necessary that I should see them again. The Emperor, at my request, has made provision for them, and I wish them well."

Despite the cold words from the princess, Cléry did have the opportunity to serve her again in Mitau, Russia. Her uncles were not wealthy, and they were reliant on the hospitality of foreign courts while exiled from France. Her oldest uncle on her father's side of the family, the Comte de Provence, had arranged for her to marry her cousin in Mitau, a small provincial Russian town, now in Latvia, where Czar Paul I had provided him with a home.

Entrance to palace in Mitau

Cléry, Hüe, and the late king's confessor, the Abbé Edgeworth, accompanied the princess to Mitau. Very little is reported of Clery's relationship with the princess at this time. This is perhaps due to the princess's unhappiness in the Baltic winters—especially since she discovered that her new husband had "very little brains and speaks in an uneducated manner."

Another indication of Cléry's fidelity to the royal family can be seen in his dedicated service to the exiled Louis XVIII, who later reigned as the king of France from 1814 to 1824. Louis XVIII began life as Louis-Stanislaus-Xavier, Comte de Provence. He was one of the three surviving grandsons of Louis XV, and the court considered him smarter and even more lovable than his dull, plodding older brother, Louis Auguste, but the rules of succession dictated that the latter would ascend to the throne as Louis XVI in 1774.

Louis XVIII (Louis Stanislas Xavier)

Louis XVIII's marriage in 1771 to the unsightly, dirty, and often foul-smelling Marie-Joséphine of Savoy was an unhappy arrangement from the beginning. The king claimed that he had sexual relations with his wife, but this could well have been just idle boasting. Marie-Joséphine herself had lesbian tendencies and formed a long-lasting attachment to one of her ladies-in-waiting, Madame de Gourbillon, a relationship that the queen's contemporaries judged to be "unnatural." It was also widely rumored in aristocratic circles that Louis XVIII had homosexual tendencies, too.

Cléry was appointed valet de chambre by Louis XVIII when he arrived, but it was a title in name only. Cléry was not required to fulfill any duties related to the title, and he was also not kept in the king's household. Instead, the king sent Cléry on numerous missions to Germany, Poland, and Russia. On one occasion, the king sent Cléry to Pyrmont in Germany in attendance upon his wife, Queen Marie-Joséphine. In April, the queen, whose health had suffered much during the long Russian winter and whose temper had probably never recovered from the indignities endured during her married life, went to Pyrmont, where she hoped to rendezvous with the unfortunate Madame de Gourbillon, who, on just being released from prison, had settled at Pinneberg, a village near Hamburg. When it was known that her mistress, the queen, was taking up residence in Pyrmont, she was asked what she intended to do there; whereupon she replied, "As long as I live, I shall be at her Majesty's orders and ready to obey her."

Louis XVIII soon discovered that the two lady friends had met again, and in order to try and separate them, the king sent Cléry, who had just followed Marie-Thérèse to Russia. Louis commissioned him to choose a suitable lodging for the queen to separate her from the scandalous relationship with Madame de Gourbillon. To Cléry's dismay after such a long and tiresome journey, however, the queen preferred to choose a new residence on her own. She refused any help from Cléry.

Cléry's wearisome and time-consuming schedule of missions on which the king sent him became not only detrimental to the aging servant's health, but to his dignity as well.

Hüe and Cléry's Rivalry

When Hüe was unable to receive a place in the princess's household in Vienna, he offered her the service of his wife, Madame Hüe. He later heard that the princess had said that she did not want another Madame Campan. In other words, the princess was revealing that she saw no difference between Madame Hüe and a common hairdresser. Hüe was understandably upset, because his wife had sacrificed family, safety, and fortune to serve the princess when she was the sole survivor in the Temple.

Madame Hüe also envied Cléry because he had received more compensation from the exiled royal family than her husband. Cléry's *Journal* was also published with the king's permission and well wishes; whereas, permission for Hüe's to publish his work was refused for various political reasons.

Madame Hüe publicly expressed her jealousy by alluding to Cléry's infidelity, indicating that Cléry had nurtured a special relationship with the revolutionary faction. Citing an article in the *Le Moniteur*, she referred to a report by the council member, Dorat-Cubières, who wrote the following:

L E

CALENDRIER RÉPUBLICAIN,

P O Ë M E,

Lu à l'assemblée publique du Lycée des Arts,
le 10 Frimaire de l'an 3 ;

Suivi d'une Ode au Vengeur, et de quelques autres poëmes
sur les victoires de la République en Italie, en Espagne, en
Allemagne ; sur la conquête de la Hollande ; sur la paix avec la
Toscane, et d'une douzaine d'Hymnes civiques ou Chansons.

Par le Poëte de la Révolution DORAT-CUBIÈRES,

AUTEUR du Voyage à la Bastille, en vers et en prose ; des Rivaux au
cardinalat, où Pasquin et Mauri, poëme héroï-comique en quatre
chants ; des cinq poëmes intitulés : les États-Généraux de l'Olympe,
de l'Europe, de l'Église, du Parnasse et de Cythère ; de l'Épître au
Grand Inquisiteur, de l'Inquisition dénoncée, de la Méprise ponti-
ficale, des Châteaux en Espagne des Émigrés, du Général Tonneau,
du Pape malgré lui, du Danger des Couvens, de la Lettre de saint
Jérôme à une Dame romaine ; de la baronne de Chantal, ou les
Dangers de la dévotion, en trois actes et en vers ; des Journaux d'à-
présent ; du Banquet des six Rois ; du Poëme des Abeilles ; des Portraits de Mirabeau, de Lepelletier, d'Athanase Auger, de Cerutti,
et de plusieurs autres ouvrages patriotiques et philosophiques com-
posés depuis la révolution.

Prix, 60 livres.

À PARIS,

Chez TESSIER, Libraire, rue de la Harpe, n°. 151,
vis-à-vis celle du Foin.

AN IV DE LA RÉPUBLIQUE.

Work by Dorat-Cubières

Wednesday morning in the Tower, Louis rose at seven thirty. He dressed quickly, picked up a book, and read for about an hour. At nine o'clock his breakfast was then brought to him. "I do not eat breakfast today," said the King. "It is Quatre-Temps (a religious fasting day)."

When the *valet-de-chambre* Cléry was asked if he was going to fast like his master, the cunning patriot said, "No, I am not fasting. I am going to eat breakfast." He then ate his breakfast right in front of Louis's nose.

Dorat-Cubières was thus insinuating that, because Cléry refused to fast and he ate his breakfast while the king was fasting, the servant was demonstrating his revolutionary zeal and being disrespectful to his master. Furthermore, resentment of the Catholic Church was an integral cause of the outbreak of the revolution.

Madame Hüe also went as far to imply that Cléry's wife had played a role in the "*Fete de la Déesse Raison*"—an atheistic belief system that was intended to replace Christianity during the revolution. This would only have created more suspicion of Cléry, despite the fact that Madame Cléry had been the queen's court musician and had even put her life in danger for relaying messages to the queen while she was imprisoned in the Temple.

Hanet summed up his brother's misfortunes when he said, "Cléry's final years were scarred with jealousy, tiresome and petty missions, and ingratitude."

Chapter 19
Cléry in Exile

Cléry's long and numerous voyages for Louis XVIII and the sorrowful dispersion of the members of his family were most wearisome. They destroyed his health.

–Clery's brother, Hanet, to his sister-in-law
1810

As soon as Cléry arrived in Wels near the town of Vienna in January 1796, he presented himself to the Princess Marie-Thérèse, who immediately sent him with a letter to Verona, Italy, where her uncle, King Louis XVIII, lived in exile. The king, knowing that the princess's Austrian relatives had plans for her, swiftly sent Cléry back to Vienna with a letter of his own. It would be in his best interest if the princess married his nephew, the Duc d'Angoulême, and it was imperative that Cléry delivered the letter in person. Although he appointed Cléry as his valet de chambre, he did not have to concern himself with the position's duties; rather, Cléry would be the king's messenger.

Cléry was able to deliver the important letter, but afterwards, the princess was heavily guarded in Vienna, and her former servants were banned from seeing her. Although Cléry was occasionally able to convey messages secretly, his service to the royals was limited for the next two years.

When the princess was finally allowed to receive Cléry, he asked her to read the journal that he had written. After reading it, she gave him permission to publish it, but there is no evidence that the princess shared her feelings and emotions after reading it. Cléry then immediately set off for Blankenburg, where the king had taken up residence. Due to Napoleon's rise in power in France and his military prowess, the king was at the mercy of European rulers for safe haven. For some rulers, having the king on their soil was a political risk.

After Louis XVIII read Cléry's journal, he added the words of Aeneas to Dido, *"Animus meminisse horret."* which translates to

"Courage to remember the horror" from the Latin. Also, as soon as Louis XVIII gave him permission to publish the journal, Cléry left for Vienna. However, the Austrians refused him a license to publish in Vienna or any of their provinces, fearing the wrath of Napoleon.

Cléry then made his way to London where he found lodgings at 29 Great Pulteney Street, Golden Square. He also soon found patrons and a publisher. His journal must have appeared in mid-1798, because there is a note in the first edition to its list of patrons dated May 25, 1798. This list, which is headed by the entire English royal family, includes many illustrious sympathizers. One of them, Walter Scott, is certain to have met Cléry, because he wrote in his *Life of Napoleon* the following lines:

> Cléry, we have seen and known, and the form and manners of that model of pristine faith and loyalty can never be forgotten. Gentlemanlike and complaisant in his manners, his deep gravity and melancholy features announced that the sad scenes, in which he had acted a part so honorable, were never for a moment out of his memory.

Cléry's journal became an overnight success, spreading throughout Europe in different languages soon after being printed. Unfortunately, although his initial earnings were substantial, Cléry's brother was still required to provide additional financial support for Cléry for the rest of the servant's life in exile and for his family that he was forced to abandon in France.

Louis XVIII was grateful. He sent Cléry, still in England, the Order of St. Louis with the following letter of recommendation:

> You have shown no less courage in the prison of the Temple than the warrior who braves death on the field of honor; and, in awarding to you the decoration which serves him as a recompense I do no wrong to the spirit of this noble institution.

There was another person who undoubtedly saw Cléry in London, and helped him with his patronage, although his name does not appear in the book's list of patrons. This was Dr. Charles Bumey of St. Martin's Street, who at once hurried off an account of his new acquaintance to his daughter and her French husband, Mr. D'Arblay, who had been adjutant-general to Lafayette. Both he and his wife were ardent royalists and, after reading Cléry's *Journal*, claimed that the mémoires "bore witness to deepest of tragedies" and that they wished for more details:

> The extreme plainness and simplicity of the style, the clearness of the detail, the unparading yet evident worth and feeling of the writer, make it a thousand times more affecting than if it had been drawn out with the most striking eloquence. What of the remaining members of the royal family? What of the tokens intended for the Queen and the Dauphin?

However, Cléry had no particulars to give about the other prisoners. He wrote in the preface to his published journal: "I shall accordingly confine myself to publishing a detail of the facts simply, impartially, and without mixing my own opinions." He also added that, although he had been an attendant to the royal family since 1782 and that he had witnessed the most disastrous events in the course of the Revolution, he would be deviating from his subject to describe them.

Jean-Baptiste Cléry

With respect to the "tokens" intended for the queen and the dauphin, the D'Arblay's were referring to the ring and locks of hair that Louis XVI gave to Cléry before his execution. Cléry promised to give them to the queen, but he was locked up in the Temple without any access to the remaining members of the royal family still in the prison. However, Cléry did explain what had happened to the "tokens" at the end of his journal. It appears that he had secretly given the ring and locks of hair to Turgy, who in turn was able to transmit the articles to the king's brother, the future Louis XVIII:

N O T E.

(*a*) Having left Vienna to go to England, I went to Blankenburg for the purpose of laying my manuscript at the King's feet. When his Majesty came to this part of my journal, he looked into his desk, and, with emotion, showing me a seal, asked me if I recollected it ?— I replied, it was the same. " If you could doubt it," continued the King, " read this note." I trembled as I took it. I recognized the Queen's writing ; and the note was likewise signed by the Dauphin, at the time he was Louis XVII, by Madame Royale, and by Madame Elizabeth. It may be imagined what I felt ! I was in the presence of a Prince whom fate tires not in pursuing. I had just parted with the Abbé *de Firmont*, and it was on the 21st of January that in the hands of Louis XVIII I again met with this ensign of royalty, which Louis XVI had been solicitous to preserve for his son. I adored Providence in its decrees, and I begged permission of the King to have this precious note engraved. I here present it to the public in an accurate fac-simile, taken from the original. (1) I attended the mass which the King caused to be solemnized by the Abbé *de Firmont*, on the day of his brother's martyrdom. The tears I there saw shed are not foreign to my subject.

(*b*) This ring is in possession of MONSIEUR : it was sent to him by the Queen and Madame Elizabeth, with some of the King's hair. The second note in the fac-simile (2) was sent with it.

Cléry Leaves England

As soon as Cléry returned from London, he was ordered to accompany the princess to Mitau, a Russian town on the Baltic Sea, where she was to marry the Duc d'Angoulême on the 10th of June 1799.

Although Cléry was on France's list of exiled countrymen, he did receive permission from King Louis XVIII and Marie-Thérèse to return incognito to Paris in 1801 to visit his family. Due to unforeseen circumstances, however, Cléry was unable to travel until 1803. Using a falsified passport and an alias, he finally reached Paris.

While in Paris, he attempted to publish a new version of his journal, but the police refused the necessary license. Cléry's request could not be considered without his journal including an acknowledgement of Napoleon's new regime. Not wanting to anger the royal family, Cléry refused to make any such changes to his work.

Under Napoleon's rule, much to Cléry's chagrin, his journal had been garbled and falsified; later he was coolly invited to append a postscript in praise of the existing government. Napoleon, always anxious to surround himself by the old servants of Louis XVI, even offered him the post of senior chamberlain to Josephine. Using former royal servants not only reflected the dictator's new power, but it was also an example of his snobbish love for all the royal trappings. When Madame Campan, former lady-in-waiting to the late queen, asked Cléry for his response, he replied: "My coach is ready, Madame, and I am ready to leave France as I speak."

Cléry's refusal is said to have irritated Napoleon immensely. Cléry left Paris immediately to return to the exiled royal family in Warsaw—for his own safety. This second and final separation, however, was even more difficult for Cléry's wife because this time he left for Poland with their oldest daughter who had been appointed to serve as Marie-Thérèse's lady-in-waiting.

Cléry spent several months in Warsaw with the royal family before returning to live in Vienna. His health was declining rapidly and worries about his eldest son in the military only increased his suffering. In 1806, he planned a trip to visit his eldest daughter and his brother in Passau, but he was overcome with rheumatism en route, and he had to return to Vienna.

In the autumn of 1808, Cléry suffered a stroke that caused paralysis. His son was called to Vienna, but he was unable to make the trip because of his duties as lieutenant in the war. In fact, Napoleon's armies were rapidly approaching Vienna.

To care for Cléry, his good friend, the Countess Rombeck, had him brought to her property in Hetzing near Vienna. In his last hours, he heard canon fire in the distance, but he knew that his son was on the battlefield there. Isolated from the rest of his family in France and the royal family that had settled in England, Cléry died on the 11th of May 1809 at the age of 51. The Countess Rombeck erected a small monument in the cemetery of Hetzing, a village near Vienna, with the simple inscription: "Here lies the faithful Cléry."

Madame Cléry died in Paris in 1811, not knowing that their son had been wounded and captured in battle, and that he ended his military service in front of a firing squad. Only their two surviving daughters would live to see the return of the royal family to France. Louis XVIII took the throne in 1814 after 23 years in exile.

Marie-Thérèse remained at Louis XVIII's side until he died in 1824. She then supported her uncle, and father-in-law, Charles X until he was forced from the throne in 1830. The Duke of Angoulême, Marie-Thérèse's husband, was bypassed for the throne when Charles X abdicated in favor of his grandson. At first, the Duke of Angoulême refused to give up his rights to the throne of France. After 20 minutes of very heated discussion, however, Charles X persuaded the Duke of Angoulême to renounce his rights.

Charles X, king of France

Marie-Thérèse, after a journey that began forty years earlier in the Temple Prison in the midst of the revolution, was again forced into exile. She died on the 19th of October 1851, just three days after the 58th anniversary of the execution of her mother, Queen Marie Antoinette. Marie-Thérèse was buried in Austria with "Queen Dowager of France" engraved on her headstone, referring to her husband's twenty-minute rule as King Louis XIX.

Chapter 20
The Final Verdict

Cléry has served as valet de chambre for the imprisoned King and the Dauphin. He was duly accepted to fulfill his duties because he had continuously shown his patriotism to the Bonne-Nouvelle section of the republic. For references he gave the names of Pétion, Manuel, Santerre, Gorsas, Grégoire, Prieur, etc. His position in the Tower has been the most awkward, the most captivating, and the most exposed to seduction and critique. In accepting the post, he had to renounce seeing his family, and he was forbidden to leave the Temple.

–Municipal representative Verdier's report to the Commune, *1792*

History has not been too kind to Cléry. Verdier's report to the Commune in 1792 alleged that Cléry belonged to the Bonne-Nouvelle section, one of the 48 revolutionary districts of Paris. Each district was armed and responsible for the arrest and trial of those who were suspected of being royalist or counter-revolutionary. The sentence for allegiance to the king was always capital punishment at the hands of the guillotine's executioner.

What is the truth? Was Cléry the loyal servant as the Countess Rombeck inscribed on his monument, or could he have been a dubious servant, a collaborator who supported the revolution?

Verdier's report also alleges that Cléry was a comrade of Pétion, Manuel, Santerre, Gorsas, and others. These city officials, however, were all known violent republicans. Antoine Santerre, for example, was one of the king's jailers who escorted Louis to the scaffold, crying to the executioner: "Do your duty!" Louis Manuel was one of the revolutionaries that led the storming of the Tuileries Palace. After missions to the Temple and becoming acquainted with the king, however, Manuel did change his sentiments, and he later became a royalist. Antoine Gorsas founded one of the most vociferous and vehement revolutionary journals, *The Courier of*

Versailles. Therefore, using these wretched men as references to gain entry into the Temple implies that Cléry was indeed an agent of the French Revolution.

While Cléry was incarcerated in the Temple Prison with the royal family, the rude Mercereau, a revolutionary who worked in the Temple as a stone mason, had reported that Cléry was "*un homme du 14 juillet.*" In other words, Cléry was "a man of the 14th of July," one of the rebels that had attacked the Bastille on that day in 1789. Finally, historians such as the author Alphonse de Lamartine only increased suspicion by writing that "Cléry was chosen to serve the King in the Temple by Mayor Pétion for his revolutionary stance."

Cléry's daughter Bénédicte, however, later condemned M. de Lamartine's statement, writing in 1847 that her father had "never been chosen by Pétion," and that before he entered the Temple Prison, "he had never shared the errors or the sentiments of the enemies of his master."

Princess Marie-Thérèse's suspicion that Cléry was an agent of the revolution haunted him for years even when he was forced into exile in Austria, and her accusation haunted his descendants even after his death. To make matters worse, his grandaughter, Madame Louise Le Besnier, who died in poverty at the age of 86 in 1896, was forced to sell any remaining souvenirs and memorabilia of Cléry, including the original manuscript of his *Journal du Temple*. The absence of male heirs made the continuation of the Cléry name impossible.

More damning to Cléry, however, was a report written by Verdier, a Temple commissioner, in early 1793:

> The citizen Cléry, currently in the service of Louis Capet and his son as *valet de chambre*, is one of the two *valets de chambre* of the Prince when he was a child. Thereafter, at the Tuileries from the 10th of August, 1792, Cléry was caught in the crossfire between the royal supporters and the revolutionaries. He then entered the Temple to serve the young Prince in the same capacity—the result of two letters written by Mayor Pétion on August 26 to Louis and to the Commune Council, stating that Cléry was a "good patriote" of the revolutionary cause.

This report is essential when considering the preconceptions that the royal family had about Cléry. The Princess Marie-Thérèse, as well as the royal family, could very well have heard these rumors and would have taken them to heart. The letter that Pétion sent to King Louis XVI would have portrayed the servant as a "bon" patriote, or rather, an enemy of the crown. The second paragraph of Verdier's report continued to align Cléry with the revolutionaries:

> Cléry was assigned to this important and delicate post by the Mayor of Paris with confidence, and he accepted the post that he well deserved. Since the 14th of July 1789, he has continuously shown his patriotism in the Bonne-Nouvelle section and he has served his time in the National Guard where he was not only promoted but he fulfilled all his duties with zeal. The citizens Pétion, Manuel, Santerre, and Grégoire all witnessed this demonstration of patriotism.

Although Verdier's report continues by praising Cléry's indifference while serving the royals, or the "enemies of France," this report is instrumental in disproving Cléry's involvement with the revolutionaries and substantiating his unfaltering loyalty to the king and his family.

Evidence Paramount to Cléry's Case

After the author's countless hours of searching for any sign that Cléry was an armed member of the Bonne-Nouvelle section, a surprising notice was found in the National Library of France (BNF). Due to the fragile state of the document, the BNF could not allow it to be photographed to be included here, but the following words are still clearly visible:

> *Grenadier Company. Roule Company.*
> *M. Cléry, 2nd Lieutenant,*
> *Faubourg du Roule Street, Paris.*
> *Section du Roule.*

The "M. Cléry" in Verdier's report was, therefore, not our dubious servant, Jean-Baptiste Cléry. The person that Verdier praised for his revolutionary zeal was actually Alexis-Fuscien Cléry, a spice merchant and resident of the Faubourg du Roule. Alexis-Fuscien Cléry belonged to an infantry company of *grenadiers* usually composed of tall, hand-picked men armed with grenades and hatchets. Verdier had gravely mistaken Jean-Baptiste Cléry for the revolutionary Alexis-Fuscien Cléry.

Moreover, we know that Cléry had never joined nor was he ever drafted or hand-picked for the military. He certainly was never a soldier in the National Guard since he had been in the royal household before and during the revolution. In fact, serving in the royal household excused young men from the draft.

The accusation that Cléry was one of the rebels organized to attack the Bastille, "un homme du 14 juillet," cannot be overlooked. The National Assembly recognized these so-called *"Vainqueurs de la Bastille"* in a special decree in June 1790 as those "citizens that have distinguished themselves at the fall of the Bastille." Their names were carefully compiled, recorded, and verified by commissioners of the Assembly with the following seal:

The list of the "Vainqueurs de la Bastille" is kept in the National Archives and contains 898 names including those of 16 widows, nine children, and two orphans. However, among the names listed in alphabetical order, there is no mention of Jean-Baptiste Cléry or Jean-Baptiste Cant Hanet.

The Final Word

Jean-Baptiste Cléry was simply the *valet de chambre* and the last servant of King Louis XVI, but he is worthy of being remembered as "*le fidèle Cléry*." The venerated king paid tribute to Cléry in his last will and testament on the eve of his execution:

> I recommend Cléry to the Prince, for whose attentiveness I have nothing but praise ever since he has been with me. Since it is he who has remained with me until the end, I beg the gentlemen of the Commune to hand over to him my clothes, my books, my watch, my purse, and all other small effects which have been deposited with the Council of the Commune.

In a touching scene just before the king was escorted to the scaffold, he took Cléry by both hands and said in a touching voice, "Cléry, I am satisfied with your services."

"Ah, Sire!" cried Cléry, throwing himself at his feet. "Why can I not die to satisfy your murderers and save a life so precious to all good French men?"

"Death does not alarm me," the king replied. "I am quite prepared, but you," he continued, "do not expose yourself. I shall ask that you be kept near my son. Give him all your care in this dreadful place. Remind him, tell him often, how I have grieved for the misfortunes he must bear. Someday he may be able to reward your zeal."

"My master, my King, if the most absolute devotion, and my zeal and my care, have been agreeable to you, the only reward I ask is to receive your blessing–do not refuse it to the last Frenchman who remains beside you."

Of Cléry's sole survivors, his daughters Madame de Gaillard and Madame de Grem, only Madame de Grem was authorized in 1817 by King Louis XVIII to use the Cléry name. However, neither she nor her sister ever conceived a male heir to carry on the family name.

The name, however, will never perish. A simple case of mistaken identity has been established as the cause of the family's humiliation and shame, and the faithful servant Jean-Baptiste Cléry who sacrificed his life in the name of loyalty can now be honored with the respect and admiration that he deserves, alongside all the heroes that France now honors.

Having approved this manuscript's defense of the "dubious" servant, the Institute of the House of Bourbon in Paris affirmed that Jean-Baptiste Cléry was truly a faithful subject of His Majesties King Louis XVI and Queen Marie-Antoinette, and that his name should be cleared of any collaboration with the revolutionary republicans.

MESSAGE FROM THE HOUSE OF BOURBON
PARIS, FRANCE

Having read "JEAN-BAPTISTE CLÉRY" the director of the Institute of the House of Bourbon affirms that Jean-Baptiste Cant Hanet, known as Cléry, was indeed the faithful servant of Louis XVI, and could not have been, as previously reported, an agent of the revolutionary factions.

Jean-Baptiste Cléry's daughter, Madame de Gaillard, had written the following lines in her letter to Alphonse de Lamartine in 1847, asking the famous author to retract his statement which tied Cléry to the revolutionaries:

Do not let it be said that the most unique example of loyalty in history has been vilified by a French historian, a man who has published such shameful defamation of character without any proof or any foundation.

Madame Gaillard's plea to clear her father's name has today finally been answered, and the ennobled daughter and all of Cléry's descendants may now rest in peace. Jean-Baptiste Cléry's honor has been restored, and he truly deserves the epitaph "Here lies the faithful Cléry."

Cléry's Memorial, Hietzing, Austria
"Ci-git le fidèle Cléry"

Sources

Armstrong, A. E. *Heroes, Philosophers, and courtiers of the time of Louis XVI*. London: Hurst and Blackett Publishers, 1863.

Biollay, Léon. *Les prix en 1790*. Paris: Librairie Guillaumin, 1886.

Beauchesne, Alcide. *Louis XVII: Sa vie, sa agonie, sa mort*. Paris: Henri Plon, 1866.

Campan, Jeanne-Louise-Henriette. *Mémoires sur la vie privée de Marie-Antoinette de Madame Campan*. Paris: Badouin Frères, 1823.

Campardon, M. Emile. *Marie-Antoinette a la Conciergerie (du 1er Aout au 16 Octobre 1793)*. Paris: Jules Gay, Editeur, 1864.

Celnart, Madame. *Manuel complet des domestiques, ou l'art de former de bons serviteurs*. Paris: A la Librairie Encyclopédique de Roret, 1835.

Cléry, Jean-Baptiste. *Journal de Cléry: suivi des dernières heures de Louis Seize*. Paris: Badouin Frères, 1825.

Cléry, Pierre-Louis. *Mémoires anecdotiques sur la Revolution Française*. Paris: Chez les Principaux Libraires, 1832.

De D****, M. Le Duc. *Mémoires de Louis XVIII, recueillis et mis en ordre par M. Le Duc de D*****. Bruxelles: J.P. Meline, 1833.

De Butenval, Charles-Adrien. *De la dîme royale de Vauban et de l'impôt sur le revenu*. Paris: Guillaumin, 1886.

De Montbrison, Le Comte Léonce. *Mémoires de la Baronne d'Oberkirch*. Paris: Charpentier, Libraire-Éditeur, 1886.

Fleury, Claude. Devoirs des maîtres. Paris: Chez Pierre Aubouin, 1688.

Eckard, Jean. *Mémoires historiques sur Louis XVII*. Paris: L'Imprimerie de Lefebrve, 1825.

Eckard, Jean. *Notice sur J. B. C. Hanet Cléry, dernier serviteur de Louis XVI*. Paris: L'Imprimerie d'Everat, 1818.

Grégoire, M. *La domesticité chez les peuples anciens et modernes*. Paris: A. Egron, 1814.

Grimm, Baron du. *Mémoires historiques, littéraires et anecdotiques tirés de la correspondance philosophique et critique adréssée au duc de Caxe Gotha, depuis 1770 jusqu'en 1790.* London: Chez Colburn, 1813.

Hare, Augustus. *Days Near Paris*. New York: George Routledge and Sons, 1859.

Hézecques, Comte de. Recollections of a Page at the Court of Louis XVI. London: Hurst and Blackett Publishers, 1878.

Hüe, Francois. *Dernieres années du regne et de la vie de Louis XVI.* London: Harper & Co., 1806.

Janet, Gustave. *Mémoires de Madame Du Barri.* Paris : Gustave Barba, Libraire-Éditeur, 1857.

Lamaballe, Marie-Thérèse Louise de Savoie-Carignan (Princesse de). *Mémoires relatifs à la famille royale de France, pendant la Révolution*. Paris: Treuttel et Würtz, 1826.

La Rocheterie, Maxime. *The Life of Marie Antoinette*. Cambridge: John Wilson and Son, 1893.

Lebon, André. *L'Angleterre et l'émigration française de 1794 à 1801.* Paris: E. Plon et Cie, 1882.

Marana, Giovanni Paolo. *Lettre d'un sicilien à un de ses amis.* Paris: A. Quantin, 1883.

Menil, René du. *Dernières années du regne de Louis XVI.* Paris: Henri Plon, 1860.

Monselet, Charles. *Histoire anecdote du tribunal révolutionaire (17 août-29 novembre 1792).* Paris: Giraud et Dagneau, 1853. Ozanam, M. L'Abbé. *Manuel des pieuses domestiques.* Paris: Jacques Lecoffre, 1847.

Par Un Ami du Trône. *Procès de Louis XVI.* Paris: Lerouge, 1814.

Pétion de Villeneuve, Jérôme, Charles-Aimé Dauban, François Buzot, and Charles Barbaroux. *Mémoires inédits de Pétion et mémoires de Buzot & de Barbaroux.* Paris: Henri Plon, 1866.

Proyart, M. L'Abbé. *Louis XVI Détrôné avant d'être roi.* London: Unknown, 1800.

Roederer, Pierre-Louis. *Chronique de cinquante jours, du 20 Juin au 10 Août 1792.* Paris: L'Imprimerie de Lachevardière, 1832.

Romer, Isabella Frances. *Filia dolorosa, memoirs of Marie Thérèse Charlotte, duchess of Angoulême.* London: Richard Bentley, 1852.

Segur, Count Louis Philippe. *Memoirs and Recollections of Count Segur.* London: Henry Colbur, 1825

Tourzel, Louise Elisabeth. *Mémoires de Madame la duchesse de Tourzel: Gouvernante des enfants de France de 1789 à 1795.* London: Remington & Co., 1886.

Verdier, P. Le. "Les reliques de la famille royale et les descendants de Cléry." *Revue des questions historiques.* Vol. 60. Paris: Bureau de la Revue, 1896.

Vigée-Lebrun, Élisabeth. *Souvenirs de Madame Louise-Élisabeth Vigée-Lebrun.* Paris: Librairie de Fournier, 1835.

ILLUSTRATIONS

(From 18th & 19th Century Publications)

ILLUSTRATIONS (Cont'd)

(From 18th & 19th Century Publications)

Floor plan of the Temple towers
Malesherbes (1721–1794)
King Louis XVI in the Temple
Louis XVI cross-examined by the Convention
Laya's play prohibited by the Convention
Louis XVI notified of trial proceedings
Louis XVI, King of France
Elisabeth, the queen, the princess, the king, the dauphin, and Cléry say farewell
L'abbé Edgeworth de Firmont
Antoine-Joseph Santerre
Louis XVI refuses to have his hands bound
Pamphlets depicting Sanson
La Force Prison
Prince Louis Charles
Prince Louis Charles tormented by Simon
View of the towers of the Temple
Marie-Antoinette awaits her execution
The Conciergerie
Trial of Marie-Antoinette
Marie Antoinette taken to the guillotine
Sketch by Jacque Louis David
Execution of Marie-Antoinette
Madame Elisabeth, the king's sister, is taken
The prince mistreated by Simon
Signature of Louis Charles Capet
The Dauphin Louis Charles
Coco, Marie-Thérèse's companion in the Temple
Marie-Thérèse being released from the Temple
Hotel du Corbeau in Huningue
Princess Marie-Thérèse of France
Cléry's Journal published in London
Entrance to palace in Mitau
Louis XVIII (Louis Stanislas Xavier)
Cléry's Memorial, Hietzing, Austria

INDEX

National Convention, *149, 157, 166, 181, 199, 200, 202*

National Guard, *62, 64, 70, 71, 109, 110, 123, 166, 265, 314, 315*

National Library of France (BNF)., *292*

Naudin, Dr., *251*

Necker, *163*

Normandy, *4, 21*

Oeil de Boeuf, 234

Palace of Justice, *143*

Palloy, *68*

perruque, 59

Pétion, *9, 66, 68, 87, 88, 89, 90, 94, 119, 198, 209, 223*

Pierre- Louis Philippe Hanet, *31*

Pinneberg, *281*

Place de la Revolution, 257

Pluche, *138*

Poland, *8, 26,* 298

Polignac, Duchesse de, *33, 41, 43, 44, 53, 55, 70*

premier valet de chambre, 27

Prieur, *290*

Princess de Guéménée, *24, 26, 28, 33, 39, 40, 41, 42, 43, 62, 84, 172*

Provence, Comte de, *171, 172, 216, 267, 299, 300*

Provence, Comtesse de, *171*

Prussia, *26, 85, 96, 117, 137*

Pyrmont, *280-281*

Queen Dowager, *289*

Racine, *102*

Rambaud, Agathe de, *77*

razors, 110, 155, 175

Richard, *243, 244, 245, 247, 323*

Rocher, 114-115

Rombeck, Comtesse, *289-290*

Rosalie, *64, 242, 244, 245, 247, 251*

Roule Company, *292-293*

Rue d'Anjou, *215*

Rue de Bièvre, *144*

Saint-Cyr, *158*

Saint-Denis, *162*

Saint-Louis, *140, 273*

sansculottes, 250, 254

Sanson, *213, 214, 215, 257*

Santerre, Antoine-Joseph, *110, 166, 203, 211, 212, 213,* 306, *311, 312, 314*

Scott, Walter, *285*

seigneurie, 20

Sénozan, Madame, *264*

September Massacres, *80, 91*

Sérent, Duchesse de, *122, 155, 235*

Sermaize, *151-152*

Sèvres, *56*

Simon, 122, 133, 231, 232, 241, 247, 261, 267, 268, 269, 270, 271, 272, 273, 277

sol, 196

Sophie-Hélène, *4, 47*

Spain, *178, 221*

Spectateur du Nord, 273

Strasbourg, *5, 288*

Swiss Guard, *76, 81, 177*

Switzerland, *62*

tabatière, 16-17

Théâtre Français, 191

Tison, 100, 108, 109, 147, 149, 162, 168, 179, 221, 230, 234, 235, 236, 237, 238, 260, 290, 296

Toulan, François, *131, 144*

Tournan-en-Brie, *225*

Marquise de Tourzel, *62, 69, 74, 126*

Trianon, *18, 21, 53, 54, 63, 172*

Tronchet, *181, 182, 183, 184*

Tuileries, 4, 60, 61, 62, 63, 67, 68, 69, 70, 71, 72, 74, 78, 81, 82, 84, 86, 87, 92, 126, 127, 131, 147, 158, 160, 175, 176, 177, 297

Turgy, Louis-François de, *54, 156*

United States of America, *216*

Vainqueurs de la Bastille, 293

Varennes, *64, 65, 66, 67, 176, 267*

Vaudeville, *191*

Vauguyon, Duc de la, *68*

Verdier, *145*

Versailles, *12*

Vienna, *5, 284, 285, 288, 291, 292, 299*

Villette, *89*

Warsaw, *288*

Widow Capet, *232*

www.ingramcontent.com/pod-product-compliance
Lightning Source LLC
Chambersburg PA
CBHW051942090426
42741CB00008B/1234